Gerotranscendence

A Developmental Theory of Positive Aging

Lars Tornstam, PhD, is a pioneer of Swedish social gerontology, who wrote the first Swedish doctoral thesis within the field of gerontological sociology back in 1973. At Uppsala University he launched the first Swedish academic courses in gerontology and did the same in Denmark during a five year stay as adjunct professor of social gerontology at the University of Copenhagen. He has also been one of the leaders of a Swedish nation-wide, cross faculty, research program *Elderly in society—Past, present and in the future*, where he himself focused his research on empirical studies of what today is labeled ageism.

Dr. Tornstam is now holding the first Swedish chair in social gerontology at Uppsala University, where he is the leader of *The Social Gerontology Group*. The wide range of research activities of this group are described in detail at the award winning web site: www.soc.uu.se/research/gerontology/

*G*erotranscendence

A Developmental Theory of Positive Aging

Lars Tornstam, PhD

 ***Springer Publishing Company***

Springer Publishing Company, Inc.
11 West 42nd Street
New York, NY 10036-8002

Acquisitions Editor: Helvi Gold
Production Editor: Jeanne W. Libby
Cover design by Joanne Honigman

05 06 07 08 09 / 5 4 3 2 1

Library of Congress Cataloging-in-Publication Data

Tornstam, Lars, 1943-
  Gerotranscendence : a developmental theory of positive aging / Lars Tornstam.
      p. ; cm.
    Includes bibliographical references and index.
    ISBN 0-8261-3134-4 (hardcover)
    1. Gerontology—Philosophy. 2. Aging—Psychological aspects.
    I. Title. [DNLM: 1. Aging—psychology. 2. Geriatrics—
  methods. 3. Human Development—Aged. 4. Self Concept—
  Aged. 5. Social Behavior—Aged.
WT 145 T686g 2005]
HQ1061.T667 2005
305.26'01—dc22   2005010133

Printed in the United States of America by Integrated Book Technology.

Contents

List of Figures   vii
List of Tables   ix
Acknowledgments   xi

Introduction   1

1 The Need for New Theories in Social Gerontology   6
The Root of the Misery Perspective
Myths Within Gerontology
The "Retirement Trauma"
The Scientific Paradigm of Gerontology
The Absolute Order of Things
The Function of Myths Within Science
Breaking the Bounds

2 Origin of the Theory and First Outline   31
The Paradigmatic Context of the Disengagement
    Theory and Its Counter-Theories
Experimental Thinking With an Alternate
    Metatheoretical Paradigm
Obstructions in the Process Towards Gerotranscendence
Conclusion

3 The Qualitative Content of Gerotranscendence   48
Gerotranscendence and Its Opposite
The Cosmic Dimension of Gerotranscendence
The Self Dimension of Gerotranscendence
The Social and Personal Relationships Dimension
    of Gerotranscendence
Obstacles and Shortcuts on the Path to Gerotranscendence
The Signs of Gerotranscendence
Development Beyond Both Disengagement and
    Ego-Integrity

4   **Quantitative Empirical Studies**   78
     Gerotranscendental Development in Retrospect
     Gerotranscendence from a Cross-Sectional Perspective
     Focusing the 65+
     Results From the 2001 (65+) Study
     Life Crises and Gerotranscendence
     The Functions of Reminiscence on Gerotranscendence

5   **Gerotranscendence in Practice**   155
     Nursing Staff's Interpretations of Gerotranscendence-
        Related Behavior
     The Impact of the Theory on Nursing Staff
     Practical Guidelines for Staff Members
     Introducing Guidelines in a Nursing Home Environment

6   **Conclusions and Summary**   187
     The Dimensions and Signs of Gerotranscendence
     The Developmental Patterns
     The Impact of Circumstances in Life
     Gerotranscendence in Practice
     Gerotranscendence Is Not Disengagement in a
        New Disguise
     Why Gerotranscendence Goes Beyond Other
        Developmental Models

Appendix: Suggested Exercises for Personal Development   *196*

References   *199*

Index   *209*

List of Figures

Figure 4.1a Cosmic transcendence.
Figure 4.1b Cosmic transcendence—women with and without children compared with men.
Figure 4.2   Coherence.
Figure 4.3   Need for solitude.
Figure 4.4   Cosmic transcendence by age and gender.
Figure 4.5   CHAID-analysis of cosmic transcendence.
Figure 4.6   Coherence by age and gender.
Figure 4.7   CHAID-analysis of coherence.
Figure 4.8   Solitude by age and gender.
Figure 4.9   CHAID-analysis of solitude need.
Figure 4.10 Dimensions of gerotranscendence and satisfaction with life.
Figure 4.11 Cosmic transcendence by age, controlling for crises.
Figure 4.12 Cosmic transcendence by age, controlling for crises and gender.
Figure 4.13 Coherence in life by age, controlling for crises.
Figure 4.14 Need for solitude by age, controlling for crises.
Figure 4.15 Reasons for reminiscence.

List of Tables

Table 4.1   Retrospective Gerotranscendence Statements in Denmark 1990 and Sweden[1] 2001, Respondents Age 74–100

Table 4.2   Correlations Between Gerotranscendence and "Confoundings"

Table 4.3   Dimensions of Gerotranscendence

Table 4.4   ANOVA-MCA Analysis of the Correlates to the Cosmic Dimension, Cosmic Transcendence as Dependent Variable

Table 4.5   ANOVA-MCA Analysis of the Correlates to the Coherence Dimension, Coherence as Dependent Variable

Table 4.6   ANOVA-MCA Analysis of the Correlates to the Solitude Dimension, Solitude as Dependent Variable

Table 4.7   Dimensions of Gerotranscendence in the Swedish 1995 Cross-Sectional Study and the 2001 Study (65+)[1]

Table 4.8   ANOVA-MCA Analysis of the Correlates to the Coherence Dimension, Coherence as Dependent Variable

Table 4.9   ANOVA-MCA Analysis of the Satisfaction With Present Life

Table 4.10   Percentages, Within Age/Gender Categories, Who Within the Last Two Years Have Experienced a Crisis in Life in Connection with . . .

---

[1]The Swedish 1995 cross-sectional study includes respondents age 20–85; the 2001 study (65+) includes respondents age 65–104.

Table 4.11   Percentage of Respondents Who Have
              Experienced One or More Crises During the Last
              Two Years
Table 4.12   Correlations Between the Experience of Crises
              and Cosmic Transcendence
Table 4.13   ANOVA-MCA Analysis of Cosmic
              Transcendence, With Age and Crises as
              Independents
Table 4.14   Functions of Reminiscence
Table 4.15   ANOVA-MCA Analysis of Cosmic
              Transcendence With Dimensions of
              Reminiscence and Other Variables as
              Independents
Table 4.16   ANOVA-MCA Analyses of Reminiscence
              Dimensions
Table 5.1   Number of Staff Members Who Have Noticed
              Specific "Behaviors" in the Residents and the
              Cardinal Interpretation of the Behavior
Table 5.2   Impact of the Theory of Gerotranscendence
Table 5.3   Correlates of the Impact of the Theory of
              Gerotranscendence

Acknowledgments

The work described in this book was largely inspired by seminars within the Social Gerontology Group in the Department of Sociology of Uppsala University, Sweden. The Social Gerontological Group comprises, in addition to the author, Gunhild Hammarström, PhD, full professor; Marianne Winqvist, PhD, certificated psychologist; Peter Öberg, PhD; Fereshteh Ahmadi, PhD; Sandra Torres, PhD; Torbjörn Bildtgård, PhD; Satu Heikkinen, BSSc; and Clary Krekula, BSSc. For further information on the work of this group, visit our homepage at: www.soc.uu.se/research/gerontology/

Introduction

Do you remember when you were ten years of age and what you, at that time, thought about those who were twenty years of age?

This question has been forwarded to several audiences as a first thread in the theory of gerotranscendence. The answers have recurrently been laughter and declarations that the twenty-year-old seemed very old indeed. Some of us admit that at age ten we wished to never grow older. Age ten was thought to be the very best in life. So, at age ten, the message was this: *If everything could just continue unchanged as it is now, life would be at its very best. What lies ahead is nothing to look forward to.*

And then we grew older and turned twenty. What did we, at age twenty, think about ourselves as ten, and what about the prospect of turning fifty? The answers to these questions were new laughter and statements about seeing oneself as very childish and immature at age ten and that becoming twenty was a pleasure rather than a nuisance. At the same time, the prospect of becoming fifty was very negative. Being twenty was felt to be the essence of life, while the thought of becoming fifty was gruesome and seen as the end of the fun. So, at age twenty, the message was now this: *If everything could just continue unchanged as it is now, life would be at its very best. What lies ahead is nothing to look forward to.*

Sure enough, those of us who have reached age fifty often praise the maturity of that time. Becoming fifty was a pleasure rather than a nuisance, and we pitied the poor twenty-year-olds, running around like hysteric mice in a maze. "Thank God for not having to suffer that age any longer." But, for sure, being eighty would be a real nuisance and a misery, including retirement shock, loss of friends, and loneliness. So, at age fifty, the message was still: *If everything could just continue unchanged as it is now, life would be at its very best. What lies ahead is nothing to look forward to.*

So, it seems, many of us have a tendency to define the present time of life as the best one and as normative for how the rest of life should be. We can understand otherwise in retrospect, but have difficulty doing so in prospect. This is, in fact, a particular aspect of something more general—the centricity patterns. We talk about, for example, ethnocentrism, and refer to a pattern where one's own ethnic group is perceived as natural and best, while other groups are defined as strange and inferior. They become "others" in an "othering" process sometimes ending in xenophobia. In the same vein there are othering processes regarding culture, social class, age, gender, and many more. This is probably one of the reasons to why, when younger, we tend to project a series of nuisances and miseries on old age, in the same vein as the ten-year-old projects misfortune as a result of becoming twenty, and the twenty-year-old projects other nuisances and miseries as a result of becoming fifty.

Not surprisingly there are severe mismatches between the nuisances and miseries we tend to project onto old age and what those who have reached advanced age tell themselves. For example, the supposed "retirement shock" seems not to be the common pattern, but rather the exception for a tiny minority (Streib & Schneider 1971; Atchley, 1971, 1999, 1980; Parnes & Nestel, 1981; Palmore, Burchett, Fillenbaum, George, & Wallman, 1985; Tornstam, 1973; Rehn, 1984; Österberg, 1982). Likewise, the assumed general loneliness among the elderly seems to be a minority problem rather than a general pattern. There are even empirical studies showing that the largest "minority" suffering from feelings of loneliness are people in the 20–29 age group, not older people (Tornstam, 1990).

However, despite the fact that the empirical data contradicts our beliefs, we seem to continue projecting these miseries onto old age. Already in 1985 Robinson, Coberly, and Paul made the observation that assumptions about retirement connected with stress and morbidity continue to flourish despite tons of contradicting empirical data. We social scientists seem so convinced of the correctness of our theories and hypotheses that we have a tendency to disregard the facts.

What we most often do when reality, as seen in empirical studies, doesn't match our theories is criticize the study in order to keep the theory. When we, for example, do not find that old people feel as lonely as our theories make us assume, we start asking questions about sampling procedures, ways of analysis, and underestimation—the sample was wrong, the analysis was made poorly, and people were reluctant to tell the truth about loneliness. That's why the data doesn't match the theory. In this way it is possible to leave the thesis of old-age loneliness intact.

But, if we for once allow the thought that our projections on old age might be erroneous and the empirical data correct, we must question the projections and the theory instead. This is exactly what the theory of gerotranscendence, the topic of this book, is about. The perpetual mismatch between theory and certain empirical data is one of the things that has led us to believe that we sometimes erroneously project midlife values, activity patterns, and expectations onto old age, and then define these values, patterns, and expectations as successful aging. Maybe our projections are not only rooted in midlife, but also in Western culture and White middle-class hopes for "success" to continue into old age.

Sure enough, the concept "successful aging" entered the field of gerontology early and is still in popular use. When scratching the surface of the concept it comes to the fore that aging successfully most often is understood as continuing to be a Western-cultured, White, middle-aged, middle-class successful person, with the typical emphasis on activity, productivity, efficiency, individuality, independence, wealth, health, and sociability. Scholars, as well as ordinary men and women may unconsciously project this specific middle-age value and behavioral pattern on old age, expressed as normative theories or facts about aging. In the theory of gerotranscendence we are questioning all this. Instead of accepting the hidden assumption that good aging is the same as continuing the midlife pattern indefinitely, we suggest that growing into old age has its very own meaning and character. By doing so, we at the same time suggest that there is a continuous development into old age. This is in contrast to much of the thinking within gerontology, where continuity and stability rather than change and development are key concepts.

In order to find and describe the hidden or overlooked developmental character and meaning of old age, we are going to listen to what old people themselves say about this, rather than relying on the statements of young and middle-aged desk theoreticians. We will then be able to demonstrate that aging certainly can involve some overlooked developmental changes related to increased life satisfaction, as described by real, flesh and blood individuals. The gerotranscendent individual, as we shall see, typically experiences a redefinition of the self and of relationships to others and a new understanding of fundamental, existential questions. The individual becomes, for example, less self-occupied and at the same time more selective in the choice of social and other activities. There is an increased feeling of affinity with past generations and a decrease in interest in superfluous social interaction. The individual might also experience a decrease in interest in material things and a greater need for solitary "meditation." Positive solitude becomes more important. There is also often a feeling of cosmic communion with the spirit of the universe, and a redefinition of time, space, life, and death.

However, gerotranscendence does not imply any state of withdrawal or disengagement, as is sometimes erroneously believed. It is not the old disengagement theory in a new disguise, as believed by some critics (e.g., Biggs, Hendricks, & Lowenstein, 2003). It is a theory that describes a developmental pattern beyond the old dualism of activity and disengagement. This book will explore this developmental pattern.

At the same time as the book gives a detailed account of the theory of gerotranscendence, it also describes how the theory was developed from the unsatisfying mismatch of common theoretical assumptions within gerontology and some empirical findings. This does not mean, of course, that all the established theories within social gerontology are useless, just that there are certain developmental patterns that they don't cover properly.

The book starts out with a discussion of the unsatisfying state of the art and what generally is needed in order to bring theory and certain empirical findings into harmony. The theory of gerotranscendence is then developed as an answer to this plea, starting out as a tentative outline in chapter 2, and followed in chapter 3 by a qualitative specification based on firsthand, in-depth interviews with individuals of a mature age who themselves have experienced the individual development in life, which we have come to call gerotranscendence.

In chapter 4 the gerotranscendence pattern is further elucidated by quantitative studies of various kinds. In chapter 5, the practical implications of the theory are brought into focus. Here you will find how the theory has been translated into guidelines for work within care settings. Finally, in chapter 6, you will find a summary of the preceding information and a conclusion. The appendix contains some suggestions for how to facilitate personal development towards gerotranscendence. This book is partly based on and further develops what previously has been written on the subject in different forums (e.g., by Tornstam from 1989 to 2003).

In order to make the book accessible for those who are not versed in research and technological matters, most of these technicalities have been placed in footnotes for those who need this information. If your interest is not academic, you can skip reading the footnotes and still acquire an understanding of the theory of gerotranscendence.

It should be carefully noted that the theory of gerotranscendence is not formulated with the aim of nullifying other theories within social gerontology. We however suggest that sometimes the old, well-known theories are just not applicable. Knowing about the theory of gerotranscendence can then be like the coin that makes the slot machine work, or like the new pair of eyeglasses that make you see the world in a new way—a theoretical tool that makes certain parts of reality comprehensible. We do not pretend that the theory of gerotranscendence is better or "normative free" in comparison with other theories, but rather that it covers certain aspects of individual aging processes which previously have not been sufficiently covered by social gerontology theory. It might be for such reasons that individuals time and again report that the theory of gerotranscendence captures much of their personal experiences of aging. In letters, phone calls, e-mails, and oral declarations after lectures, such testimonies have been given by a considerable number of individuals, ranging from retired university professors, a former ambassador, and a couple of novelists, to very ordinary, retired, white-collar workers and other working folk. These spontaneous testimonies tell us that the theory corresponds to the experiences of aging that a number of individuals have actually had.

CHAPTER 1

The Need for New Theories in Social Gerontology[1]

With this chapter, with its touch of critical gerontology, we hope to give the reader un understanding of why the idea of a new theory forced itself to the fore. Even if the chapter aims at demonstrating some insufficiencies in the common theories of social gerontology, it is not the same as arguing that all other theories are inadequate, just that they have obvious blind spots. But, as a starting point, let's listen to Eva, a former nurse whom we will learn to know better later on, who describes her changes in attitude towards life and herself in the following way:

> Using an analogy, earlier I used to feel that I was out on a river being carried away by the stream without being able to control it. Even if I wanted to go ashore, I couldn't control it; I was carried away both from pleasant and unpleasant things. But today I feel like the river. I feel like I'm the river. I feel that I'm part of the flow that contains both the pleasant and the unpleasant things.

She seems happy and satisfied with her life today and describes how she has come to change much of the understanding of herself and her life. She has discovered some self-infatuation with her younger self, at the same time as her sources of joy in life have changed:

> Well, earlier it may have been things like a visit to the theater, a dinner, a trip. I wanted certain things to happen that I was a little excited

---

[1]This chapter builds, with permission, in part on what previously was published in Tornstam, L., 1992a, The Quo Vadis of Gerontology; On the Gerontological Research Paradigm, *The Gerontologist, 32*(3), 318–326.

about. . . . My best times [now are] when I sit on the kitchen porch and simply exist, the swallows flying above my head like arrows. Or a spring day like this when I can go to my nettle patch and pick nettles for soup.

Eva pointed out that she is not at all religious. Nevertheless, she has come to accept science and faith as equal:

Some people stick with a natural science theory and other people stick with a religious theory. One theory is just as good the other. Some things are unanswered.

In relation to other people, Eva also has become a different person. Her need for positive solitude has increased, and she has become more restrictive in her choice of friends and company. She has abandoned the big circle of friends:

. . . I think it's more fun to . . . go to an older woman that I know, sit and talk to her. I get much more out of this than going to parties and being with a lot of people where you really don't talk so much with people.

How shall these changes be understood? Are they part of a negative withdrawal or a developing wisdom? Let's have a look on what theories in social gerontology have to offer.

The most useful practical tool for understanding is said to be a good theory. No surprise then that theoretical renewing is asked for repeatedly. In a description of the theoretical state of the art Bengtson, Burgess, and Parrot (1997) concluded that we still have some distance to go. More attention should be given to theory. At the very beginning of this new century this plea is still advocated as in, for example, a book with the title *The Need for Theory—Critical Approaches to Social Gerontology* (Biggs, Hendricks, & Lowenstein, 2003).

Theorizing within social gerontology has been organized regarding content and theoretical level as well as historical development (see, for example, Estes, Binney, & Culbertson, 1992; Bengtson, Parrott, & Burgess, 1996; Bengtson, Burgess, & Parrott, 1997), but this is not the place to account for this. It is sufficient to say that we are going to deal with theorizing on the micro to intermediate level, and with a developmental perspective focusing on the individual. It might also be mentioned that regarding the efforts to label and systematize theories, the theory of gerotranscendence has been placed in a box with the label "critical theory" (Bengtson, Burgess, & Parrott, 1997).

When theories are the target of discussions, however, we sometimes refer to different entities. Some of us only count as theories such a set of propositions (axioms) from which invariance hypotheses can be derived and tested quantitatively. We are then referring to formalized theories. Other definitions of a theory focus on the fact that a theory always is a way of comprehending reality, not necessarily by means of any system of formal axioms and hypotheses, but rather as a shorthand for understanding or characterizing a phenomenon. In the latter case, the way of classifying and understanding reality is more important than the set of axioms and hypotheses used to formalize this understanding. Stevens Barnum (1990) is an example of those having a definition close to the latter position, while Galtung (1969) exemplifies a position closer to the former, formalized understanding of what a theory is.

Our own opinion is that a theory first and above all has the mission to offer ways of understanding and comprehending reality. Forgetting this and focusing on the formal aspects only might lead to a fruitless and mechanical manipulation of details. So, when we take a look at some theorizing within social gerontology in what follows, it is with a focus on which ways of understanding reality the theories offer, not "if" or "how" these understandings are formalized.

Among the many ways of understanding what aging is about on the individual level, more or less overlapping perspectives can be mentioned. The following list of some common approaches is introduced for the purpose only of illustrating that we see different things depending on which pair of theoretical glasses we use. For a fuller description of the different theoretical approaches you will have to consult a general textbook on theories in social gerontology.

- The *pathological* perspective, which, according to common interpretations, more or less equates aging with disease, and interprets various behaviors in old age as manifestations of a physical or mental pathology. Already Aristotle described the aging process as a pathological affliction of the body (the classical metaphor *Senectus ipsa morbus*).

- The *activity* perspective (see Hooyman & Asuman Kiyak, 1988; Kelly, 1993), which according to common interpretations assumes that all kinds of physical and social activity is beneficial for the aging individual, and that lack of this can result in maladjustment.

- The *disengagement* perspective (Cumming, Newell, Dean, & McCaffrey, 1960; Cumming & Henry, 1961; Cumming, 1963), which, according to common interpretations, assumes an inherent and natural drive to disengage mentally and socially when growing old.

- The *continuity* perspective (Havens, 1968; Atchley, 1999), which, according to common interpretations, assumes a positive and natural urge to continue the midlife lifestyle and identity into old age.

- The *developmental* perspective as described by Erikson (1950, 1982), which, according to common interpretations, assumes a positive development of the identity into old age.

- The *Mask of Aging* perspective (Featherstone & Hepworth, 1991), which, according to common interpretations, assumes an increasing distance between the real inner self and the betraying aging body.

- The *masquerade perspective*, where, according to common interpretations, a masquerade in old age becomes part of a coping strategy to maintain identity as a means of keeping one's options open (Biggs, 2003, 2004).

- The *SOC perspective*, where, according to common interpretations, the behavior is understood as ways to cope with the difficulties in old age by means of Selection, Optimization and Compensation (Baltes & Baltes, 1990).

The interesting thing with the above and other perspectives is that the same behavior can be understood quite differently depending on which perspective you take. A lack of interest in participating in parties, as described by Eva, can be understood as differently as a symptom of a beginning dementia (the pathology perspective) or as a way to cope with reduced mobility by means of selecting where and how often to go to parties (the SOC perspective).

As mentioned in the introduction, it might be that our "understanding" of aging and how it ought to be, the normative part of the "understanding," is quite affected by our own position in life and society, and not randomly selected from the above mentioned and other possible perspectives. This should, however, not be any surprise, since sociology of science have taught us that science in general and social science, in particular social gerontology, never is absolute or final. It is selective and relative.

This relativity exists on several different levels. One level has to do with how the general ideas about aging and elderly people are relative to our own position in life, as described in the introduction to this book. Another level has to do with how the empirical knowledge is directed by the choice of theoretical points of departure. A third level has to do with how the choice itself of theoretical points of departure is relative to cultural and historical relationships. With illustrations from a number of studies, we will show how poorly many of the research findings correlate with our theoretical assumptions, and how difficult it is, despite this, to abandon the theoretical points of departure that we have chosen. We will argue that the usual theoretical points of departure for gerontological research only represent a narrow corridor in a theoretical field, which actually is much broader. We will also argue that it is not just by chance that we choose these very theoretical points of departure. The ways we chose to construct old age in our theories are directed not only by our own position in the life cycle, but also by an overflow of predominant, general values from society into science.

A national Swedish gerontology research project back in the 1970s, "The Elderly in Society," started with some theoretical points of departure that were partly new at that time. The most central of these was one which came to be called the *resource perspective*, which quickly gained great popularity. This perspective is close to what today is known as the *salutogenic* perspective (Antonovsky, 1987). As opposed to the, at that time, prevailing way to "construct" old age as a misery and old people as a burden, we were encouraged to see older people as resources. This new *resource* perspective would not only expose a number of popular public myths about the elderly, but would also call our attention to our own theoretical constructions within the discipline of gerontology.

The consciousness that the understanding of aging can be constructed from both a misery perspective and a resource perspective released new knowledge early in the research process. In the first research report from the project we (Tornstam, 1981) could show how younger people overestimated the problem-reality of the elderly, compared with how the elderly themselves defined it. The omission of the everyday reality of the elderly was guided by a misery perspective, rather than anything else. Further information of the same kind was presented later (Tornstam, 1983a) where it was shown that knowledge about the actual conditions of the elderly was vague and that it had a quite pessimistic coloring.

THE ROOT OF THE MISERY PERSPECTIVE

Why do our pictures of the elderly look the way they do? Why do we frequently depict the elderly as sicker, feebler, and more miserable than they are in reality? Above all, why do we still, in gerontology, nurture myths related to these negative images? The sociology of knowledge and the sociology of science give us some useful clues.

In the contemporary sociology of knowledge there is evidence that science is not as "scientific" as was once believed. Even if it had long been known that that the direction and speed of scientific development was related to the society in which it was developed, it was later accepted that the core content of science—the concepts, the theories, and the way of interpreting data—was also related to the society around the sheltered scientific community (Young, 1973; Lemaine, et al., 1976).

Much of the very substance of science is nothing but "common sense," which, imported from the surrounding society, becomes an integral part of recognized scientific practice (Elliot, 1974). Holton (1973) argued that all scientists import, from the surrounding society, basic presuppositions that inform and guide their work. They commit themselves to assumptions of conflict or consensus, development or equilibrium, or to a misery or resource perspective. These presuppositions are often taken as "givens," and can be looked upon as an unconscious overflow from society to science. In the following we are using the term *overflow* to refer not only to the input of basic presuppositions from society to scientific theory, but also to the fact that such basic presuppositions affect the way in which empirical research is carried out and interpreted.

As a typical example of this phenomenon, Mulkay (1979) analyzed the development of the Darwinian theory and concluded that it was based to a large extent on what he termed "informal thinking." The major interpretations proposed were not based directly on observation of biological phenomena. Rather they were taken over from practical activities and from the wider realm of philosophical, theological, and social debate to provide the framework within which the observations were given scientific meaning. Sometimes, as in the above-mentioned case, the overflow from society to science turns out to be fruitful; sometimes it can badly distort science, as in the case of Lysenko, described by Joravsky (1970). Based on dubious genetic research on vegetables, Lysenko came up with the suggestion that acquired qualities could be inherited. An idea which was appealing to the political leaders in the old U.S.S.R., who saw a possibility to create socialist individuals from birth. Lots of resources were invested in Lysenkos's research before the bubble burst in the mid 1960s. Today the name Lysenko stands for politically directed pseudoscience.

Gerontology, too, can be seen to participate in the use of societal overflow in formulating its theoretical points of departure. As Gubrium and Wallace (1990) pointed out, there are striking parallels between ordinary people's way of thinking about age and aging and the theoretical products of professional peers. Estes, Binney and Culbertson (1992) make a similar observation when they point out *functionalism* as a very powerful ideology affecting gerontology. Functionalism is " . . . *rooted in American traditions of individualism, self-reliance, and independence, and posits that cohesion and social harmony are* natural" (p. 51). Bengtson, Parrott, and Burgess (1996) conclude that there has not yet been any definable paradigmatic shift in gerontological theorizing. They herein include the very first steps towards the theory of gerotranscendence.

Our thesis is, however, that the overflow of functionalistic presuppositions, values, and "common sense" from white middle-class, middle-aged Western European society explains, in part, why gerontology nurtures some very persistent theoretical assumptions, even when the empirical reality contradicts the theories. As Hickey (1992) observed, there is quite much of the same in the way gerontologists have addressed their issues, despite seemingly new approaches and developments.

The Hidden Contempt for Weakness

White, Western, middle-class, middle-life society has, since the Reformation, been characterized by an overwhelmingly strong performance orientation. Productivity, effectiveness, and independence are prestige words.

What happens to those in our society who do not live up to the ideal of productivity, effectiveness, and independence? The Norwegian philosopher, Harald Ofstad (1972), has in a thought-provoking book, *Our Contempt for Weakness*, described what happens. Quite simply, we come to look down upon and hold in contempt those who are unproductive, ineffective, and dependent. To the extent that this applies to ourselves, we will do the same. We will regard ourselves with self-contempt. It is here we find the basis for contempt towards unproductive, ineffective, and dependent old people, and a basis for the mismatch between theory and empirical findings.

However, the value patterns of our society have several different cultural sources. One is the old Hebrew tradition, where age and wisdom are held in high esteem. This is in conflict with the value patterns that generate contempt for the elderly. Ofstad suggests that we tend to "solve" this conflict by hiding the contempt, or by changing it into something that allows it to be united with the respect for the elderly found in the Hebrew tradition.

What happens, according to Ofstad, is that we transform the contempt into a condescending pity. We feel so sorry for the poor, feeble, sick, and lonely old people. We feel so sorry for them to the extent that we force ourselves to "construct" them in a way that confirms that we are right when we feel sorry for them. It is a well-known psychological fact that we often perceive or construct reality in congruence with our need to apprehend it, rather than as it really is. We have a need to perceive the elderly as feeble and weak, in order for us to feel sorry for them. Thus, the false image of the elderly as miserable is produced, and we "solve" the problem of our contempt for unproductive, ineffective, and dependent old people. In other words, the myths—seen from this perspective—have the function of solving the problem of our contempt for weakness in the elderly.

If among the general population there is a value dependent tendency to adopt a misery perspective towards elderly people, we should not be surprised to find the same tendency within gerontology.

MYTHS WITHIN GERONTOLOGY

That the researcher also has a tendency to regard the elderly from a misery perspective was demonstrated by Åkerman (1981), who carried out a historical research project among elderly persons in a depopulated parish in northern Sweden. He had expected to find abandoned and lonely old people, but instead found well-integrated old people having a rich social life with good contact with their children. The expectations he had corresponded poorly with the reality he met, and he was sufficiently open to note the difference. In the conclusion of the research report Åkerman wrote:

> Our study has shown that the isolation and the fairly pitiable situation that is often conjured up in the press and on the radio and TV by no means seems to afflict all elderly people, even in a depopulated village. Contacts between the generations in our area of investigation have been unusually many and have been unusually intensive. On the whole, there seems to be reason to vigorously retouch the picture of pensioners as a marginalized group in society. (Åkerman, p. 43)

In the following, we will give a couple of examples of central "misery myths" within the discipline that have proved to have a very great vitality during the years. We will also try to further explain why the vitality of these myths is so great, and what is needed in order to reach a breakthrough in theoretical social gerontology.

The Supposed Effects of Modernization

The expectations Åkerman carried with him into his research project are not only derived from general mythical ideas about the elderly, but also from a well-established theoretical background which, at the same time, constitutes an example of how firmly entrenched these theoretical points of departure are, and how difficult they are to revise, even if the empirical reality contradicts the theories. The theoretical background in question focuses on the supposed conditions in the old peasant society, and the negative effects that the modernization of society by industrialization and urbanization is supposed to have had. But, for example, the concept of the happy, extended or three-generation family as the dominating pattern in the old peasant society has, however, been refuted relatively early from several quarters. Hansson (1980) referred to studies that show that neither in Sweden nor in other European countries has the percentage of house-holds with more than two generations ever gone beyond 7 percent, except in exceptional cases. In a convincing analysis, the English historian, Peter Laslett (1976), had earlier arrived at a similar conclusion in regards to England.

Contrary to the common assumption that the processes of industrialization and urbanization distanced older people and their children from each other, empirical studies have repeatedly shown that today's elderly, in general, stand out as being well integrated in society, and as having good contact with their children, with only a small minority being socially isolated (Babchuk & Beates, 1963; Shanas, 1968; Hess, 1972; Roos, 1975; Tornstam, 1978; Atchley, 2000). However, despite numerous empirical studies that contradict the mythical pictures, these myths seem to have a life of their own, unperturbed by contradictory research results. Even scholars find it difficult to abandon these myths. It may be that we hang on to our favorite theories in more ingenious ways.

Being conscious of the contradictory research results, Hareven (1978) once made the assumption that the good social integration and the good contact between the generations, that actually exist today among the elderly, are a result of the structural conditions in society that existed earlier. The idea is that the negative effects of industrialization and urbanization are not immediate, but instead make themselves felt after a couple of generations. In this respect, Hareven built on the theory of cultural lag formulated by Ogburn (1922).

This is an example of the ingenious way the researcher can save his or her favorite theory. Hareven's message was that the theory is correct, but that the effect that the theory presupposes has not had time to make itself apparent. The present good social integration and contact between the generations that gerontological studies document are taken to be a remnant of the good relations that existed earlier in society. Now, it just happens to be that these earlier conditions, at least in Europe, were not good at all. Historians have shown that the earlier conditions for the elderly rather could be characterized by poverty and heart-rending conflicts between generations, and by a poor social integration for the elderly (Gaunt, 1983; Odén, 1991, 2002).

It appears that we researchers have some difficulties in questioning the popular theoretical points of departure. Instead of doing so, we discover more and more ingenious ways of thinking in order to "preserve" our theories. So, not surprisingly, within the Swedish research program, "The Elderly in Society," we were also guilty of clinging to this favorite theory about the negative effects on the elderly of industrialism and urbanization. In the same way as Hareven did, we (Tornstam 1983b) referred to the theory of cultural lag in order to "explain away" the good social integration and the good contact between the generations which earlier empirical studies have shown. In fact, the purpose of one of the partial projects within the research program was to examine the effect industrialization and urbanization have had on solidarity between the generations. A hidden hypothesis was that if one just studies the conditions sufficiently and ingeniously, the negative effects will come to the fore. Without presenting a detailed account of the project in question, we would like to quote the conclusion that Hammarström (1986) arrived at after careful analysis:

> The main tendencies in the study that has been carried out are, thus, that macro-structural changes, such as changes on the labor market and urbanization and industrialization, hardly seem to have had an effect on relations between generations within the same family. (Hammarström, p. 229)

THE "RETIREMENT TRAUMA"

We have already pointed out that in Western society we strongly value productivity, effectiveness and independence. We also value ourselves and others in terms of our and their productivity, effectiveness and independence. When the overflow of these values is combined with role theory, it is not difficult to understand why gerontologists have focused on the importance of working life, or rather the negative effects of ceasing to be gainfully employed.

Many gerontologists have put forward the hypothesis of the negative effects of retirement, in regard to both psychological well-being and physical health. Even if the discussions sometimes have tried to take into account both positive and negative aspects of retirement, the very frame of reference has mostly taken its point of departure from negative aspects. Retirement has been described as a trauma with numerous negative aspects (Burgess, 1960; Miller, 1965; Maddox, 1968; Blau, 1973; Lowenthal & Robinson, 1976; Bradford, 1979; Bernard, 1982). The following quotation is typical:

> *In addition to his source of income, a man's job means a point of personal and social anchorage with considerable significance, both for the emergence and maintenance of a satisfactory self-identity and for the experience of adequate intercourse with his family and peers. Thus the argument has followed—and with considerable justification—that any tampering with the work role, the great balancing factor in life, runs the risk of creating a profound alienation and disequilibrium among the affected individuals. In an environment characterized by a religious devotion to work and peopled by individuals dedicated to conspicuous production as an important means of self-identification and self-justification, retirement would be expected to have social as well as economic significance. (Maddox, 1968, p. 359)*

The trauma of retirement is, however, not a general pattern, as we like to imagine. As early as 1971, Streib and Schneider presented a longitudinal study where 1,969 persons were followed into retirement. Among other things, they studied the subjective life satisfaction both before and after retirement, and did not find any appreciable differences. Atchley (1971, 1980), Parnes and Nestel (1981), and Palmore, et al. (1985) are examples of the many who have arrived at similar conclusions. Streib and Scheider bravely held that prevailing role theory did not seem to be applicable in the later life cycle, but that despite this, researchers continued to base their hypotheses on this theory, perhaps in order to acquire "scientific" arguments in order to bring about sociopolitical changes.

In the third edition of *The Encyclopedia of Aging*, Ekerdt (2001) concluded:

Early conceptions about possible retirement adaptation, developed while the retirement role was still gaining popular acceptance, foresaw retirement as a stressful transition and a "crisis" for personal identity. Research reports from longitudinal studies of workers' experience before and after retirement concluded instead that there is likely to be continuity of well-being and activities over the transition from work to retirement. . . . Contrary to the widely held notion that retirement often has negative consequences for health, epidemiological studies have consistently demonstrated that the event of retirement does not influence the risk of decline in physical or mental health. (p. 889)

Interestingly enough, the theoretical descriptions of the negative effects of retirement seem to persist, despite the findings of a number of empirical studies that contradict the theoretical assumptions and the growing knowledge within gerontology. It may even be that some writers try to rescue the "retirement shock" in a more intriguing way, almost touching on the concept of "false consciousness" on behalf of people who might have positive preretirement attitudes. Townsend (1986) thus wrote:

Those reaching retirement age do not welcome retirement as warmly as they thought they would or others suppose. Many who have retired deeply regret their inactivity or loss of status. . . . The satisfaction often expressed by many retired people turns on closer examination to be more an assertion of hope, or what they think is expected of them, than a true representation of what they feel. (p. 25)

Against the above background, it is illustrative how we also in Sweden have cherished the idea of the traumatic effects of retirement. At the laboratory for stress research between 1976 and 1978, a good thousand office workers were asked questions about their health and well-being immediately prior to retirement and about a year and a half after retirement. The analysis of the data was carried out within the framework of the research program, "The Elderly in Society," and was reported by Rehn (1984).

In the study, questions dealt with attitudes about retirement, financial situation, leisure-time activities, and social relations, and about medically treated illness and subjective medical problems. The idea behind the longitudinal study was to capture and describe the consequences of the "retirement shock." The results of the analysis showed, however, that these effects mainly were conspicuous by their absence. The dominant pattern revealed little or no changes in conditions before and after retirement. When there were changes, they were most often for the better. Regarding attitudes towards retirement and being retired, Rehn (1984) concluded:

> *The attitudes of the respondents to retirement were, in most cases, positive. Most of them also felt that retirement had come at the right time, and that it had been easy to get used to being retired. In the longitudinal perspective, the trend was such that even more felt that retirement was something positive, came at the right time and was easy to adjust to afterwards than in advance. (p. 5)*

In the *1985 Handbook of Aging and Social Sciences* Robinson, Coberly, and Paul made the observation that the assumptions of various miseries related to retirement seem to prevail in spite of contradictory evidence. It seems as if every new gerontologist starts out with the assumption of the existence of a "retirement shock," and gets surprised when empirical data contradict theory. Some then, as in the above Townsend example, explain the data away as wishful thinking on behalf of the respondents, while others accept the data as valid, and move towards new lines of thought, but still prefer to focus on the minority with problems, rather than asking the question why we bring with us all the misery expectations. In the preface to his book on continuity theory, Robert C. Atchley (1999) wrote:

> *For more than 30 years I have been interested in how people adapt to the changes associated with aging. I began my research in gerontology in 1963, with a study of how retirement influenced the self-concepts of retired women. . . .*
>
> *I . . . predicted negative effects for the self when women retired and thus no longer had a work identity. But [. . .] I was thoroughly impressed with the positive adjustment I found among both retired women schoolteachers and retired women telephone operators. . . .*
>
> *The observation that most people carried their occupational identity over into retirement and thus maintained their identity led to a preliminary statement of a theory of identity continuity (Atchley 1971). . . .*
>
> *Although in my studies only a very small minority of people experienced social withdrawal, declining morale, or declining physical health as a result of retirement, anecdotal and clinical reports still stress negative outcomes of retirement. I continued to be curious about the mechanisms that might cause people to have difficulty adapting to retirement. (p. ix–x)*

Thus, empirical studies do not reveal any general retirement shock pattern. If one wants to "rescue" the theory of the retirement trauma, one can, of course, argue that people under-report the problems they have, or that, when it regards longitudinal studies, the space of time between retirement and the follow-up measurement had been too short for the negative effects to make themselves apparent. This is the same time lag argument as Haraven (1978) used when trying to explain away the lack of empirical support for the assumption of the negative impact of modernization. If it was only one single longitudinal study at hand, such an "explanation" might possibly be accepted. However, since empirical reality time and again yields results that conflict with the assumption of the retirement trauma, we ought to turn our gaze from the explanations that have to do with "errors in methods" to explanations that have to do with "errors in theories."

But, in light of the above, it may not appear altogether surprising that very current studies also tend to focus on adaptive problems, health hazards and risks related to retirement, rather than applying a possible salutogenic perspective where the causes of health and well-being in retirement come to the fore. An example is a recent study by Angel, Buckley, and Sakamoto (2001), where the focus is on "nativity as a risk factor for poor physical and emotional health for an ethnically diverse population making the transition into retirement." The focus perpetually is on the presumed traumatic aspects of retirement.

The above reported dramatic differences between theoretical predictions and empirical research findings are just examples. The list can be made longer. Further examples would, for example, deal with failed intervention attempts that were based on the assumption that pensioners lack meaningful occupation, or the popular, but incorrect, notion of widespread loneliness among particularly old people.

However, in light of the subject of this book, the contradictory results within gerontological research have become so overwhelmingly troublesome that they generated an urge to examine the basic assumptions in the gerontological research paradigm.

THE SCIENTIFIC PARADIGM OF GERONTOLOGY

At first glance, it might appear that the theoretical points of departure within gerontology are considerably varied and essentially different, often diametrically opposed. When we replaced the misery perspective with the resource perspective in The Elderly in Society research program, we liked to see it as a completely new and different theoretical perspective. Our view is, however, that the misery perspective and the resource perspective can be referred back to the very same overflow of presuppositions and to the very same basic scientific paradigm, and that the resource perspective (as we applied it) may be nothing other than the old misery perspective in a new, ingenious, theoretical disguise.

It has been stressed that stereotyped ideas about aging and elderly people are linked with the need to categorize and systematize the reality that surrounds us (Tornstam, 1983c). The same is true, of course, for science in general and gerontology in particular. Scientific theories can be understood as special ways of categorizing and systematizing reality to make it understandable and to create order in life. Sometimes this need for order and understanding leads to oversimplification, which can partially explain a persisting tendency to focus on homogeneity and central tendencies in studies of aging rather than on variance and heterogeneity.

There was a time in the history of science when people thought there was a final way of categorizing reality, an order that was the final and correct one. In their book, *Science, Order and Creativity*, Bohm and Peat (1987) describe how the idea about the true order within the "firm" sciences evolved from classical antiquity to our time. As far back as the fourth century B.C., Aristotle wrote about an eternal order where everything had its given place in the natural scheme of things. During the Middle Ages, these ideas had such a strong impact that they became the basic foundation for religion, philosophy, and morality—indeed, for the whole white Western social order. These ideas came to be the central, basic assumptions upon which other scientific theories and assumptions about society rested. Within the theory of science we call these central and fundamental assumptions a scientific paradigm.

The conception of the world and the view of science in classical antiquity were to undergo the dramatic changes that Kuhn (1962) calls "scientific revolutions," even if later research within the sociology of science was to show that the changes were nor as abrupt as the word implies. Characteristic for such scientific revolutions is that the evidence against the old, basic assumptions has begun to become so overwhelming and troublesome that science finds itself in a crisis. Excuses made for troublesome research results no longer hold, and the paradigm changes in a painful but inevitable process.

The classic example of the significance of such a scientific revolution is when, in the 17th century, Newton and Galileo could crush the scientific paradigm that had been in existence since antiquity. In the Middle Ages people believed that the Earth was the center of the universe. All the other planets, including the sun, moved in orbit around the Earth in what was called the Ptolemaic system. Based on this cosmic system, this paradigm, theories within religion, physics and astronomy were formulated. When Copernicus suggested that the Earth and the other planets were in orbit around the sun, his hypothesis was nothing less than a revolutionary shift of paradigm. Not only the image of the cosmic system but all scientific theories were changed by this shift. When Copernicus suggested that the sun was the center, it caused so much fear and aggression that Galileo almost paid with his life when he advanced his ideas. Despite this extreme reaction the image of the cosmic system and all scientific theories were changed.

Along with Einstein's theory of relativity at the beginning of the previous century, another revolutionary change took place within physics: Newton's assumptions about the absolute nature of time and space were questioned. The theory of relativity demonstrated that time was not something absolute that moves through the universe with the same speed, but that the concept of time is dependent on the timeframe of the observer himself.

Along with quantum theory, another revolution took place within physics, whereby the entire mechanical world view was questioned. Assumptions about unambiguously defined paths of particles were questioned now, and new relativistic concepts about quantum conditions and energy levels were introduced. The whole idea from antiquity about the absolute and natural order of things has been replaced by a new insight that everything is relative. The so-called exact or firm sciences have become relative. Thus, a series of crises within physics developed and renewed the construction of scientific theories. Gerontological theory, we believe, is in need of and on the verge of such a transformation.

THE ABSOLUTE ORDER OF THINGS

In order to make a new orientation possible within gerontological theory, we must make visible the overflow of presuppositions from society and the borders of the paradigm that are now predominant. In our earlier discussion, we indirectly glimpsed these borders because a number of empirical studies had stumbled upon them.

Without getting into a discussion about the development and changes in the positivist view of science from the 18th century philosophers, David Humes and Auguste Comte, and the 19th century philosopher, Karl Popper, we would like to argue that gerontology, by and large, bears the mark of traditional positivism, even if some late efforts in a "third wave" of social gerontology have given some room to critical gerontology, in which the theory of gerotranscendence has been counted. We use the term *positivism* here in a generic sense, in the way the term has often been used in the modern criticism of, among other things, social research. More precisely, we mean that the following characteristics still constitute the borders of substantial parts of the prevailing research paradigm for gerontology:

1. We essentially regard the elderly as research objects. As researchers we define concepts and formulate theories, and it is the *behavior* of the elderly that, above all, interests us. By behavior, we are referring not only to activities of different kinds, but also to emotional reactions like life satisfaction.

2. The way in which we choose to define concepts and formulate theories is not in accordance with some natural order, but is only one of many possible ways. The way we choose to define concepts and formulate theories is affected by an overflow of presuppositions from society to gerontology. This overflow is sometimes strong enough to make us cling to our theories even when our data contradict them.

3. In particular, there is an overflow of mid-life values found in society at large, particularly among White Western, middle-class males (from whose ranks the majority of researchers have come), which means that our choice of conceptual delineations and theories carries the (sometimes hidden) stamp of values that emphasize productivity, effectiveness, and independence. We assume that old age implies the continuity of mid-life values. Yet, these values may become less important to us as we age.

4. The points of departure we choose lead to certain theories being predominant within gerontology rather than others. Examples of such theories are the *interactionist* efforts that are reflected in role theory and activity theory, and in the so-called *social breakdown syndrome* that during certain times has been very popular within gerontology.

5. We force upon the elderly our own value-dependent theories, which at the same time means that deviations from the theoretical predictions are looked upon as being abnormal, pathological, or whatever term we decide to use. It could, of course, be argued that all theories are value dependent, with the theories of gerontology being no exception. But, in the case of gerontology (as in other fields) the values imposed by the theorists are not necessarily the values held by the research objects themselves.

6. The experiments we undertake are unwittingly manipulative in the sense that their purpose is to bring about that which we—with our (often hidden) value-dependent, theoretical points of departure—define as normal or healthy behavior.

We can illustrate the above points with many gerontological research projects. For example, in the longitudinal research project described earlier (Rehn, 1984), where a survey was made of people immediately before retirement and a year and a half afterwards, the researchers, in effect, carried out a quasi-experiment, in which retirement constituted the experimental "manipulation." We wanted to see how the "subjects" reacted to this manipulation. These subjects could just as well have been rats or rabbits since in no way could they influence the theoretical construction of the experiment or its practical application. The researchers alone defined the concepts and variables that were regarded as important to study in relation to the retireees. Many of these had to do with the presence of medically treated illnesses and subjective symptoms of illnesses. The researchers tended to adopt a perspective whereby retirement was not only seen as a stress factor (which, of course, is a natural thing to do in a laboratory for stress research), but was also medicalized and its effects made into an illness.

The values that lie behind this way of looking at retirement and its effects stem from the aforementioned cultural emphasis on productivity, effectiveness, and independence. *The value of work* lay behind the whole investigation and it was the negative effects of losing this "candy" that were looked for. It is probable that work has a special value for the younger and middle-aged researchers involved in a project like this, but this does not necessarily mean that other people, in other age groups, attach the same value to work.

The emphasis on productivity, effectiveness, and independence makes itself felt in another way in investigations of this kind. Old people are expected to be active—mentally, physically, and socially. They are expected to exercise, to be responsible for their health. To the extent that we researchers think that old people are not sufficiently active or responsible for their health, we start intervention programs in order to make our "guinea pigs" behave the way we want them to. Juul-Jensen (1984) once wrote about gerontological researchers in this respect:

> *We not only interest ourselves in what we shall do as young people in order to retain our vitality and health in old age. We speak, in one way, on behalf of the elderly. We profess to know what it is that can secure a meaningful life for the elderly, marked by the striving of the individual to realize himself to the end. . . . We see in front of us the image of the vigorous citizen, who—with a smile on his lips—realizes his life, while he runs into death. One cannot avoid the following criticism: researchers make the catastrophic mistake of depicting a value, an ideal for a younger group in modern industrial society, as though it could be the fundamental value for old people in general. (p. 113)*

We place our own theoretical cap over the heads of old people without thinking that our own points of departure for assessment are relative. "Passive" pensioners who do not share a "normal" interest in career work, leisure-time activities, and keep-fit measures are regarded as problematic and in need of activation. And, in order to achieve this activation, we start experiments that will make the elderly behave the way we and our theories would like them to.

Behind the elegant resource perspective, a misery perspective is hidden in a new guise, where responsibility for the misery of aging becomes the responsibility of the individual. If one is not active and does not keep fit, then one has only oneself to blame. If one reaches old age in illness and isolation, then one has "not taken care of" oneself during one's life and is deserving of contempt. There is a risk that the healthy and successful old people will be admired at the same time that we look down on those who have not made the most of their talents. A new ideal of productivity and effectiveness is emerging, namely, *to properly manage one's life, and to actively participate in preventive activities of various kinds.*

Of course it is an advance to have changed the perspective from one where passive elderly people are cared for to a perspective where the initiatives and resources of the elderly themselves are utilized. However, a new problem is hidden here. When we emphasize the importance of the initiatives and the resources of the elderly themselves, we may also shift too much of the responsibility for the conditions of aging over to old people themselves. It becomes a private matter for the traveler whether the final station is comfortable or miserable. At the start of the Swedish Elderly in Society research program, we formulated the overall goal thus:

> *The research problem for the interdisciplinary project—from an overall perspective—has been set in such a way that it is a matter of finding solutions to how long it is possible to postpone the transition for aging people from an independent, active group to a dependent group. For the individual, such a lengthened period of activity would mean a richer and more substantial life; for collective groups and families living together, a new resource in regard to time and experience and for society a possibility of keeping health costs down. Fundamentally, in such a case, the purpose of medical and social intervention will be to stimulate continued activity and to prevent pathological changes. (Tornstam, Odén, & Svanborg, 1982, p. 9)*

This clearly shows not only that the fundamental points of departure for our entire research program are based on values that emphasize independence and activity, but that there is also an economic interest. The use of the initiatives and resources of the elderly were put forth as a way to save society money for their care—at a time when the high cost for the care of the elderly appeared on the political agenda. This is, at the same time, a good example of another general phenomenon in science. As described by Mazur (1973) and Nelkin (1975), scientists often align their science with the political debate, which is another aspect of the overflow from society to science.

THE FUNCTION OF MYTHS WITHIN SCIENCE

What is it that keeps scientists, in general, and gerontologists, in particular, tied in a predominant paradigm with such strength that time and again we adhere to our theories even if they are undermined by empirical findings? Uncovering the ties, from micro to macro levels, that restrain us in this way is the first step to freeing ourselves from them.

Our Human Lack of Perfection

Part of the explanation as to why we cling to old, well-worn concepts and theories has to do quite simply with the fact that, as gerontologists, we are just ordinary people with common limitations and shortcomings.

Anthropologists know that people, in general, find it very difficult to see the distinguishing characteristics of the culture they are living in. One sees one's culture as being something that is self-evident, and one tends, instead, to look upon foreign cultures as being exactly that—foreign. From this perspective, the myths we have within our discipline are nothing else but the distinguishing characteristics of our culture, which give us a feeling of security and order in our everyday lives.

Another well-documented human shortcoming is the fear of change. It often feels more secure to be able to trust something familiar and lasting, instead of embarking upon the new and untested. There is certainly a strong resistance to arguing against what one understands to be established conditions. One technique for opening these locks can be to construct a more anthropological view within gerontology, or to involve anthropologists who are given the task of freely analyzing the culture within our discipline as though it were a newly discovered foreign culture in the depths of the rain forests of South America. It is a positive sign that the Gerontological Society of America at the beginning of the 1990s opened an informal section of humanists, with a more critical and humane research approach.

Distinguishing Characteristics of the Scientific Society

The scientific society, like other types of societies, operates with quite a few control and ejection mechanisms. Storer (1966) talked about an internal police system in science. It is necessary to keep within the established frameworks if one wants to avoid reprisal. Anarchistic elements are not really taken seriously since they go beyond the established borders of the research society. But perhaps we ought to give these kinds of anarchistic elements support instead of expelling them. This is very difficult to do, however, since the myths found within the discipline have the function of consolidating and closely knitting together the scientific society, as we know it.

The Solidification of the Status Quo

When we have argued that the chosen theoretical points of departure actually constitute reflections or overflow of the ideals that are strongly emphasized in parts of our Western society, we are hinting at another function of the mythical pictures within the discipline. Quite simply, it is a question of confirming and strengthening these ideals, solidifying and asserting the "correctness" of certain norms and the modus operandi of our society. By carrying out "scientific studies," we produce support for our culture's strong work orientation and our glorification of productivity, effectiveness, and independence. Also, as Olsen (1982) has argued, most gerontological theories imply an individual adaptation to the existing social arrangements of old age. As put by Gubrium and Wallace (1990), the theories analytically reproduce and empirically confirm ordinary, old-style liberal or conservative sentiments, not radical or existential ones. The flow goes back from science to society in a presupposition-confirming way, and gerontological theory is at risk of being petrified.

"Scientific" Arguments for Desirable Sociopolitical Measures

Many gerontological researchers have embarked upon this research area for humanitarian reasons; the author of this book being no exception. We have—often quite rightly so—felt that the elderly have been treated badly, and we want to contribute to making improvements in various respects. By research contributions of different kinds, we wanted to illustrate the different ways in which the elderly have a difficult time so that politicians and other decisionmakers would have strong arguments for making certain sociopolitical changes. With such a fundamental point of departure for the scientific work, it is not difficult to understand why the descriptions of aging and the conditions of the elderly easily led to a "misery perspective." Making various miseries visible is usually the best argumentation for new sociopolitical measures, and the myths within the discipline serve the purpose of making "scientific" arguments for the desired changes. Gerontological research shows quite a few examples of interpretations of reality seen from a problem-elevating perspective, the purpose of which has been precisely to bring about sociopolitical changes or other kinds of changes intended to improve the conditions of the elderly.

Now, of course, we do not argue that it is reprehensible to try to make visible the problems that are visited upon on the elderly. This should continue to be one of the tasks of gerontological research. However, the problem arises when we go over to being advocates for the elderly to such an extent that we start to manipulate our science. In certain cases such a manipulation can take place consciously and premeditatedly by holding back research results that do not fit, or by presenting them in a way that serves the goal one wishes to attain. In other cases we unconsciously choose concepts or theories that agree with the purpose of making problems visible and bringing about change.

We would like to dare make the statement that for most gerontologists there is a point of departure of this kind. We have a basic humanitarian wish to contribute to improvements being made for the elderly. This desire has certainly been stimulated by a research policy emphasizing that research should be "relevant to society" in the sense that it should be converted into practical measures as fast as possible. In this case, useful, practically-applied research has been emphasized in preference to basic research.

Once again it must be repeated that there is nothing wrong with this type of incentive to gerontological research. However, at the same time, it must be understood that this incentive presents a problem. It is difficult to prevent the choice of research paradigm from being directed by the mentioned incentive. The choice of conceptual apparatus and theoretical points of departure are chosen so that they fit the purpose of making visible problems and bringing about changes. This might take place at the expense of other choices of perspective, which, from the point of view of basic research, can be more interesting.

The sum total of this problem is that the individual gerontologist must ask himself the questions 1) to what extent is the humanitarian motive a driving force in the research, and 2) in what way does it guide the choice of conceptual limitations and theoretical points of departure. Overall, we gerontologists must try to think a little more freely and boldly in order to widen the theoretical perspective of our discipline. We must dare to question the "sacred cows" that our traditional theories constitute and break the bounds of our theoretical corral.

BREAKING THE BOUNDS

One way of breaking the bounds of the predominant gerontological paradigm might be quite simply to reverse the gerontological research paradigm in order to see which concepts and theories would then come to the fore. Such a reverse paradigm should not be seen as the new indisputable one, but rather as an intellectual tool that might help us to see things we have not seen earlier, and to teach us how to break out of the traditional paradigm.

An experimental reverse gerontological paradigm might look like this: It is not the researchers who define concepts and theories in the first place, but the elderly themselves. Concepts and connections take their form from the way old people themselves structure and discern reality. This leads to a different research effort whereby the elderly cease to be research objects and instead become co-creating subjects. As earlier suggested by imaginative gerontologists (e.g., Neugarten, 1977; Coleman, 1990), the phenomenological research effort comes to the fore. The phenomenological research effort, like modern physics, has as its starting point the insight that there is no single truth, nor any absolute natural order of things. Here, one strives to get new images to emerge from reality. Above all, one tries to free oneself from the limiting conceptual world of the researcher in order to, instead, attach greater importance to the conceptual world that is defined by others—e.g., by the research objects themselves (Spinelli, 1989). As expressed by Coleman (1990), the researcher, rather than in the positivist tradition looking for causal or mechanistic explanations of observed behavior, ought to be encouraged to seek a fuller description and understanding of behavior and consciousness by elaborating the meaning that it has for the individual. May we suggest that this could take the following form:

1. We consciously choose to try to replace the overflow presuppositions with alternative ones, and let these alternative prepositions direct the conceptual and theoretical development. In practice we would allow ourselves to play with the thought that ineffectiveness, unproductiveness, and dependency are guiding values. This could result in focusing on concepts such as rest, relaxation, comfortable laziness and play, and creativity and wisdom.

2. If the strong emphasis on the points of departure for the role and activity theories is toned down, then theories with their points of departure in, for example, philosophy and anthropology can come to throw new light on gerontological research.

3. With a reverse definition of what is regarded as normal or pathological, there will be new tasks of understanding, for example, why some elderly people hang on to the mid-life ideal of productive work and self-punishing exercise programs, and why we, in various keep-fit programs place sole responsibility on the individual, thus creating a sense of failure in those reluctant or unable to meet our expectations.

Without an attempt to break free from the traditional, sometimes mythical gerontological presumptions, it might quite possibly be that we carry out research work and care that, in certain cases, are incompatible with the metatheoretical paradigm that defines reality for aging individuals in the real world. Perhaps we force upon some elderly people a paradigm that they, themselves, no longer inhabit.

Of course, it is not easy to free oneself from the paradigm that one is used to and to change the metatheoretical conditions for the scientific work. Just to discern the borders of the paradigm one is working within can be as difficult as it is for a fish to become conscious of the water in which it swims. Therefore, we cannot claim to be able to offer the new "quantum theory" of gerontology. The theory of gerotranscendence is, however, an attempt to renew some of the traditional ways of thinking while working within the framework of the above principles for breaking theoretical boundaries.

CHAPTER 2

Origin of the Theory and First Outline[2]

The theory of gerotranscendence was, as described in the previous chapter, born of the uncomfortable knowledge and insight that not only much of the empirical data didn't match the prevailing theories, but also that certain theoretical attempts had been furiously discarded. Maybe the baby had been thrown out with the bathwater?

When Cumming, Newell, Dean, and McCaffrey (1960) first published their tentative disengagement theory of aging, followed by an elaboration (Cumming & Henry, 1961), the theoretical gerontological discussions turned into something like a riot. The theory assumed an intrinsic tendency to disengage and withdraw when growing old, which was supposed to go hand in hand with the tendency of society to reject aging individuals. The individual was, according to the theory, supposed to gradually cut his/her bonds with society and, to an increasing extent, turn inward. This two-way process was supposed to be, both for the individual and society, inevitable and functional. As a preparation for death, the individual and society were thought to gradually disengage from each other. This disengagement does not, according to the theory, involve dissatisfaction or mental problems on the part of the individual. On the contrary, since disengagement was supposed to be a natural process, it was associated with satisfaction and inner harmony. According to this theory, disengagement is a culture-free concept, but its specific expressions are invariably culture bound.

---

[2]This chapter builds, with permission, in part on what previously was published in Tornstam, L., 1989, Gero-transcendence: A Meta-theoretical Reformulation of the Disengagement Theory, *Aging: Clinical and Experimental Research*, Vol 1, Nr. 1: 55–63; Milano.

In principle, the disengagement theory generated three types of hypotheses. The first hypothesis states that all societies, in one way or the other, push the aging individual away. The second hypothesis states that the individual, motivated by intrinsic forces, disengages from society. This individual disengagement is both social and psychological. Social disengagement refers to the reduction of social interaction and the reduction of social roles and the amount of time spent in each role. Psychological disengagement refers to the reduction of ego involvement, interest, and emotional involvement in other people and society as such and, in its place, a disengaged turning inwards. The third hypothesis assumes that the individual, despite social and psychological disengagement, continues to experience a high degree of life satisfaction, happiness, and contentedness. This third hypothesis also implies indirectly a decrease in satisfaction if the natural process of disengagement is violated and old people are forced into various activities. Thus, the main premise of the activity theory—that activity leads to satisfaction and contentment—was disputed by the disengagement theory.

The disengagement theory not only ran counter to the widely accepted activity theory, but also to the personal values held by many gerontologists, and their wishes for what reality ought to be like—a continuation of their middle-aged, middle-class Western lifestyle. And, additionally, as many gerontologists enter the field of gerontology with a mixed humanistic and scientific approach—having the feeling that old people are treated badly and wanting to study this scientifically—it is not surprising that the theory of disengagement was perceived as threatening and uninviting. From a humanistic point of view, the very word *disengagement* has negative overtones. Consequently, much time and effort were spent during the 1960s and 1970s to refute or modify the theory theoretically and empirically. The author of this book indeed participated in this campaign.

A series of modifying or alternative explanations to the empirically observable pattern of disengagement was offered. The theory in its original raw shape was apparently unacceptable. As the empirical data neither supported, nor totally refuted the theory (which was also the problem with the theory of activity), the theory could be disarmed by modification. Cumming (1963) herself modified the theory by stating that the process of disengagement is not universal but dependent on personality types.

All three hypotheses mentioned above have been the target of research for many gerontologists. Everyone seems to agree with the statement that Western societies reject old people. This agreement is also the only indisputable support for the disengagement theory. The second hypothesis, which states that the individual disengages socially and psychologically, has been dismissed by almost every gerontologist. Most gerontologists, including the author of this book, agreed that individual disengagement was non-existent, and even if some "disengagement behavior" existed, it was dependent on something other than an intrinsic drive to disengage (Desroches & Kaiman, 1964; Videbeck & Knox, 1965; Kapnick, et al., 1968; Palmore, 1968; Thomae, 1969; Tornstam, 1973).

Many gerontologists have been particularly interested in testing the third hypothesis and focusing the causes of life satisfaction and contentment in old age—activity, disengagement, or something else. Lowenthal and Boler (1965) argued, for example, that the lack of sufficient support for the hypothesis that activity leads to well-being and contentment must be understood in terms of *deprivation*. A voluntary reduction of the social network and social engagement differs from an involuntary reduction. Havens (1968), on the other hand, gave prominence to the continuity of life patterns as the cause of life satisfaction and contentment in old age; the important thing is neither activity nor disengagement, but *continuity*. Tissue (1971) presented ideas similar to those of Lowenthal. The cause of dissatisfaction is the discrepancy between the social network the individual has and the one he/she would like to have. Lowenthal and Haven (1968) pointed to the fact that the research usually fails to distinguish between the quantitative and qualitative aspects of social interaction. If we only measure the quantity of social interaction we end up with weak correlations between interaction and satisfaction.

Finally, social gerontology was supplied with a new model which completely reduced the disengagement pattern to social psychology. Kuypers and Bengtson (1973) took their point of departure from a model formulated by Zusman (1966) and introduced the concept of a social breakdown syndrome. Zusman's model described the process by which the individual's social environment interacts with his/her self-perception in the production of a negative spiral—a social breakdown. Kuypers and Bengtson transferred the model to social gerontology and presented at the same time a model of social reconstruction, which described how the negative disengagement pattern could be broken. If some kind of "disengagement behavior" could be observed, it was the result of an externally produced social breakdown spiral, which, by proper means, could and should be reverted. The original disengagement theory had now been given the coup de grace.

After this, the disengagement theory was referred to almost with disdain. Hardly any gerontologist dared to state anything but that the theory was false. The defeating of the disengagement theory was buoyed by an almost "religious" conviction of its incorrectness. This emotional vindication of the incorrectness of the theory resembles other "isms" (Communism, Protestantism, racism, etc.) where, after some time, devotion to the ism veils the reality. This possibility contributed to a curiosity to take a new look at the theory—with a new metatheoretical perspective—to see if the outcome might throw some light on the aforementioned discrepancies between gerontological theory and empirical findings.

This curiosity was sustained by some indicators suggesting that certain theoretical aspects might have been hidden in the shadow of the disengagement theory. One such "unscientific" indication was a personal conversation with the Polish gerontologist, Jerzy Piotrowski, with whom the author of this book had the pleasure of collaborating during a research period in Warsaw in 1975. While discussing with him the disengagement theory and its countertheories, we were both of the opinion that the disengagement theory was incorrect. Our discussion was renewed at the 11th International Congress of Gerontology in Tokyo in 1978. On this occasion Piotrowski suggested that the disengagement theory perhaps did trail some theoretical strength behind it after all. Maybe we had thrown the baby out with the bath water was Piotrowski's suggestion. When asked what new evidence could be presented to support this opinion, Jerzy stated, "The evidence comes from within myself."

Other indications came from subjective reports of staff members working with old people. On several occasions they reported having very mixed feelings when trying to "activate" certain old people. They maintained that activity is good, but they nevertheless confessed feeling that they were doing something wrong when they tried to drag certain old people to various forms of arranged social activity or activity therapy. They felt as if they were trespassing on something they rather ought to respect and leave alone.

Even other, more "solid" indications, as mentioned earlier, contributed to the suggestion that the disengagement theory perhaps did trailshadow some theoretical strength behind it. In particular, it was at that time, my personal study of experiences of loneliness among Swedish inhabitants age 15 to 80 years (Tornstam, 1988) where it was shown, contrary to general assumptions, that the degree of loneliness decreased with every consecutive age group, despite their role losses and other losses. It was the young respondents, not the old ones, who reported the highest degrees of loneliness. It was also shown that the positive effect of social interaction with other people, as a remedy for loneliness, decreased for every consecutive age group.

THE PARADIGMATIC CONTEXT OF THE DISENGAGEMENT THEORY AND ITS COUNTER-THEORIES

Although the old disengagement theory and its counter theories seem to be very different, they flourish within the same paradigmatic framework. This framework is a rather common positivist one, in which the individual is regarded as an object directed by internal and external forces and the researcher is mainly interested in the behavior of the individual. It is also the researcher who defines the key concepts and what is considered "normal."

Also typical for these kinds of theories is the assumption of a common and shared definition of reality and the existence of general invariances or "laws"—sometimes qualified a bit by, for example, describing how the disengagement process can be slightly different for people with different personalities.

What was missing in order to make both disengagement theory as well as the theory of activity correspond with the empirical reality was the lever of a paradigmatic shift. To illustrate the point and in order to open the mind for doing something similar in gerontological theory, we will use two well-known and clear examples from other fields.

Everybody is familiar with the classic psychological double picture, in which you see either two faces turning toward each other—or a chalice. Depending on one's perspective, one or the other of the pictures appears. What is background in one of the versions becomes foreground in the other. When the observation paradigm is changed in this way, the picture of the reality under observation also changes. In science there are many examples of how the picture of reality was modified when the theoretical paradigm was changed. The classic example of the importance such a change can bring is when the Ptolemaic cosmology was substituted with the Copernican system, as earlier described. When Copernicus suggested that the Earth and the other planets were in orbit around the sun, his postulate was nothing less than a revolutionary shift of paradigm. Not only the picture of the cosmic system but all scientific theories were changed by this shift.

In a much more modest way, such a paradigmatic shift is necessary for a new theoretical understanding of aging. A few gerontologists have in fact approached such a shift. Hochschild (1976), for example, argued that the patterns of "engagement" or "disengagement" must be phenomenologically understood. What is lacking when it concerns the disengagement pattern is an understanding of the meaning the individual imparts to "engagement" or "disengagement"—not the meaning the gerontologist attributes to it.

Gutman (1976) did, in fact, move towards such a phenomenological description of the "disengagement pattern." In a cross-cultural study of Americans, Navajo Indians, low- and highland Maya Indians, and Druzes, TAT-tests of young and old men were compared. The TAT is a projective test, where ambiguous drawings are shown, and the tested person asked to tell what is going on in the drawing. When telling this, the person projects his or hers own values, expectations, and definitions of reality into the picture.

Gutman found a common pattern in all societies: young men demonstrated what was called *active mastery* in their projections of the TAT-pictures, while the old men demonstrated *passive mastery* or *magical mastery*. For example, young men projected more competitiveness and aggressiveness into the pictures, while old men projected more solidarity, understanding, and harmony.

At the same time as Gutman observed this cross-cultural tendency toward passive mastery and magical mastery in old men, he also observed that this tendency was socially anchored among the Druze, but not among Americans. In the Druze culture the tendency toward passive mastery and magical mastery were found to be connected with leadership, activity, and engagement. In America the same tendencies were connected with social inactivity. In conclusion Gutman summarized:

> . . . it is the movement toward passive and magical mastery that appears to be universal, not the movement toward disengagement.

Gutman was moving toward a paradigmatic shift but ultimately stopped himself by creating a dichotomy between disengagement and the universal tendencies of passive and magical mastery. His perspective remained traditional, since the behavior of the individual also was interpreted as a functional instrument for mastering a new situation. The behavior was seen as a coping strategy—not as a developmental qualitative difference in how young and old men define reality. To reach a new understanding we have to switch to quite another kind of metatheoretical paradigm.

EXPERIMENTAL THINKING WITH AN ALTERNATE METATHEORETICAL PARADIGM

To find way to a new meta-theoretical paradigm we shall leave the ordinary positivist way of thinking and instead, as an intellectual experiment, turn to the exotic and strange frame of reference offered by Eastern philosophy. We are going to contrast our understanding of the world with what a Zen Buddhist would probably have. This does not in any way mean the advocating of Zen Buddhism as misunderstood by some (e.g., Jönsson & Magnusson, 2001). It is just an example of turning our ordinary way of thinking upside down in order to get a new view of things—a technique suggested earlier in this book. So, the following is experimental thinking, based on guesses of how Zen Buddhists possibly might construct their world.

The Zen Buddhist probably lives within a cosmic world paradigm where many boundaries are diffuse and permeable. He probably looks upon Westerners as limited and trapped in an obsessive, materialistic pattern. When we, with our metatheoretical perspective, observe the Zen Buddhist lost in meditation, it is not unlikely that we end up labeling him as "disengaged." We would almost certainly do so if we did not know that he was a Zen Buddhist.

According to the metaperspective held by Zen Buddhists, however, it is not at all a matter of disengagement. The Zen Buddhist lives in a world that is defined differently from ours. In this world much of the difference between subject and object is erased. The statements made by a Zen Buddhist are often difficult to understand from the point of view of our metatheoretical paradigm—for example, that you and I not are separate objects but parts of the same entirety. Past, present, and future are not separate but exist simultaneously.

It should be mentioned that this way of thinking is not totally foreign to Western philosophy—even if it has been virtually nonexistent within gerontology. In his theories of psychology, C. G. Jung (1953) described the *collective unconscious*, referring to the fact that in our minds we have inherited predispositions that are reflections of the experiences of earlier generations. The collective unconscious embraces structures and predispositions that unify both generations and individuals. There are no boundaries between individuals, generations, or places. Some of Jung's followers believe that you can get in touch with this collective unconscious through meditation. Much of the initial train of thought regarding gerotranscendence did, in fact, arise from an early lecture of Jung (1930), where he stated that the meaning and the tasks of old age are quite different from the meaning and the tasks of mid-life. In the first part of life the task is getting acquainted with and socialized to society, whereas the task in old age is getting acquainted with yourself and with the collective unconscious. Much of this can be understood as a transcendental change in the definitions of reality. In modern language a de- and re-construction of the reality—much in line with what might be regarded as strange and odd with a Zen Buddhist. In his 1930 lecture Jung also stated that is a tragedy in our part of the world that the developmental tasks of the second half of life seem unknown to most people. We lead our lives with the erroneous apprehension that continuing with the tasks of the first half of life is all there is. As a consequence many of us meet our death as only half-developed individuals, exhibiting signs of depression, despair, fear of death, and disgust with ourselves and others, together with a feeling that life has been uncompleted or wasted. Jung's lecture implies that other (non-Western) cultures might be better aware of the special developmental tasks of the second half of life.

At any rate, here we can find a link between Eastern and Western philosophy. Erich Fromm (1960) points to other links between Western psychiatry and Zen Buddhism. We mention this since venturing into a foreign, strange metaworld might feel safer if we can hold hands with a couple of well-known Western philosophers.

However, the Zen Buddhist would probably never agree to being labeled as "disengaged." Rather, he would call himself *transcendent* in the sense that he lives in another, more boundary-free world compared with most of us from Western societies. His engagement is substantial, but according to a definition other than ours. That is why we might reach the conclusion that before our very eyes we have an individual who is ignorant of the world and disengaged.

Now, let us suppose that, without thinking about it, we become more and more like the Zen Buddhist, figuratively speaking, when we age.

Suppose that, without knowing anything about Zen Buddhism or transcendence, we reach a certain degree of transcendence. Some of us might even reach a high degree of transcendence—entering a new metaworld with new definitions of reality. These definitions might seem to be much less restricted than the "normal" definitions held by social gerontologists. Then we would end up with a remarkable situation in which researchers with one paradigm try to study individuals who are living according to another one—just as if Ptolemy, working from his paradigm, should try to describe and interpret the theories of Copernicus.

Let's suggest that aging, or rather living, implies a process during which the degree of transcendence increases from young adulthood and on. If looking at the full age range we might even find a U-shaped correlation with age. As small children we live in a world with a higher degree of transcendence, where the borders between you and me, now and then, fantasy and reality, are permeable. Gradually these borders are established according to the rules and definitions given by our culture. Later on, in young adulthood, these borders again become permeable and the degree of transcendence increases. The kind of transcendence we experience as small children could be termed *paedotranscendence* as distinguished from the *gerotranscendence* we can reach in old age. This, however, in no way implies that gerotranscendence means returning to childhood. Instead, we suggest that the condition of gerotranscendence is reached by a process where all the experiences in earlier life are included. Therefore, at the same time we suggest that the process towards gerotranscendence is generated by normal living. Let's also suggest that this process is intrinsic and culture free, but modified by specific cultural patterns.

In principle, it might be assumed that the process towards gerotranscendence, after young adulthood, is a life-long and continuous one. In practice, however, this process might be both obstructed and accelerated. The process toward gerotranscendence might, for example, be accelerated by a life crisis, after which the individual totally restructures his/her metaworld instead of resigning him/herself to the former one. This accelerated restructuring of the metaworld has been described in many cases of young individuals facing death as a result of a fatal disease. It should be emphasized that, in our interpretation, this is not the same as a defense mechanism, which always functions within the former metaworld. As we see it, both the classic defense mechanisms and the processes of coping take place within a given metatheoretical framework, whereas gerotranscendence refers to a shift away from this framework.

It is presumed that the process toward gerotranscendence also can be impeded. It is most probable that certain elements in our culture, for example, hinder this process. Social gerontologists themselves might contribute to its obstruction. We shall return to this question later. If we, however, accept the idea that the process towards gerotranscendence can be both obstructed and accelerated, we will as a consequence find many different degrees of gerotranscendence in old people. Not everyone will automatically reach a high degree of gerotranscendence. It is rather expected to be a process, which, at very best, culminates in a new gerotranscendent perspective.

The idea of a life process which optimally ends with gerotranscendence recalls the developmental model formulated by Erik H. Erikson (1950, 1982). According to this model the individual develops through seven stages and, if all goes well, ends up in an eighth stage, which Erikson calls *ego-integrity*. At this stage the individual reaches a fundamental acceptance of his/her own life—regardless of how good or bad it has been. The individual looks back and feels satisfied with the past. Erikson's eighth stage and what is referred to as the stage of gerotranscendence differ on this point. In their interviews with Gutman (1976) the old Druze males, who by our terms had reached the stage of gerotranscendence, did not look back on their past lives with pure satisfaction. Rather, they considered themselves as ignorant when they lived in the former meta-world and were reluctant to look back at this immature period in life with proud satisfaction only.

According to Erikson's theory, if the individual does not reach the eighth stage of ego-integrity, he/she experiences despair and fear of death. The positive personality characteristic during this eighth stage is wisdom, while its negative opposite is disgust and contempt. The individual who reaches this eighth stage also recognizes ego-integrity in others who have come to the same destination. Erikson is, however, rather vague when describing what the wisdom in this eighth stage really constitutes. It may be that Erikson, as do others who talk vaguely about wisdom, intuitively have come close to what here is referred to as gerotranscendence—without understanding the metatheoretical shift of paradigm that is necessary in order to reach a new comprehension, as suggested by the experimental thinking on gerotranscendence.

With the intellectual input from Eastern philosophy and the above discussion, a basic metatheoretical suggestion can now be formulated: The enlightened maturity which, at very best, accompanies the process of aging, or rather the process of living, might be described as a shift in metaperspective—from a materialistic and rational perspective to a more cosmic and transcendent one, normally followed by an increase in life satisfaction.

The development towards gerotranscendence might, as a preliminary suggestion, include the following:

- an increasing feeling of cosmic communion with the spirit of the universe

- a redefinition of the perception of time, space, and objects

- a redefinition of the perception of life and death and a decrease in the fear of death

- an increased feeling of affinity with past and coming generations

- a decrease in interest in superfluous social interaction

- a decrease in interest in material things

- a decrease in self-centeredness

- an increase in time spent in "meditation"

The increasing feeling of cosmic communion with the spirit of the universe might be experienced as being a part of a flow of energy which is coursing through the universe. Likewise, the perception of time might come to change from our normal linear view. Not only the perception of the velocity of time, but also that of the past, present, and future can be expected to change. In fact, our normal perception of time is only one of several possibilities as postulated by the theories of Einstein and Bohr, who punctured the notion of linearity as the only way to understand time.

The change in the perception of objects might include an elimination of the boundaries between "you" and "me" and between "us" and "them." An impression of being "one" might perhaps appear instead. As a consequence, the degree of self-centeredness would probably diminish. To a certain extent the enclosed self may become disaggregated and substituted with a cosmic self. Individuals might no longer look upon themselves as especially important. Maybe they perceive themselves as part of a cosmic flow of energy, in which the flow of energy, and not its individual parts, is the important thing. This might also involve a redefinition of the perception of life and death. It is not individual life but rather the total flow of life that is important. With such changes in the definitions of the metaworld it would be understandable that the fear of death would decrease and that the feeling of affinity with past, present, and coming generations would increase.

With the above assumed changes in the definitions of the world, it is easy to predict a decreasing interest in superfluous social relations and material goods. The individual who has experienced these changes may look with pity on many younger people who are obsessed with social engagements. Instead, time might be spent on what is more important, e.g., meditation and philosophizing. This does not necessarily imply a social withdrawal, although that may prove to be the case in our society, as suggested by Gutman (1976), since few roles conforming to gerotranscendence are provided and no guidance for entering the later part of life is given.

It is interesting how Chinen (1985, 1986), in an analysis of fairy tales which include older protagonists, found that the central motif in these tales is transcendence. Chinen proposed that the fairy tales represent guidelines for the developmental sequence of old age and identified processes of religious, social, and psychological transcendence. After reviewing over 2500 fairy tales, Chinen found that very few from Western societies had an older protagonist. Instead, the Western fairy tales predominantly featured young protagonists. In Eastern and some Slavic countries there seem to be normative fairy tales supporting the process towards gerotranscendence, while in the Western countries no such phenomenon can be observed. Drawing on this finding, we suggest that the stress on youth in the Western fairy tales, as well as in society as such, may obstruct the process towards gerotranscendence—simply by overshadowing the developmental tasks of old age. The existence of such tasks becomes invisible.

Chinen (1989a) also provided an example of how the new insights of old age can be achieved, under favorable circumstances, through a gradual process of change. Chinen analyzed the changing attitudes towards their science of two outstanding scientists, Ludwig Wittgenstein and Alfred North Whitehead, both still active and respected scientists and philosophers in their old age. Both of them changed their view of science from a rather rigid and self-assured positivism in their younger years, to a more pragmatic attitude in mid-life, and finally to a transcendent outlook in their old age. In their younger years, they were sure about things and convinced that, given sufficient research, everything could be given scientific explanation. In mid-life, they began to accept the thought that possibly everything may not be explainable in scientific terms. And, in their old age, both evidenced a radical transcendence of the borderlines between scientific disciplines as well as an acceptance of nonscientific explanations. To Chinen's observation it could be added that there are other examples of well known scientists who have developed in a similar way, Sigmund Freud, Carl Jung, Albert Einstein, and Niels Bohr, to name a few.

The personal development of these "atypical" scientists is mentioned as an example of how personality and perception of the world undergo changes, under favorable circumstances, in individuals who, to a great extent, have been able to go their own way without being hampered by others. Chinen (1989a) holds that this development is seen in individuals who either are given the chance or have within them the power to develop freely. Many of us, however, meet obstacles to such a free development.

OBSTRUCTIONS IN THE PROCESS TOWARDS GEROTRANSCENDENCE

In Western culture we might possibly be at risk of being regarded as odd, asocial, mentally disturbed or even disengaged if we change our perceptions of the world in accordance with a gerotranscendental development. In most Western cultures there are no roles or arenas where such a view of reality fits. In the Druze world, however, as described by Gutman (1976), there were roles and arenas available within, for example, religion and religious ceremonies provided a social arena for the wise chiefs and shamans.

Everyone in Western culture "knows" that it is activity, productivity, efficiency, individuality, independency, wealth, health, sociability, and a "realistic" view of the world that counts. By considering this as "fact," we are making a moral and normative judgment. As a result, we may impede the process towards gerotranscendence by making the individual feel guilty about his/her developmental change away from parts of this. Supported by interactionist gerontologists, staff members and relatives of old people may obstruct a natural process towards gerotranscendence. The attitude is that old people who are "turning inwards" or "withdrawing" to something we do not understand, must be reactivated. Inevitably, even old people participate in this obstruction as they, like everyone else,

recognize that it is mid-life activity, productiveness, and social commit-
ments that count in our society. We should therefore not be surprised
to find old people who feel guilt in connection with their own development
toward gerotranscendence; they may even apologize for having reached
a different view of life and living.

One hypothesis is that, paradoxically, obstruction of the gerotranscendental process may possibly precipitate a real syndrome of social breakdown. Hindered in their own personal development, and assaulted by
feelings of guilt, individuals may regress to a former developmental stage
and undergo a syndrome of social breakdown. This is very much in line
with Jung's sad observation that lots of people in our society grow old
unknowing of the special developmental tasks of later life, and thereby
come to develop depression, despair, fear of death, disgust with themselves
and others, together with the feeling that life has been wasted.

The works of several of the scholars quoted above (Jung, Hochschild,
Gutman, Erikson, Chinen) point in a vague way towards a developmental
process which, by and large, has been neglected by gerontologists. Other
indirect evidence for the claim that gerotranscendence is part of a normal
process is suggested by Peck (1956, 1968). In a study of approximately
one thousand businessmen he focused on developmental crises during
middle and old age.

Peck's description of how these subjects deal with aging implies a
right or good way in the sense that this way seemed connected with more
happiness and life satisfaction in old age. In line with Erikson (1950) he
pointed to a number of developmental crises that may result in either a
positive constructive outcome or a negative one. He did not, however,
say much about the general developmental process behind the different
ways of handling the crises in the second half of life.

According to Peck, the following crises occur in the second half of life:

1. *Ego differentiation or job preoccupation.* Some people seem to be able
   to reorient their lives in such a way that their identity is no longer
   dependent on the previous work role. Many other things replace the
   importance the job had earlier in relation to the perception of the
   self. Others seem unable to let go of their earlier work career. Ego
   differentiation is regarded by Peck as the natural and good solution
   to this developmental crisis, but something prevents certain people
   from reaching this stage.

2. *Body transcendence or body preoccupation.* Some people become increasingly preoccupied with their bodies in the second half of life. They

are attuned to every little new ailment and make it a major problem in life. Others seem to transcend the body in the sense that they know all about their physical condition and take proper care, but are not focused on it as if it were the hub of universe. Peck indirectly states that body transcendence is the natural development, which for some reason is thwarted for many people.

3. *Ego transcendence or ego preoccupation.* In the same way as the body, the ego should be transcendent in old age. Peck claims that the knowledge of one's own aging and the inevitability of death should prompt a reorganization of the ego, causing the elderly to live in a more generous, unselfish way. This should induce an acceptance of death. For various reasons, many people seem unable to reach such a stage. Instead they develop the type of ego preoccupation and fear of death described by Erikson as despair.

When Peck (1956) uses the term *transcendence* he means something like "overcoming" pains of the body or fear of death and the future, an adaptation to or coping with a deteriorating life situation. Our interpretation is, again, that what Peck actually found were aspects of the general process towards gerotranscendence, which in our society is obstructed by our value patterns and notions of how life in old age should be. We suggest that the "good choices" cited above are reflections of a successful gerotranscendental process. Behind the bad choices are obstructions in the process of gerotranscendence.

CONCLUSION

In this chapter we have suggested that human nature—the very process of living—encompasses a general tendency toward gerotranscendence, which is, in principle, universal and culture free. To reach gerotranscendence might be to reach wisdom. Our hypothesis is that the process toward gerotranscendence is continuous, but can be either accelerated or obstructed. If all goes well, we will reach the final stage of gerotranscendence, but much in our society impedes the process. In Western societies the process toward gerotranscendence might often be accompanied by guilt. It may be that social gerontologists contribute to such an obstruction, for example, by misinterpreting gerotranscendence as negative disengagement. From our perspective, however, gerotranscendence is never negative. It could instead be the highest level of human development and, as such, supremely positive. Of course this statement contains a normative component—an idea of what natural and good personal development should be like. In this respect our theory is no different from others, for example, the theory of activity or Erikson's developmental theory. But, it is different, and it offers a new understanding of aging.

Different and seemingly conflicting theories can very well be valid at the same time. It is, for example, true that light can be described both as "particles" and as "waves." Both these perceptions of light are true, based on different scientific paradigms. In the same way, the suggested theory of gerotranscendence can be true at the same time as the activity theory. The latter is true within its own metatheoretical paradigm. In other words, we do not deny the applicability of other theories. They are valid and applicable to individuals who have the same view of life as the theories. They are, however, less applicable to individuals who have moved on to a new comprehension of life—a new metaworld.

This leads us to a major challenge for future empirical and practical gerontology—how to decide whether an individual is demonstrating a negative withdrawal within the mid-life metaworld, or is in the process of transforming this metaworld into a new one, in the process toward gerotranscendence. The very first and most important step is, of course, to recognize if there is something called gerotranscendence. The next step is to discover its characteristics.

As in Jung's theory of the individuation process, gerotranscendence is regarded as a possible final stage in a natural progression towards maturation and wisdom. It defines a reality somewhat different from the "normal," mid-life reality which we often tend to project on old age. Even if Bernice Neugarten and colleagues (1964) early on wrote about the contemplative nature of the inner lives of old people and Clark and Anderson (1967) described how older people turn away from the competitive values of mid-life, many theories have, as earlier described, been based on the assumption that "good aging" equals continuity and preserving mid-life ideals, activities, and definitions of reality. The theory of gerotranscendence takes a perspective that emphasizes change and development.

The term *gerotranscendence* has been chosen because many of the related changes, crises, or developmental characteristics described by others involve various ways in which elderly people break through old boundaries or transcend developmental crises when moving on to a new stage in life. Thus, in this context, the word *transcendence* is used in this simple sense, not in the religious or metaphysical sense.

This chapter has reviewed the beginning of the theory of gerotranscendence. The following chapters report on the search for empirical evidence and elucidation.

CHAPTER 3

The Qualitative Content of Gerotranscendence[3]

Ihe it was stated earlier in this book that we need to reach a phenomeno-logical understanding of aging from the individual's inner perspec-tive, rather than it being observed, defined and understood from the perspective of the scholar. It is the aging individual's subjective meanings attached to activities, values, goals in life, and understanding of aging that we need if gerontological theorizing is going to be renewed. This chapter reports on such a phenomenological and qualitative step on the road towards the theory of gerotranscendence.

The outcome is based on in-depth interviews with 50 people recruited after a lecture on some early tentative ideas about the theory—basically corresponding to the content of the previous chapter in this book. After a newspaper interview with the author of this book about the ideas behind the theory a lecture announced in the newspaper article attracted no less than 500 people, most of them in the second half of life, but also a handful of younger ones.

After the lecture the question was asked if there was someone in the audience who might recognize something of the ideas presented in their own personal development, and if they were willing to be interviewed about their developmental experiences. The 50 people who volunteered, between 52 and 97 years of age, were interviewed some months later by

---

[3]This chapter builds, with permission, in part on what previously was published in Tornstam, L., 1997a, Gerotranscendence: The Contemplative Dimension of Aging, *Journal of Aging Studies*, 11.2:143–154; Tornstam, L., 1996a, Gerotranscendence—a theory about maturing into old age, *Journal of Aging and Identity*, 1:37–50, and Tornstam, L., 1999b, Late-Life Transcendence: A New Developmental Perspective on Aging, in Thomas, L. E., Eisenhandler, S. A., eds., *Religion, Belief, and Spirituality in Late Life*, New York: Springer.

a collaborating psychologist. So, this was a self-selected group of people who, not only from the very beginning felt attracted by the ideas of a personal development continuing into old age, but also recognized such a development in themselves, and were willing to be interviewed about it. The interviews, carried out in 1991, were semistructured, i.e., some theoretically generated themes were discussed but the conversations had an open format. For each theme, the goal was for the interviewer to guide the conversation as little as possible.

The interviews, lasting from one to three hours, were tape-recorded and transcribed, i.e., they were listened to several times, and their essential parts were identified and written down. The resulting 1,250 pages of text constitutes the empirical basis for the present analysis.

Each interview began with an open theme where the respondent simply was asked to tell about changes in attitudes and perspectives during life. Had anything changed since mid-life, and in such case what had changed? This was followed by specific themes generated by the preliminary theory outline. The analysis as well as the following presentation are organized in terms of some major categories obtained during the open-theme interviews. The open theme generated three main dimensions of gerotranscendental change: 1) the *cosmic dimension*, 2) the *self dimension*, and 3) the *dimension of social and personal relations*.

It is interesting to note that Achenbaum and Orwoll (1991) have reached similar dimensions in a psychogerontological analysis of *The Book of Job*. Job's struggle towards wisdom is described as developmental changes in the *transpersonal, intrapersonal,* and *interpersonal* dimensions. This is a coincidence that came to our knowledge when the main dimensions of gerotranscendence were already established.

GEROTRANSCENDENCE AND ITS OPPOSITE

Among the 50 respondents, some two or three, as exceptions, came to the lecture and agreed to be interviewed, not because they had experienced any development towards gerotranscendence, but because they felt that the developmental idea was interesting even if they could not identify any such change in themselves. Thus, the present material offers the possibility to demonstrate the qualitative content of gerotranscendence by comparing a gerotranscendent and a nongerotranscendent individual. In the following, then, a contrast is made between a respondent who seemed to have developed a lot even during late life, and a respondent who seemed to be trapped in the definitions of the first half of life.

Eva—Who Has Come a Long Way Towards Gerotranscendence

Eva, formerly a nurse, was 69 years old at the time of the interview. Though not from a poor family, she had a difficult childhood; her upbringing was strict and brutal. She was married and has three adult children. She experienced a deep crisis in connection with her divorce a number of years ago. She said about that:

> *I don't think a person should ask for crises, but I think that we learn something from the crises we go through.*

In answering the open question about whether she has changed her attitude towards life and herself, she described a rather radical change in perspective:

> *Using an analogy, earlier I used to feel that I was out on a river being carried away by the stream without being able to control it. Even if I wanted to go ashore I couldn't control it; I was carried away both from pleasant and unpleasant things. But today I feel like the river. I feel like I'm the river. I feel that I'm part of the flow that contains both the pleasant and the unpleasant things.*

In contrast to the earlier experience of being a powerless object thrown back and forth in "the river of life," Eva now perceives herself as a part of the flow of life itself. The boundary between herself as an object and the universal life has been transcended. Eva came back to this type of change several times during the interview. Now she feels that she "participates in a wider circle, in humanity."

Her perception of time has also changed. Eva now sees time as circular rather than linear. She realizes now that she, in fact, has always lived in a circular time frame without understanding it. According to Eva, this is particularly true of women:

> *I mean, she gives birth after 9 months, she has her monthly periods, she hangs out her wardrobe in the spring and brings it in the fall, and so on. There are a lot of examples of circularity in women's lives.*

Eva's circular time also implies that "one always lives with the past and the future" as she put it. One lives in different times simultaneously. In other words, Eva has transcended the boundary that we normally draw between past, present, and future. She also has strong links with her ancestors, "because I [literally] live very much in the time of my ancestors' generations, too." About her feeling of kinship with earlier generations she said:

> *That's immortality. The genetic chain that coils.*

In this coiling genetic chain, Eva sees a form of eternal life. It is only natural that she does not fear death:

> *No, it's quite a natural part of life.*

In her formulation of "immortality in the coiling genetic chain," Eva in a way combines science and faith (or mysticism), a unification of scientific genetics and the immortality of mysticism and faith. The boundary between science and mysticism is transcended. Eva pointed out that she is not at all religious. Nevertheless, she has come to accept science and faith as equal:

> *Some people stick with a natural science theory and other people stick with a religious theory. One theory is just as good the other. Some things are unanswered.*

With this complete change in her attitude towards life, Eva has also noticed that the sources of joy in life have changed:

> *Well, earlier it may have been things like a visit to the theater, a dinner, a trip. I wanted certain things to happen that I was a little excited about. . . . My best times [now are] when I sit on the kitchen porch and simply exist, the swallows flying above my head like arrows. Or a spring day like this when I can go to my nettle patch and pick nettles for soup.*

It is not only the definitions of "the cosmic dimension" that have changed for Eva. Her perception of who she is and wants to be has also changed. She has discovered sides of herself that she is now trying to change:

> *. . . I wanted to keep things to myself. I wanted my inner space, my integrity. I used to think that integrity depended on keeping as much*

as possible secret, on not giving yourself away. Also in my relationship to my husband I thought I wanted something that was my own. I think that has changed a lot. Feeling that my integrity doesn't depend on that. It would have helped my marriage a lot if I'd realized that earlier.

Opening up her enclosed self to the outer world, Eva has achieved an ability to watch herself from the outside. Describing her change she said about her old self that:

I couldn't see myself from the outside.

Now watching her old self from the outside she can see a good deal of self-infatuation:

It was all narcissism. I remember as a girl, lying on the beach touching myself, touching and kissing my skin. Playing with a friend's hair. I mean, it was all narcissism. This has changed a lot. I'm not the slightest bit worried about my belly or bad skin or the wrinkles in my face. It means nothing to me, nothing at all.

In this statement, Eva not only demonstrates her new insights into herself, but also that she has transcended conventions about the body. She does not deny that her body is changing. It does not scare her. She has no need to separate body and mind in the way that many aging people do, i.e., to look at the aging body with disgust, claiming the exchangeability of the mind or the self. Separating body and mind has almost become the norm for the aging human being as well as for the gerontologist. In her book The Ageless self, Kaufman (1986) has introduced this separation between body and mind as part of the normal aging process. The self does not age, only the body. In this perspective, then, Eva's aging is not "normal." For Eva, changes occur in both body and mind. There is a self-developing in an aging body. Eva not only accepts, but enjoys, this development. Neither does she participate in the masquerade, as suggested by Biggs (2003, 2004), where masking the aging body with clothing, cosmetics, or surgery becomes part of a coping strategy to maintain identity.

Also in relation to other people, Eva has become a different person. She is more open to other people today. At the same time, she has become more restrictive in her choice of friends and company. She has abandoned the big circle of friends:

. . . I think it's more fun to . . . I go to an older woman that I know, sit and talk to her. I get much more out of this than going to parties and being with a lot of people where you really don't talk so much with people.

Being with a lot of people used to involve a good deal of make believe and disguise which Eva has now abandoned:

I somehow walked around and played "the discreet charm of the bourgeoisie,"[4] and I did it well. . . . I adjusted a great deal to the roles people expected me to play. I have been a very well-behaved little middle-class girl, but I'm not anymore.

Having the courage to be herself, Eva today dares to say and do things that she did not dare to earlier out of fear of breaking the rules and embarrassing herself:

I'm old enough and wise enough to dare to do dumb things.

However, when asked if it has become easier with age to make wise decisions and give good advice to other people, Eva answered:

Well, it's easier to make both dumb and wise decisions, but there is one thing that I find easier today. That is to refrain from giving good advice.

For Eva, the previously clear difference between good and bad advice has been transcended. Eva thinks that deciding what is good and what is bad is not as easy as it previously seemed to be, particularly where other people are concerned. Eva is happy and satisfied with her life today. She radiates satisfaction with life.

Greta—Who Seems to be Stuck in Her Development

A person who does not radiate any real satisfaction with life is Greta. Greta is a former schoolteacher, 72 years of age at the time of the interview. She grew up in a quiet and safe middle-class environment, but her mother died when she was only 13 years old. Greta has been a widow for several years and has two adult sons. She also had a daughter, but the girl died

---

[4]Alluding to Luis Buñuel's movie, *The Discreet Charm of the Bourgeoisie* (1972).

at 15 years of age. Her husband, who was very domineering, died when the children were in their first school years.

Thus, like Eva, Greta has gone through difficulties in her life, but she does not seem to have been able to turn them into something positive. Instead, the crises in her life have been compounded. Answering the open question about whether she may have changed her attitude towards life and herself, she just told about how meaningless life became after she retired:

> *I thought that as a senior citizen I would be active, have adventures, but this just hasn't happened. It's like my feet have been knocked out from under me. I'm surprised that I gave up that easily. I quickly fell into a life as a senior that is rather pointless for me. . . . I miss my work a lot. I miss the satisfaction of working.*

Greta has not experienced any considerable changes in perspective when it comes to her perception of herself and the surrounding world. Rather, she seems to cling firmly to middle-age ideals and definitions of reality. She evaluates herself within these frames of reference and arrives at discouraging conclusions:

> *When I watch myself it's mostly disappointing. Now I'm rather disinterested, unfortunately. I feel that I've used up my supply of . . . I'm afraid I have used up my supply of interest in other people and things like that.*

As Greta told her story, it sounded as if she had given up. Her interests and perspectives had not changed very much, they had just ceased. About her relationships to other people, Greta said:

> *I've had an enormous social network but it's also . . . I think I have . . . I'm not interested anymore. Disengaged and disinterested.*

Perhaps the cause of her disinterest is that she is still stuck in the patterns of middle-age. Measured in terms of middle-age performance ideals, neither Greta herself nor other senior citizens are worth much. Greta was to the point when she said:

> *I'm not fond of seniors but, of course, I don't need to be.*

It is evident that Greta includes herself in the category of people that she does not like. Greta is not satisfied with her life.

The comparison between Eva and Greta might lead to the conclusion that Eva has succeeded, in the terminology of Erikson, Erikson, and Kivnick (1986), in attaining ego integrity in the face of despair, while Greta has not. But, there is more to it. Instead of just attaining a balance between ego integrity and despair, Eva transcends such opposites.

For example, Eva's whole perspective has changed from floating powerlessly in the river of life to being the river itself. She is not just balancing the possible despair of being even more powerless in old age, she transcends it. Eva has also transcended the conventional way of perceiving her body. She has no need to separate body and mind. Again, this means more than just balancing or coping with an ageless self in an aging body. Instead, she transcends the duality.

THE COSMIC DIMENSION OF GEROTRANSCENDENCE

Time and Childhood

Earlier we saw that Eva had changed her definition of time. The change in the concept of time is one of the dimensions subsumed under the heading "the cosmic dimension." The interviewer introduced the time concept theme in the following way:

> Some people say that they have gradually come to a concept of time that is different from the one they had before. They say that, in early life and adulthood, they had a very clear idea of what is today and what belongs to yesterday, but that it has changed and they feel like they are able to be in two time periods at once. Their past may be present so strongly that they almost live in it, at the same time as they live in the present. Is this something that you recognize?

A few of the respondents answered "yes" to the specific question, but the majority slid over to reports on how childhood has come more alive in their older days.

The fact that people, irrespective of any transcendence of time, begin to think more about childhood experiences and places is well illustrated by the 86-year-old woman who said:

> You go back to childhood almost daily. It comes without reflection. I talked to a good friend about this . . . We both go back to the town where we grew up [in our thoughts] . . . Childhood means much more than one thinks, I go back to it all the time.

A 79-year-old woman expressed a similar view saying that it both pleases and scares her: "Now I'm almost 80 and now I dare to remember my childhood." She added:

> The older you get, the more you remember of your childhood. There's a dangerous trap in this. I have heard about that all my life.

Thus, when she realized that recalling the experiences of childhood was beginning to mean a lot to her, she became frightened. She interpreted it as a negative sign of her own aging. She had not come up with this negative interpretation herself. She said: "I have heard about that all my life." Thus, the pleasure that this woman finds in recalling her childhood is offset by the negative interpretation of returning to childhood that she has internalized.

The Connection to Earlier Generations

The descriptions of transcendence of the time dimension and the importance of childhood in several cases drifted over to another theme, namely the relation to earlier generations of people. A 72-year-old man describes how the distance to the 17th century has decreased:

> If we take the 17th century, it used to be (earlier, in my younger years) tremendously distant, but today I don't think that the 17th century is all that far away. It is somehow as if it has come nearer. And everything in history has come nearer.

A 65-year-old woman, during the conversation about time and childhood, told of an experience of kinship with earlier generations:

> . . . I particularly remember one night, I looked out and saw the moon . . . suddenly I got the thought that it was the same moon and the same sun that the Greek philosophers describe, it was just as if . . . you know, such a strange feeling that . . . I can't explain . . . a feeling of kinship . . . yes, that's it.

We also recall that Eva perceived "the coiling genetic chain" as her immortality. In both these cases, the feeling of kinship and affinity with earlier generations has been expressed in more general terms. In one case as a general kinship with previously living people, in the other case as a definition of immortality.

In the interview the interviewer introduced the theme in a way that more directly related to the respondents' own ancestors:

> *Some people say that, during the course of life, they experienced a change in how they feel in relation to their ancestors. It's a kind of increasing kinship with those who lived earlier, a feeling that you are a link in the chain of generations. Have you experienced this?*

This theme provoked many reactions in the respondents. The most prominent was the many reports about the wakening interest in genealogy. Several respondents had begun to seek their roots in this tangible manner.

When describing their feelings of increased kinship with earlier generations, respondents used expressions or metaphors showing that the kinship with ancestors has a very strong appeal. "It's the desire under the elms, you know," said a 65-year-old woman referring to an old movie classic.[5] "Yes, yes, it is almost a religious feeling," said a 71-year-old man.

Life and Death

The theme concerning life and death was introduced in the following way:

> *Some people experience changes during life in relation to the questions of life and death. Somebody who has feared death in his or her youth can get rid of the fear later in life. Others have always feared death. How do you feel about this?*

There were various types of reactions to this question, but the common denominator was that the respondents did not, in general, fear death. They may fear dying, that it will be extended and painful, but not being dead. Some have had this feeling all their lives while others have achieved it later in life.

A 58-year-old man formulated an attitude that comes back in several interviews:

> *. . . much of life may be preparation for dying. It is in the character of maturation. I think it comes completely by itself. I don't live in order to die, I want to live. But implicit in maturation is a greater and greater capacity for dying. Some kind of preparation. I think that eventually one dies quite naturally.*

---

[5]The Desire Under the Elms (1958) by director Delbert Mann.

This attitude, and consequently a decreasing fear of death, had come gradually during life. A couple of respondents describe a more sudden disappearance of the fear of death in connection with "near death experiences."

Irrespective of how people have come to terms with death, our interviews indicate the great importance this seems to have for gerotranscendence and positive maturation in old age. None of the respondents who either feared death or avoided the question showed any signs of development towards gerotranscendence.

Mystery in Life

This theme, focusing the acceptance of the mysteries of life, was introduced in the following way:

> Some people say that they have come to accept that there are things in life that can not be explained with science or reason, things that must be left incomprehensible, part of the mystery of life. Do you recognize this?

Several respondents recognized this and many pointed out that it had been a gradual change during life. An 85-year-old woman said:

> I guess I have taken for granted [earlier] that science knows what it talks about. But now I have realized that there is an awful lot beyond the reach of human knowledge [and] especially senses, that we can't know anything about.

The same woman said that there may be "knowledge categories" that are quite different from those that we are used to.

A related thought was expressed by the 71-year-old man who thinks that what we can understand is limited by language. Language constrains us to a certain form of understanding, he says, and implies that transcending the barriers of language gives rise to new forms of understanding. He gives as examples music and painting, which may allow forms of understanding beyond those that can be expressed through language. This statement corresponds with Gamliel (2001) who observed that a group of people at a house for the elderly used to gather in silence before dinner:

> Sitting together silently, they transcended the borders of past and future time to live in a "sacred present" or a "limbo time." By ignoring movements and sounds around them, they also transcended space . . . The

silence transcends the barriers of language, probably yielding to new insights.

Transcendental Sources of Happiness

The respondent quoted above had discovered music as a "gateway" to new insights. Similar experiences were related by a 77-year-old man who, however, kept them at a distance in front of the interviewer.

> *. . . one is, of course, a little softer now than before in certain situations. Above all, pretty music. The tears flow almost, well, my eyes get moist at least. There are other situations, too, . . . like drama and music. It wasn't like that before. But now it's a block that's breaking down . . . you experience it as a sort of euphoria, feeling of happiness. It has come during the last few years.*

Regarded superficially, it may seem as though the man has simply become more interested in music or just has become more soft-hearted. The real meaning of this new source of joy can go deeper, however. The respondent himself says that it is a block that is breaking down. His experience of music borders on something that has previously been sealed off. Now, however, this block is released.

When the interview touched upon the joys of life and how these may have changed, there were many answers that can be seen as related to the example above. The transcendent Eva and many others said that earlier it was the more spectacular events that gave joy in life, but that now it is more a question of small and commonplace things. These are often, as in the case of Eva, events and experiences in nature. Not that the opportunities for spectacular events have vanished, it is the perspectives that have changed.

Instead of assuming that such changes are adaptations to decreasing possibilities in life, one must accordingly ask whether the increasing interest in the small everyday experiences of nature does not have a deeper significance. A 58-year-old man describes what this may be about:

> *I see trees, buds, and I see it blossom, and I see how the leaves are coming—I see myself in the leaves.*

The experience of nature evokes the feeling of being at one with the universe, which is called *at-one-ment* in the Eastern tradition. The increasing significance of these small everyday experiences of nature could therefore be interpreted as a way in which the barrier between the self and the universe is transcended.

Almost all respondents who have children and grandchildren stressed their importance. This well-known phenomenon, too, can be given an interpretation in terms of the concept of transcendence. Through children and grandchildren the barriers between the present and the future as well as between life and death are transcended. "The coiling genetic chain" is present in the children and the grandchildren. This chain provides the opportunity to participate in life on earth in the future.

THE SELF DIMENSION GEROTRANSCENDENCE

The first outline to the theory of gerotranscendence assumes that the individual self is gradually changing and developing. In this regard, the theory contrasts sharply with theories that assume that the self, like the perception of the self, is constant and ageless. In our interviews, we have approached the question of the constancy or variability of the self and the perception of the self in aging using several conversation themes.

Self-Confrontation

The constancy of perception of the self is partly dependent on the degree to which we discover the hidden aspects of our personality, what Jung calls *the shadow*. This theme was introduced in the following way:

> *Some people say that, during the course of life, they have begun to discover sides of themselves that they hadn't known before, both positive and negative. Do you recognize any of this in yourself?*

Our respondents reported that they had discovered both positive and negative sides of themselves in their older years. An 85-year-old respondent discovered a literary talent. It can also be a question of previously unknown personal characteristics. One respondent discovered that she is actually a cheerful, light-hearted person, while another respondent realized that she is more serious than she had once thought. Still another respondent said that what he had earlier considered positive carefulness in his personality was in fact an exaggerated pedantry.

The latter case is not about discovering new qualities in oneself but rather about *redefining* qualities that were already known. Another example of this redefinition of qualities is given by a 72-year-old man, a former labor union ombudsman, who used to think that his driving force was engagement and empathy, but who now understands that it was pure performance anxiety that drove him.

The most common discovery or redefinition, however, is about relationships to other people. Respondents described an egocentricity that they had previously been unconscious of. The 69-year-old woman who earlier in life thought that she had an unselfish interest in her children, has now discovered that it was really about something else:

> *I have been much too domineering. . . . I kind of forced myself on them in a way.*

Another respondent said, along similar lines:

> *I talked very egotistically about how I was doing. It was me all the time. . . . I never listened to my children. Today I can listen.*

Decrease in Self-Centeredness

In connection with the theme about self-confrontation, several respondents gave descriptions of how the perspective of the confined self had been transcended. In addition, this topic was introduced as a special theme using a somewhat different approach:

> *Some people say that they have changed their view of themselves during life in such a way that they no longer see themselves as being as important as before. Is this something that you recognize?*

Considering the indoctrination of the people of this generation in Scandinavia with the theses of the Jante Law (first thesis: Don't think that you are important! [A. Sandemose, Danish-Norwegian writer]), it is not surprising that many reacted to this question by saying that they never felt important. The conflict between the egocentricity of early life and the self-denial of the Jante Law was also described by a 60-year-old woman:

> *Well, I guess I have always liked to be in the middle of things, I always talked a lot and expressed my opinion, but I never tried to be important.*

This new insight during old age may be, in the best case, about realizing that one is not really as unimportant as the Jante Law implied nor as unimportant as one felt. A 62-year-old woman formulated this insight in the following way:

> *I always had low self-confidence . . . always felt insufficient. It's only when looking back, in hindsight, that I can see that what I have achieved is not so bad.*

Thus, for the people we interviewed, there has hardly been any inflated self-importance to transcend. Rather, it has been a question of struggling to establish a level of confidence that feels appropriate.

Self-Transcendence

The reactions to the self-confrontation theme illustrate, among other things, that people have come to see certain egotistical features in themselves, and replaced them with a higher degree of altruism. This type of change—from egoism to altruism—has been called self-transcendence by Chinen (1989b). The wishes and needs of the self are transcended in favor of other people's needs and wishes.

In interviews, this type of change was introduced in the following way:

> *If one thought in earlier life "I'll do this for myself," it has turned out later in life that one is more likely to do things for others. There has been a shift from doing things for oneself to doing things for others. Is this something that you recognize?*

Even if the respondents during the earlier part of the interview spontaneously related their previous egoism, this introduction usually generated another reaction. The transcendent Eva seems quite sincere when saying that she always gave the well-being of the family priority over her own wishes and needs. In fact, all women giving an opinion on this theme answered similarly. Among the male interviews there are descriptions that are closer to the type of change referred to in the theme. An 85-year-old man said:

> *When I did things to improve myself . . . I did it for my own sake, because it gave me satisfaction, but also because it was to the benefit of the family. They were always in the picture. But I don't feel that way now. I must say that everything I do now is in order to help others.*

Even if this man recognized the shift from egoism to altruism, there is also in this male report a description of a lifelong altruism. So, among these men and women there seems not to be any real egoism to transcend, as implied in Chinen's (1985) afore mentioned analysis of the didactic messages of fairytales, where self-transcendence was a central motif.

Ego-Integrity

We tried to approach the eighth and last stage of development described in Erikson's (1950, 1982) psychological model of development using a theme introduced in the following way:

> *Some older people say that they feel that their life has now become a whole—even if their earlier life may have been uneven and chaotic. They have the feeling that the pieces of life's puzzle have fallen into place and formed a coherent pattern. Is this something that you recognize?*

The stories told by our respondents were very similar to Erikson's description of the last and eighth stage of development. A 65-year-old woman said:

> *Earlier I thought that . . . if it weren't like this, if I had had a little more money, then things may have been different. But now I think . . . this is my life after all, and it didn't turn out all that bad.*

A 62-year-old man said that the feeling of wholeness and coherence in life that has come lately is not stable. When alone, he often experiences the ego-integrity that Erikson speaks about. Under the pressure that he sometimes experiences with other people, this feeling of wholeness disappears. Many respondents told about the difficulty to achieve, or preserve, the experience of ego-integrity. In the case referred to above, tranquility and solitude is a prerequisite for the appearance and, in the best case, consolidation of ego-integrity.

THE SOCIAL AND PERSONAL RELATIONSHIPS DIMENSION OF GEROTRANSCENDENCE

A pilot assumption of the theory of gerotranscendence has been that what can superficially be interpreted as social disengagement could be understood as changes in point of view, shifts of emphasis, and redefinitions of the meaning of social relations. Guided by these assumptions, we have included the following themes in our interviews.

The Importance of Social Contacts During Different Phases of Life

Given the assumption that the nature and importance of social contacts can change character during the course of life, the following theme was introduced:

> Some people say that their interest in other people changes character during the course of life. One becomes more selective and prefers deeper relationships with a few people rather than more superficial relationships with many people. Is this something that you recognize?

Some respondents said that they had not changed at all in this regard, but an even greater number of respondents said that they had. "Those superficial things that were fun when I was younger are not fun in the same way anymore," said a 79-year-old woman. The waning need for glamorous social company is well illustrated by the following statement by an 86-year-old woman:

> I used to dance at the spring ball, I enjoyed it enormously. Now it's a tremendous difference. Now a few friends are quite enough, that's for sure. So [now] I have a much greater need for solitude. It's striking. It's extremely sufficient to meet and . . . just a few people, to sit down and talk. . . . One doesn't need so many.

The increased need for positive solitude, in contrast to loneliness, is evident in the above quotation as in the reports of many other respondents. A 77-year-old man said:

> I appreciate solitude more now. You know, you become fed up with company faster. And you feel that a lot of talking is just nonsense. . . . You long for home and a good book instead, or to put on a record.

It appears clearly in these and other interviews that we are not dealing with a kind of passive withdrawal, as a young observer may easily think. It is rather about changes in the importance of social relationships. We shed the company and activities that lack content, we become more selective, preferring literature or music, or a few friends. Not because of lack of possibilities, but of choice.

Sometimes, a former professional life has forced people into social patterns that they never asked for and that they can easily give up. An 85-year-old man showed his relief through a symbolic act:

As long as I was working I had to go to different things. Then I had both tails and a tuxedo. Tails were required at some dinners, at others a tuxedo. The day I retired I got rid of both the tails and the tuxedo.

The latter quotation is not about a redefinition of the importance of social contacts. The man had always disliked the big parties, but only after his retirement could he reconcile interest and behavior.

Social Masks

An insight that increases with maturation is assumed to be that certain social interactions are merely role playing, where the role does not necessarily fit the actor very well. This theme was introduced in the following way:

Some people say that they have become more and more conscious about the fact that interaction with other people is a masquerade, role playing. Some have gotten the inclination to throw off their mask or role. Is this something that you recognize?

The transcendent Eva said that she was good at playing "the discreet charm of the bourgeoisie," but that she had now changed behavior. She claimed explicitly that it is a question of maturation. Another 60-year-old woman said:

I don't think that older people need to wear masks. It's just so clear that everyone is allowed to be himself. I don't have anyone to answer to, it doesn't matter if they think I'm strange. . . . I think that's a great relief, you know.

Many respondents mentioned that the new capacity to "be oneself" is related to an increased self-confidence. Earlier, there was the tendency to fear not being accepted and to hide behind the kind of role offered by, for example, work or motherhood. "It feels like I don't need to take on any role because I'm confident in myself," said a 69-year-old woman.

Some people who tell about the increasing inclination to "be oneself" still stress the necessity of playing roles in various situations. "Out in society, of course, we play our roles and wear our masks," said the transcendent Eva. Several respondents had similar thoughts. Roles are necessary for life to function, and can be played easily even when they are not "genuine." Those respondents had discovered and accepted the difference between the self and necessary roles. As we can see, these reports poorly match the idea of Biggs (2003, 2004), who suggests that more and more of a masquerade accompanies aging. Now, it may well be that the masquerade is a sign of not developing in a gerotranscendental way, of being hampered in development, since our respondents, who might be regarded as examples of those who have developed in a gerotranscendental way, reject the masquerade.

Emancipated Innocence

A frequent theme in many of the open theme reports was an almost roguish delight in breaking away from the role expectations or social conventions that were earlier seen as compelling. A 68-year-old woman related:

> *Now I don't care a bit about what people think. . . . I dare to go out biking or walking in [X-town] wearing torn stockings, I couldn't do that before. . . . Sometimes I think, but I really can't do this, you know . . . but I do it anyway.*

The delight in doing things that one did not earlier dare to do falls most closely into the theme that we, following Chinen (1989a), have called *emancipated innocence*. It refers to a capacity to break away from certain social conventions. A new kind of innocence and spontaneity is added to adult judgment and rationality. This allows important feelings and questions to be expressed regardless of the barriers of social conventions.

A special quality of this new attitude seems to be that people can admit that they do not know about something without feeling embarrassed. It is not only a question of not caring about making a fool of oneself, it also involves the recognition that an admission of ignorance is far from foolish. A 60-year-old man said:

> *Previously I had to read the newspaper in order to keep up with what was going on, in order to have something . . . well, people should not be able to attack me because I didn't know this or that. Today I read the newspaper only when I feel like it. . . . I no longer have the need to pretend to know more than I do.*

This change is connected with other, parallel changes. A 72-year-old man associated his new capacity of emancipated innocence with his decreasing interest in his own prestige:

Since I don't care about prestige anymore I don't feel it's such a big deal to make a fool of myself once in a while . . . I used to take that very seriously, if I said something stupid at a meeting or something like that.

Summarizing the messages from our respondents, the increased capacity for emancipated innocence was associated with a) practice and experience, b) personal maturity, c) a redefinition of what constitutes foolish behavior, and d) less need for prestige, coupled with a greater degree of self-confidence.

Attitude Towards Material Assets

In both spiritual and worldly contexts, owning property is described as an obstacle for spiritual or political growth and freedom. Religions describe asceticism as one of the paths to insight and wisdom. Similar advice is often given by political revolutionary movements. In a discussion of power and dependence, Blau (1964) argues that revolutionary ideologies frequently include an ambition to reduce materialistic needs, in this way decreasing the power of an adversary offering materialistic goods, and keeping the revolutionary spirit alive.

The common denominator of these attitudes is that focusing on material assets has a stagnating, pacifying, and petrifying function. Less focus on material assets, on the other hand, is said to promote both spiritual and revolutionary growth. This thought is also found in some of the folk tales analyzed by Chinen (1989b). The path to wisdom is easier when material needs are transcended.

Quite in line with this theoretical point of departure, a 72-year-old man spontaneously described how his not insignificant fortune restricts him:

It's tiresome to own . . . one becomes locked up, one isn't free when one owns. . . . Many say the opposite, but that's wrong. The more you own, the more you have to take care of, to manage, to watch out for. Now I have as much as I'm interested in. I have put up a limit at SEK 500,000 [approx $70,000]. I don't want more. I was on my way up, but I said "no," and went down.

This man has in no way turned his back on material possessions, but he has realized that owning things limits his freedom and has therefore set a limit. A 57-year-old woman expressed an almost identical view telling how she has come to experience her art collecting of 20 years as a burden.

She argues that "the later part of the journey through life should be made with lighter luggage," having enough for a modern definition of the necessities of life, but not more. One should eat and drink well, but not stockpile money, said a 79-year-old woman. We might call it a kind of *modern asceticism.*

The insight expressed in the above statements is that an economic buffer is good to have, but that the volatility of material assets makes saving beyond that meaningless. Many show a tendency to try and reduce the number of "things" they own. "I'm an expert in getting rid of things," said an 80-year-old woman.

Everyday Wisdom

It is often thought that practical everyday wisdom or common sense increases with age. This was the point of departure when the following theme was introduced:

> *Some people think that it has become easier and easier to make wise decisions and help others to make decisions. What is your experience of this?*

A number of respondents answered in a way that makes one assumption in our question explicit, namely, that it is possible to distinguish between wise and unwise decisions. The respondents often reached the conclusion that it has become more difficult to identify the boundary between wise and unwise.

Given the experience that the boundaries between right and wrong, wise and unwise are transcended, the consequence for everyday wisdom is to refrain from giving advice or helping others to make decisions. The transcendent Eva said that what she had learned above all was to refrain from giving good advice. In a similar vein, an 80-year-old woman said:

> *I guess I used to think that I always made good decisions and gave good advice, too. I have been in a situation where I have had to give a lot of advice. . . . I had no problems with it. How is it now? I guess I must say that I avoid giving advice. I suppose I have learned that what I think is wise for me can be very unwise for others.*

Another way of expressing this new approach is in terms of an increased broadmindedness, tolerance, and humility in response to other people's behavior. Tolerance and acceptance of other people's views have increased. A 78-year-old man said that:

> . . . I guess I used to have strong views of everything, but I don't today.
> I understand that it's not . . . it is not so simple, it depends.

In the case of an 88-year-old woman, broadmindedness had gone so far that she, with a bit of ironical distance to herself, said, "In the end, I don't see any criminals, either."

In summary, in these reports everyday wisdom is expressed by avoiding both giving good advice and helping people make decisions. The origin of this form of everyday wisdom is the transcendence of the boundary between right and wrong accompanied by an increased broadmindedness and tolerance.

OBSTACLES AND SHORTCUTS ON THE PATH TO GEROTRANSCENDENCE

Since, according to the theory, the development towards gerotranscendence can be obstructed as well as facilitated, it is reasonable to assume various catalysts and obstacles to be described in the interviews. This was also the case. These catalysts and obstacles are described in the following.

Owning as a Burden

One obstacle was identified in the above thematic survey—unnecessary material assets. Even if none of the respondents advocated pure asceticism, several spontaneously argued that owning too much may be burdensome and binding. Others, elaborating on the same theme, recommended that the latter part of the journey through life should be made with "light luggage." In addition, there were descriptions of how this has been achieved by giving away a good deal of property and adopting a simpler life. A 60-year-old woman, who did just that, said:

> I want to own as little property as I can. I have simple china, simple
> knives and spoons. I want it that way. I don't want it the way it used
> to be. It's great fun if the kids can use it. . . . Some of it is packed up,
> I don't want to unpack it. I think living simply is nice, but I wish I was
> living out in the country.

This quotation not only reflects a longing for comfortable simplicity—what we called earlier *modern asceticism*—but also a longing for the country life. The interview revealed that the attraction was the refreshing ascetic solitude near nature. This could be a side effect of the current "back to nature" trend, but we could just as well refer to parallels from other time periods and other cultures. In the Indian religion, since the ancient Vedic culture more than 3000 years ago, there have been ideas about how to live in order to achieve purification of the soul and eventual attainment of nirvana. Tilak (1989) describes how, during the Dharma Sastra period (200 B.C.–200 A.D.), life is explicitly organized in four phases, each with different content and meaning. These phases are: 1) the student, 2) the housekeeper, 3) the hermit, and 4) the wanderer. Characteristic of the latter two periods is the giving up of material goods. During the hermit phase, the old man, possibly accompanied by his wife, is expected to give up his house and lands, join other hermits in the woods and lead a simple life. During the last phase, the wanderer or beggar phase, he has given up all earthly goods and wanders alone from village to village.

Tilak holds that the idea of these phases still remains in the normative cultural heritage in India. A modern version of the hermit phase, for example, may consist in an old man or woman periodically isolating himself or herself in a room to meditate. This behavior, thanks to the living cultural heritage, is neither misunderstood nor opposed.

It must be understood that none of our interviewees aimed at anything like the extreme poverty and isolation described in the old Vedic tradition. Rather they wanted to live a modern, comfortable, but simple life, understanding the trap inherent in excessive owning.

Positive Solitude

The modern asceticism described above also contains a prominent element of what we call *positive solitude*. The need for and the pleasure of contemplative solitude are evident in most of our interviews. There are at least two reasons for this. One reason is that solitude seems to be necessary in order to achieve and consolidate one's ego-integrity. The other reason is that one has become more selective in terms of activities and social interactions. The man who preferred to read a book or listen to a record expressed part of these two aspects at the same time. While he experienced social interaction with certain other people as tiresome and meaningless, there was also a new need for the joy and stimulation offered by solitary activities.

The need and search for positive solitude is not the same as ultimately choosing loneliness over interaction with others. Rather, the need for positive solitude comes and goes. A woman said:

> *I need periods of solitude, then it feels good to work things out and maybe change my behavior. And I feel that those periods make me feel well and that I need them. Other people can't understand that perhaps.*

This woman eventually touches on a question which is not unessential, namely other people's lack of understanding of the importance of positive solitude. The Swedish language lacks a cognate of the primarily positive English word *solitude*. This may be a further reason why the positive need for solitude may be misinterpreted in terms of negative disengagement, depression, apathy or resignation. Of course, this kind of loneliness exists, too. It has been exemplified by Greta who appears to have stopped in her development towards gerotranscendence. The point is that we probably misinterpret some people's need for a positive solitude as signs of depression or negative withdrawal.

Life Crises

The theoretical discussion of the concept of transcendence emphasizes the possible role of life crises as catalysts. Life crises may contain the *kinetic energy* that make the development towards gerotranscendence accelerate.

Our interviews contain several examples in which crises have contributed to an accelerated development towards gerotranscendence. An 80-year-old woman described how the death of a close friend a couple of years ago had changed her and helped her to develop:

> *I guess I was a noli me tangere type. This means "don't touch me." . . . Now I think that I have come closer to people, I understand people better, I am more open to them, I notice that when I give of myself, I get something back. So I have come closer to people than I used to. . . . This change was triggered when he died 2 years ago. When I realized that one must give and not only take.*

A 68-year-old man told us, in a similar way, about how his heart disease and operation opened him up to thoughts that he had not had before. A book that would not have interested him before became the gateway to a process of change:

I think there is so much in these new things that I have learned that makes things fall into place. You just lose the fear of death, and then there is so much to learn, and there is a lot to be done there . . . so I'm in the middle of a process where I have a lot to learn.

The life crisis changed the direction of this man's life not only through the power of the crisis itself, but also by preparing him for new thoughts and impressions. In this way, crises can be said to have a double effect.

One way of understanding life crises in this context is that they consist of upheavals that challenge or question the foundations of one's concept of reality. The death of a close relative, for example, undermines ideas of immortality, the notion that "it won't happen to me," and the idea that it is never too late to change. In scientific terminology, we would say that crises might challenge, question, and undermine basic ontological assumptions, replacing them with new ontological assumptions.

Bridges and Landings

Our respondents gave several examples of what could be called mediating links or bridges to different aspects of gerotranscendence. The transcendent Eva talked about how experiences of nature—swallows flying like arrows over her head, picking nettles for soup—give her life meaning. This can be understood both as part of her gerotranscendence and as a bridge to it. The development towards gerotranscendence seems to be stimulated by small experiences of nature. Also, the 59-year-old man's ability to see himself in the leaves on the trees can be interpreted in the same way.

The transcendent quality of experiences of nature offers a new way of understanding the increased interest in nature and gardening expressed by many older people. Old people's interest in their gardens is often interpreted in other ways, seen as a sort of therapy or a way to fill up their otherwise idle lives.

Apart from experiences of nature, our interview material also contains descriptions of experiences of music and drama as parts of or bridges to gerotranscendence. In the section on sources of happiness, a 77-year-old man related how experiences of music had become more important and more emotional for him. This statement can be interpreted in several ways. The man himself said that it was a barrier that had been broken down. In our terminology, we would say that it was the barrier between music and emotion that had been transcended, or that music helps in transcending a number of barriers. Music becomes a bridge to a transcendent experience of the whole. In such an interpretation, the increased emotional element stands out as something positive, as an indication that certain barriers have been demolished. Using other frames of reference, the same report could be interpreted as pathological. The increasing emotionality, the softening up, becomes a symptom of a disintegrating personality. The latter interpretation is the most common in the geropsychiatry literature.

However, if the experiences of nature and music are considered in parallel, certain similarities can be seen that clearly indicate their transcendental character. Both cases deal with experiences that appeal more to the emotions than to the intellect. The dimensions of experiences of both nature and music are relatively free. Their limits are set subjectively; they are not limited by predetermined categories. The relative freedom from boundaries, frames, and rules that characterize these experiences can thus become bridges to new ways of defining existential categories.

THE SIGNS OF GEROTRANSCENDENCE

Summing up the messages from the qualitative interviews, our selective group of aging individuals display in various degrees a series of characteristic signs of their development. These signs belong in three different dimensions:

The Cosmic Dimension

- *Time and childhood.* Changes in the definitions of time and the return of childhood. The transcendence of borders between past and present occurs. Childhood comes to life—sometimes interpreted in a new reconciling way.

- *Connection to earlier generations.* Attachment increases. A change from link to chain perspective ensues. The important is not the individual link (life), but rather the chain (stream of life).

- *Life and death.* The fear of death disappears and a new comprehension of life and death results.

- *Mystery in life.* The mystery dimension in life is accepted.

- *Rejoicing.* From grand events to subtle experiences. The joy of experiencing macro cosmos in micro cosmos materializes, often related to experiences in nature.

The Dimension of the Self

- *Self-confrontation.* The discovery of hidden aspects of the self—both good and bad—occurs.

- *Decrease of self-centeredness.* Removal of the self from the center of one's universe may eventuate. However, if self-esteem from the beginning is low, it may rather be a question of struggling to establish a level of confidence that feels appropriate.

- *Development of body-transcendence.* Taking care of the body continues, but the individual is not obsessed with it.

- *Self-transcendence.* A shift may occur from egoism to altruism. This may be a special matter for men.

- *Ego-integrity.* The individual realizes that the pieces of life's jigsaw puzzle form a wholeness. This may be a delicate state, demanding tranquility and solitude.

The Dimension of Social and Personal Relationships

- *Changed meaning and importance of relations.* One becomes more selective and less interested in superficial relations, exhibiting an increasing need for periods of solitude.

- *Role playing.* An understanding of the difference between self and role takes place, sometimes with an urge to abandon roles. A new comforting understanding of the necessity of roles in life often results.

- *Emancipated innocence.* Innocence enhances maturity. A new capacity to transcend needless social conventions.

- *Modern asceticism.* An understanding of the petrifying gravity of wealth and the freedom of asceticism develops. Having enough for a modern definition of the necessities of life, but not more.

- *Everyday wisdom.* The reluctance of superficially separating right from wrong, and thus withholding from judgments and giving advice is discerned. Transcendence of the right-wrong duality accompanied by an increased broadmindedness and tolerance ensues.

DEVELOPMENT BEYOND BOTH DISENGAGEMENT AND EGO-INTEGRITY

Drawing on our interviews it must be made clear that the development towards gerotranscendence cannot be regarded as any uniform development that characterizes all aging individuals. We should rather talk about it as a developmental possibility, where the precise form of the gerotranscendence can differ from individual to individual. Also, there are several pathways to gerotranscendence. It may be that the *seed* of gerotranscendence is within us all, but needs proper watering to grow. In today's society, we probably lack much of the proper watering, which also means that the proportion of individuals who reach high degrees of gerotranscendence is quite small.

Nevertheless, in our interviews, mainly based on individuals who may have come further than others, some rather distinct dimensions and aspects of gerotranscendence did crystallize. This does not mean that every subject was characterized by all these aspects. Some of the aspects of gerotranscendence, as summarized above, were recognized by most of the interviewees, while some were recognized by just a few.

The need for and the pleasure of contemplative *positive solitude* is highly evident in our interviews. This call for positive solitude as described by our respondents is, however, not the same as loneliness and disengagement. Rather, it is part of a development wherein they have become more selective. This eventually touches on a question that is essential, namely, that the developmental changes described by our interviewees could be given different interpretations. One set of interpretations stems from traditional gerontological theories, while other interpretations are rooted in a different paradigm as offered by the theory of gerotranscendence.

The decreasing interest in participating in certain social and personal relationships could, from a traditional perspective, be regarded as a negative disengagement, or as part of a social breakdown syndrome. But, at least among our respondents, the meaning of this behavior must be interpreted quite differently—as part of a positive developmental change. In the same vein, *emancipated innocence* could be regarded as a mental breakdown symptom, even though our interviews suggest it should be interpreted as part of a positive transcendence of futile social conventions.

Our interviews show that these and other aspects of gerotranscendence form, for the individual, coherent developmental patterns, of which high degrees of life satisfaction and absence of depression and neurotic symptoms are parts. The conclusion must be that the traditional interpretations have a limited scope. Sometimes traditional interpretations of behaviors such as those mentioned above may be appropriate, sometimes they may be totally wrong. A new understanding, as offered by the theory of gerotranscendence, might at times be more intelligible.

The developmental perspective in the theory of gerotranscendence is certainly very different from the old disengagement theory, but what about its relationship to Erikson's (1950, 1982, 1986) model of personal development?

The argument here is that gerotranscendence goes beyond Erikson's theory. In both cases the process of aging is regarded as a developmental process, which, at very best, ends with a higher state of maturity—in Erikson's case, ego-integrity, in ours, gerotranscendence. In Erikson's theory, the ego-integration primarily refers to an integration of the elements in the life that has passed. The individual reaches a fundamental acceptance of the life lived, regardless of how good or bad it might seem from the outside. In this way the ego-integrity described by Erikson becomes more of a backwards integration process within the same definition of the world as before, while the process of gerotranscendence implies more of a forward or outward direction, including a redefinition of reality. After reading a description of the theory of gerotranscendence, Joan M.Erikson, wife and co-worker of Erik H. Erikson, wrote in a personal communication (1995) to the author of this book:

> *When I got 91 myself, I became aware of the inadequacy of the words "wisdom" and "integrity," feeling that they in no way represented what I was experiencing as an elder. . . . So boldly I revised the Eighth Stage . . . including a Ninth and Tenth Stage, which even attempt to deal with "gerotranscendence."*

In 1997 an extended version of *The Life Cycle Completed* (Erikson, 1997) was published with new chapters on gerotranscendence and a ninth stage of development, written by Joan M. Erikson.

So, it seems evident that gerotranscendence goes beyond both disengagement and ego-integrity, while it perhaps, in line with Baltes (1993), could be argued that when our respondents talk about an increased broadmindedness and a tendency to avoid simple distinguishing between right and wrong, this could be understood within the first of Baltes's three metacriteria of wisdom, which are: 1) *Relativism*, the development away from ideological positions associated with dogmatism, rightness, and lack of tolerance; 2) *Life-span contextualism*, the defense against the predominance of the present in the conduct and interpretation of life; and 3) *Management of uncertainty*, the development away from the hegemony of determinism and rationality.

These criteria seem close to some aspects of gerotranscendence. But, while the aspects of gerotranscendence go beyond our "normal" paradigmatic world, Baltes's criteria remain within it. When, for example, Baltes describes relativism as a metacriterion of wisdom, he is only describing a behavior or a mode of thinking, while the theory of gerotranscendence understands this on a new paradigmatic level. The relativism described by Baltes is only a specific, manifest aspect of the general tendency to transcend boundaries and old forms of understanding reality, which is the essence of gerotranscendence.

CHAPTER 4

Quantitative Empirical Studies[6]

I n this chapter we examine three different quantitative studies that elucidate the theory of gerotranscendence. The first to be described is the *1990 Danish Retrospective Study*, in which 912 Danish men and women, age 74–100, in a mail survey were asked retrospective questions about gerotranscendence-related developments in life.

The *Swedish 1995 Cross-Sectional Study* supplements the above study by including younger respondents (age 20–85) in an effort to describe the level of gerotranscendence in individuals of different ages. In this study 2002 Swedish men and women age 20–85 responded to a mail survey.

The *Swedish 2001 (65+) Study* was a mail survey of 1771 Swedish men and women, where questions generated in the above studies were further addressed focusing on individuals age 65–104.

Some of the questions that will be addressed below rely on more than one of the above studies. You may refer to the above brief descriptions whenever you need to keep track of what is what.

GEROTRANSCENDENTAL DEVELOPMENT IN RETROSPECT

It is evident that a substantial minority of people in the second half of life recognize developmental changes of a gerotranscendendental kind *in*

---

[6]This chapter builds, with permission, in part on what previously was published in Tornstam, L., 1994, Gerotranscendence—A Theoretical and Empirical Exploration, in Thomas, L. E., Eisenhandler, S. A., eds., *Aging and the Religious Dimension*, Westport: Greenwood Publishing Group. (pp 203–225); Tornstam, L., 1997b, Gerotranscendence in a Broad Cross Sectional Perspective, *Journal of Aging and Identity* 2:1: 17–36; Tornstam, L., 1997c, Life Crises and Gerotranscendence, *Journal of Aging and Identity* Vol 2:117–131; Tornstam, L., 1999a, Gerotranscendence and the Functions of Reminiscence, *Journal of Aging and Identity* 4(3):155–166.

themselves. The respondents in the qualitative study described earlier were, however, a self-recruited and selective group of individuals. Do the gerotranscendental experiences described by these individuals match the experiences of ordinary men and women? An initial answer to this question will be given by the quantitative study described below. Before diving into this empirical pond, it might be interesting to learn how this first quantitative study came about.

When the very first ideas of the theory of gerotranscendence were presented to some gerontology colleagues in Denmark, where the author of this book worked at the time, they were quite skeptical. One of them, however, later became supportive when he learned that individual old people in Denmark, who had heard about the ideas, spontaneously confessed that they could recognize themselves in the thought patterns and characteristics attributed to gerotranscendence. The support from this Danish colleague came in the form of an offer to participate, with a limited number of survey questions, in a study that was just about to be launched, the results of which are reported below.

Questions for the First Quantitative Study

At the outset, the study intended to give answers to the following questions:

1. *The question of recognition, which* focuses on whether old people in general actually recognize the kind of changes suggested by the theory of gerotranscendence.

2. *The question of distribution, which* assumes that gerotranscendence is a variable, where some individuals demonstrate high degrees of gerotranscendence, others low degrees. How to define these groups?

3. *The question of gerotranscendence and social activity, which* focuses on a difference that distinguishes this theory from the disengagement theory. The theory of gerotranscendence does not necessary imply social withdrawal.

4. *The question of gerotranscendence and coping patterns, which* is related to the previous question. How do individuals with high degrees of gerotranscendence cope with problems in life. If gerotranscendence were the same as disengagement, we would predict a passive or defensive coping style. But, since the theory regards the state of gerotrans-

cendence as a mature state of development, approaching wisdom, we expect other coping patterns, perhaps even several different simultaneous coping strategies.

5. *The question of gerotranscendence and life satisfaction, which* builds on the theory's assumption that the development toward gerotranscendence is a natural developmental process associated with an increase in life satisfaction. People who do not reach gerotranscendence are expected to score lower on life satisfaction.

6. *The question of accelerating or retarding the process of gerotranscendence, which* builds on the theory's assumption that certain life crises can accelerate the process, as for example when severe illness can make an individual redefine reality. Traditionally, such changes are looked upon as defense mechanisms, but the theory of gerotranscendence regards such changes as real changes in the metastructure, not as defense mechanisms. The theory also assumes that individuals who are not hindered by the restrictive norms or values inflicted on them, or who have enough personal resources to withstand such constraints, more easily reach gerotranscendence.

7. *The question of gerotranscendence as possibly related to confoundings like mental illness, depression and consumption of psychotropics.* At seminars, when the tentative theory was presented, critics suggested that the state of gerotranscendence could be a reaction to, or correlated with, depression and mental illness, since its "symptoms" show some similarities. Also, as critics suggested, the consumption of various psychotropics might cause the same "symptoms." Our hypothesis was, on the contrary that gerotranscendence is negatively correlated with depression, mental disturbances, and consumption of psychotropics. Again, this follows from the assumption that development toward gerotranscendence is a natural positive developmental process, which is followed by contentment, satisfaction, and, consequently, reduced need for psychotropics.

Method and Measures

This study was based on a mail survey of 912 individuals remaining from a panel of 1261 representative, noninstitutionalized Danish men and women who participated in a longitudinal study with data collections in 1986 and 1990. Details of the sampling and data collection procedures are described by Holstein, Almind, Due, and Holst (1990).

In 1990, when the questions related to gerotranscendence were asked, the mean age of the 912 respondents was 79, ranging between 74 and 100 years.[7]

The degree of gerotranscendence was approximated by a series of 10 items derived from the theory and after a selection procedure that included qualitative interviews and tests on old people not included in this study. When the offer to participate with questions in this quantitative study came, the qualitative study described in the previous chapter was only in the planning stages. Some test interviews had been made, but the detailed results accounted for in the previous chapter were not available.

In the questionnaire, we posed the following question: "We now want to ask you whether your view of life and existence is different today, compared to when you were 50 years of age. Please read the following, and decide what you think of the statements below." For each of the statements, the respondent had two response alternatives: Yes (I do recognize myself in the statement) or No (I do not recognize myself in the statement). The statements and the proportion of respondents recognizing the content of the statements within themselves, are given in Table 4.1, which also gives the corresponding data for a replication of the survey in Sweden eleven years later.[8] The analysis below is based, however, on the original Danish data, when not otherwise specified.

Since the theory of gerotranscendence suggests different types of changes which may reflect different dimensions of gerotranscendence, the answers to the 10 items were analyzed with an exploratory factor analysis.[9] The factor analysis separated two factors of gerotranscendence. The first factor was labeled *cosmic transcendence*, since it clearly defines a type of transcendence connected with changes in the perception or definition of time, space, life, and death. The second dimension was labeled

---

[7]The distribution of men and women was, of course, uneven, with 64 percent women and 36 percent men. This corresponds identically with the total distribution of men and woman 74+ in the whole of Denmark at that time. Also, the age distribution within the age range of the respondents is very close to the corresponding age distribution in the whole of Denmark. Among the men, the age distribution is identical. Among the women, the younger ones are over-represented by two percent and the older ones were correspondingly under-represented.

[8]The Swedish data have been age selected from a larger study, the 2001 (65+) Study, and were weighted in order to match the age range and age distribution in the original Danish study.

[9]A principal component analysis with varimax rotation.

TABLE 4.1   Retrospective Gerotranscendence Statements in Denmark 1990 and Sweden[1] 2001, Respondents Age 74–100

	Percent Recognizing Content of Item		Factor Loading	
	Denmark 1990	Sweden 2001	Denmark 1990	Sweden 2001
Cosmic transcendence				
Today I feel that the border between life and death is less striking compared with when I was 50 years of age	60%	68%	.75	.43
Today I feel to a higher degree how unimportant an individual life is, in comparison with the continuing life as such	55%	52%	.72	.51
Today I feel a greater mutual connection with the universe, compared with when I was 50 years of age	32%	28%	.68	.74
Today I more often experience a close presence of persons, even when they are physically elsewhere	36%	36%	.67	.71
Today I feel that the distance between past and present disappears	42%	52%	.64	.63
Today I feel a greater state of belonging with both earlier and coming generations	49%	57%	.61	.41
Ego-transcendence				
Today I take myself less seriously than earlier	60%	73%	.77	.68
Today material things mean less, compared with when I was 50	74%	81%	.76	.74
Today I am less interested in superficial social contacts	53%	71%	.59	.66
Today I have more delight in my inner world, i.e., thinking and pondering, compared with when I was 50	57%	65%	.54	.48

[1]Swedish data selected from a larger study (n = 1.770) and weighted in order to match the age range and age distribution in the original Danish study. Unweighted number of Swedish respondents 74–100 years of age = 1.215.

ego-transcendence, since it is connected with changes in the perception of the self and relations with other people, and it includes both the qualitatively derived dimensions of the self and the social relations. The two extracted factors were almost exactly replicated eleven years later in the Swedish 2001 (65+) Study. The exception is the statement about the border between life and death, which in the Danish but not the Swedish study had a very strong factor load in the cosmic transcendence factor. Otherwise the similarities between the two studies in two different countries, eleven years apart, are striking.

It might be noted that the two factors generated by the quantitative analysis correspond with the two different tasks of old age, as described by Jung (1930), i.e., knowing about the universe and knowing about the self.

For the measurement of the two types of gerotranscendence mentioned above, two standardized additive indexes based on the items in each dimension were constructed.[10]

Social activity was measured by an additive index summing up the frequency of visits to other people in their homes, visits by other people to the home of the respondent, contacts with relatives (other than children and grandchildren), contacts with other friends, and leisure activities outside the home. The reason for excluding the contacts with children and grandchildren from this index was that only those social activities where the older people themselves had more of a choice in initiating contact were to be included. Earlier research has shown that contact between old people and their children and grandchildren tends to be made on the initiative of the latter (Hill, et al., 1979; Teeland, 1978).

Life satisfaction was measured by a single item, where the respondent, using a five-point scale stated how satisfied or dissatisfied he or she was with overall life at present.

An old age depression scale was constructed on the basis of five items, where the respondents, using a three-point scale were asked to agree or disagree on whether they: 1) feel lonely, 2) find the time passing slowly,

---

[10]This was according to Galtung's (1969) recommendations on procedure. Essentially this procedure involves a uniform trichotomization of each item before adding the response values up to an index. This procedure is done in order to reach an approximative rank-order Likert scale. The Cronbach's alpha for the six items in the cosmic transcendence scale is .81, and for the ego-transcendence scale .75, which is satisfactory (Bohrnstedt & Knoke, 1982). The above refers to the original Danish study, which is further analyzed in the following.

3) have a feeling of being forgotten, 4) have a feeling of being superfluous, and 5) feel old.[11]

Psychological strain was assessed by an index adding the number of present symptoms in the following list: sense of fatigue without any cause, insomnia, nervousness, anxiety, and depression.

A special *coping pattern typology* was based on four items, where the respondents, using a four-point scale, had to agree or disagree on what they do when they have problems or worries.[12] The items form a dimension of *defensive coping*, and a dimension of *offensive coping*. These two dimensions are not negatively but positively correlated.[13] This means that we do not find any support for the assumption that people have *either* an offensive *or* a defensive coping style. Rather we find that different combinations of both offensive and defensive coping are used. For this reason we have constructed a coping pattern typology based on the two dimensions. *Low copers* (32 percent) are those who are below average on both the offensive and the defensive coping dimensions. *Multicopers* (28 percent) are those who are above average on both dimensions. *Defensive copers* (14 percent) are high on the defensive coping dimension, but low on the offensive. *Offensive copers* (26 percent) are high on the offensive coping dimension, but low on the defensive.

The respondents in this survey were also asked whether they had experienced specific listed problems in coping during the last 12 months preceding the measurement in 1990. In this analysis we are using the answers to whether the respondents had experienced the loss of a close person or not, and if so, whether this trauma could be dealt with or not. On a four-point scale, those respondents who had experienced the loss of a close person were asked about the degree to which they themselves could solve the problems connected with the loss. The response alternatives ranged from "such problems cannot be solved" to "I could do a lot myself to solve the problems."

Results

Please note that when not specifically stated, the analysis refers to a cross-sectional analysis of the first 1990 Danish retrospective study.

---

[11] The Cronbach's alpha of this scale is .77.

[12] The behaviors in question were; "Trying to forget and pretend that nothing has happened," "Doing something to chase the worrying thoughts away," "Discussing with persons who are close to me how to solve the problem," "Concentrating completely on how to solve the problem." An exploratory factor analysis reveals these four items to form two dimensions.

[13] (eta = .33 p < .001).

Recognition

As to the initial question of recognition it must be noted that quite high proportions of the respondents recognize in themselves the content of the various statements. It is interesting that such a high proportion as 42 percent (in Sweden, 52%) recognize in themselves such a "strange" phenomenon as the disappearance of the distance between past and present. Several of the statements were recognized by many respondents. This fact can be regarded as a validity confirmation of the measurement. The statements apparently correspond with developmental changes people recognize in themselves.

Distribution

When it comes to the age distribution and the degrees of gerotranscendence, the theory certainly assumes a correlation with age. The degree of gerotranscendence is expected to increase with age. In this study, however, neither cosmic transcendence nor ego-transcendence show any correlation with the age of the respondent. Nor are there any gender differences in these respects. Controlling for both gender and age at the same time shows the same result.

The lack of age differences can be understood as a result of the study population and the methodology we have used. The sample is quite homogeneous, with all respondents above the age of 74. The methodology implies a retrospective technique, where the respondents compare the present situation with the situation at age 50. Those who have experienced developments in the direction of gerotranscendence might well have done so before the age of 74. As we are going to see in a later section of this book, the expected age correlation will appear when a larger age span is the target of analysis and age groups are compared as to the extent to which they have developed towards gerotranscendence.

Gerotranscendence and Social Activity

On the question about social activity and gerotranscendence we find a positive correlation between cosmic transcendence and social activity[14] and a positive, but not statistically significant, correlation between ego-transcendence and social activity.

The above-mentioned correlations are not in themselves overwhelming in magnitude, but they are theoretically very interesting. If changes

---

[14]$(eta = .17, p < .001)$

toward gerotranscendence were to be aspects of social withdrawal and disengagement, we would expect to find a negative correlation with social activities. Since we do not find such correlations, but rather the opposite, we have a quantitative empirical indication that the concept of gerotranscendence is something different from the old concept of disengagement or part of a breakdown syndrome. Gerotranscendence goes with self-decided activity, not with withdrawal.

Coping Patterns

Further, if gerotranscendence were the same as disengagement or part of a breakdown syndrome, the predicted coping patterns would be an increasing proportion of low copers and defensive copers, with increasing degrees of gerotranscendence. We find the opposite. With increasing degrees of cosmic and ego-transcendence, we find increasing proportions of offensive copers and multicopers.[15]

Two differences between respondents with high and low degrees of cosmic transcendence are especially interesting. First, the proportion of lowcopers is considerably higher among the respondents with a low degree of cosmic transcendence (41 percent) compared with the respondents with a high degree of cosmic transcendence (26 percent). Second, the proportion of multicopers is considerably higher among the respondents with a high degree of cosmic transcendence (33 percent) compared with respondents with a low degree of cosmic transcendence (22 percent). The same type of differences are found when comparing respondents with high and low degrees of ego-transcendence, even if the differences in this case are not as pronounced. These findings contradict the assumption that gerotranscendence is the same as or part of a negative disengagement or a breakdown syndrome. Instead we find a pattern where high degrees of gerotranscendence are combined with more coping, more offensive coping, and more multicoping.

Also, we find that one of the gerotranscendence measures is related to the degree to which the respondents have a positive view of the possibilities of solving problems connected with the specific trauma of losing a close person. Among the respondents who had experienced such a loss

---

[15]The correlation between the degree of cosmic transcendence and the coping pattern is eta = .16, p < .001. The correlation between the degree of ego-transcendence and the coping pattern is eta = .13, p < .05.

during the last 12 months preceding the measurement in 1990, the respondents with the higher degrees of cosmic transcendence had a more positive
outlook on the possibility of solving the problem.[16] No such relationship
was found with ego-transcendence however.

Life Satisfaction

The data show positive correlations between life satisfaction and the
degree of both cosmic[17] and ego-transcendence.[18] The higher the degree
of transcendence, the higher the life satisfaction. These correlations are,
however, somewhat modified when you take the degree of social activity
into consideration. The degree of social activity correlates with life satisfaction[19], and when both the degree of social activity and the degree of
cosmic transcendence are introduced as independents in an MCA analysis[20]
with the life satisfaction as dependent, we can conclude that both types
of gerotranscendence show a remaining correlation with life satisfaction.[21]
This also applies when we control for the degree of social activity, even
if social activity, generally speaking, seems to be the more important
predictor of life satisfaction.

The intercorrelations between social activity, gerotranscendence, and
life satisfaction however show a theoretically quite interesting pattern.
The original correlation between the degree of social activity and life
satisfaction decreases when we take gerotranscendence into consideration.
The higher the degree of cosmic transcendence, the weaker is the correlation between social activity and life satisfaction. In other words, *the more
transcendent the respondent, the less essential is the degree of social activity
for life satisfaction.* The modifying effect of ego-transcendence on the
correlation between social activity and life satisfaction shows the same
tendency, though it is not as obvious (see Tornstam, 1994, for details).

---

[16](eta = .21, p < .05)
[17](eta = .16, p < .001)
[18](eta = .12, p < .05)
[19](eta = .36, p < .001)
[20]ANOVA-MCA is a multivariate variance analysis that allows nominal data as independent
variables. As with ordinary regression analysis, the beta values show the explanatory power after
the introduction of other independent variables.
[21]The explanatory power of cosmic transcendence decreases somewhat (from eta = .16 to beta
= .12), while the explanatory power of social activity decreases from eta = .36 to beta = .28.
When ego-transcendence is introduced as an independent variable, together with social activity,
the explanatory power of ego-transcendence remains constant (eta = .12, beta = .12) as does the
explanatory power of social activity (eta = .36, beta = .30).

Also when the satisfaction with social activity is analyzed in relation to the degree of social activity, we find that the degree of gerotranscendence has the same modifying effect—the more transcendent the respondent, the weaker the correlation between the degree of social activity and the satisfaction with social activity. Again, this is especially pronounced when we control for the degree of cosmic transcendence.

In summary, we find a new pattern where a high degree of transcendence— especially cosmic transcendence—is related to a higher degree of both life satisfaction and satisfaction with social activity, at the same time as the degree of social activity itself becomes less essential for life satisfaction at the higher levels of gerotranscendence.

Also in the longitudinal perspective, there is a connection between gerotranscendence and the change in life satisfaction. Since the 1990 Danish retrospective study is part of a longitudinal study, we have information about the degree of life satisfaction at two points in time, 1986 and 1990.

As expected, most respondents report the same degree of life satisfaction at both points of measurement. When changes occurred, however, they were correlated to the degrees of both cosmic and ego-transcendence. Those who rated low on gerotranscendence in 1990 were more likely to have decreased in life satisfaction between 1986 and 1990. Those who rated high on gerotranscendence in 1990 have been stable in life satisfaction between 1986 and 1990.

The causal interpretation of the above finding is somewhat difficult, since the degrees of gerotranscendence were measured only in 1990, while the longitudinal changes in life satisfaction refer to the changes between 1986 and 1990. If, however, the measure of the two types of gerotranscendence is tapping a developmental process starting before both measurements (as implied by the phrasing of the items), one causal interpretation could be the following: The reason that we find a correlation between gerotranscendence and life satisfaction in a cross-sectional analysis might not be that a high degree of gerotranscendence produces higher life satisfaction, but rather that, to a certain extent, it prevents decreases in life satisfaction. This is however nothing but an hypothesis, which needs to be tested in a longitudinal study where both gerotranscendence and life satisfaction are measured at several points in time.

Facilitating or Obstructing Gerotranscendence

The process of gerotranscendence can, according to the theory, be accelerated, facilitated or obstructed in different ways. One assumption was that major crises in life might facilitate the restructuring of the definition of reality, as implied by the theory. One such crisis, used as a test variable in this context, is the death of a spouse or another close person. In this material[22] 203 respondents (22 percent) had experienced such a loss during the 12 months preceding the data collection in 1990. When the respondents who experienced such a loss were compared with the ones who did not, we found the degree of cosmic transcendence to be somewhat higher among those who experienced that loss.[23] No such differences were found as to the degree of ego-transcendence. It seems reasonable to assume that it was the crisis of losing a close person that caused an increase in the degree of cosmic transcendence.

We also found that the degree of cosmic transcendence is correlated with the type of work the respondent had before retirement, and with social class. Respondents who had white-collar work or were metropolitan entrepreneurs had somewhat higher degrees of cosmic transcendence than others[24]. Also, the degree of cosmic transcendence was found to be higher among the respondents in the higher social classes[25]. The common denominator in these observations might be that the respondents with the higher degrees of cosmic transcendence had led less restricted lives with higher degrees of personal freedom. Their personal development was less hindered by limiting rules or values.

This interpretation is in line with the reasoning of Chinen (1989a) who, as described earlier, analyzed the scientific works of Ludwig Wittgenstein and Alfred North Withed, and found that their way of working became more qualitative and "transcendent" in their later years.

In summary, we do find some evidence that the degree of cosmic transcendence might be affected by both life crises and other facilitating or restricting factors. It should be observed, however, that this statement is only valid for cosmic transcendence. The empirical findings, however, support the assumption that the development of gerotranscendence is not only dependent on pure *age development*, but is also affected by *social-matrix factors* and *incident-impact factors*. Social position, including type of work, is an example of a social-matrix factor. Illness and perceived crises in life are examples of incident-impact factors.

---

[22]The 1990 Danish retrospective study.
[23](eta = .11, p < .01)
[24](eta = .15, p < .001)
[25](eta = .12, p < .05)

Mental Illness, Depression, and Use of Psychotropics

One important question to be answered by the empirical data was whether the state of gerotranscendence might be related to, confused with, or caused by mental illness, depression, or consumption of psychotropics. Table 4.2 summarizes our tests of this hypothesis.

The old age depression scale does not correlate with either cosmic transcendence or ego-transcendence. That the complete set of items in this scale was used only at the 1986 measurement poses a methodological problem. Hence, the correlation refers to the depression value in 1986 and the gerotranscendence values in 1990. Two of the specific items in the old age depression scale were used, however, in 1990. Neither of these (feeling lonely, feeling old) correlated with the gerotranscendence scales. It therefore seems reasonable to suggest that gerotranscendence is not to be seen as a depression correlate or defense reaction caused by old age depression. The same conclusion holds concerning psychological strain. The psychological strain scale does not correlate with any one of the gerotranscendence measures.

Nor is the assumption that the use of psychotropics is related to gerotranscendence supported by our data. The only statistically significant correlation in this respect is the negative correlation between the use of psychopharmacological drugs[26] and the gerotranscendence scales. In both

TABLE 4.2 Correlations Between Gerotranscendence and "Confoundings"

	Cosmic Transcendence	Ego Transcendence
Old Age Depression Scale (1986)	$.06^{ns}$	$.02^{ns}$
Feeling Lonely (1990)	$.03^{ns}$	$.06^{ns}$
Feeling Old (1990)	$.04^{ns}$	$.01^{ns}$
Psychological Strain Scale (1990)	$.01^{ns}$	$.03^{ns}$
Use of Sedatives or Hypnotics (1986)	$.02^{ns}$	$.01^{ns}$
Use of psychopharmacological drugs (1986)	$-.07^*$	$-.10^{**}$

$^*p < .05$
$^{**}p < .01$
^{ns}not significant

---

[26]Psychopharmacological drugs are distinguished by their potency from such milder psychotropics as sedatives, which are used to combat insomnia and anxiety. The more potent psychopharmacas would more likely be employed to control neuroses and psychoses.

cases the correlation indicates that respondents who used psychopharma-cological drugs in 1986 had *lower* degrees of both cosmic and ego-transcen-dence in 1990. If any causal conclusion should be drawn from this, it should be that the consumption of psychopharmacological drugs is a hindrance to achieving gerotranscendence.

One Step Ahead

This chapter has brought us another step closer to an empirical illumina-tion of gerotranscendence. From the answers to the items included in the gerotranscendence measures it can be concluded that the items touch upon something that is recognized by the respondents. Significant propor-tions of the respondents recognize in themselves the changes expressed by the items. From the initial description of the theory it should be obvious that the points of departure for the theory of gerotranscendence are quite different from the interactionist theories and the "activity the-ory." But is gerotranscendence something new and different from the old concept of disengagement? Several of the results described in this study indicate that it is.

First, the very content of the statements forming the gerotranscen-dence scales is different from the disengagement concept. While "disen-gagement" only implies a turning inwards, "gerotranscendence" implies a new definition of reality.

Second, while disengagement is connected with social withdrawal, our data show gerotranscendence to be positively correlated with social activity, at the same time as a greater need for solitary "philosophizing" is experienced. But, and most important, the social activities positively correlated with gerotranscendence are activities where more of the initia-tive for activity rests with the individual.

Third, the coping patterns of the respondents with high degrees of gerotranscendence certainly do not correspond to what would be pre-dicted by the theory of disengagement, nor by the assumption that gero-transcendence is an aspect of a social breakdown syndrome. Instead of reporting passive or defensive coping strategies, we find that respondents with high degrees of gerotranscendence make greater use of "offensive" and multicoping patterns.

Fourth, we have found a new pattern where a high degree of especially cosmic transcendence is related to a higher degree of both life satisfaction and satisfaction with social activity, at the same time as the degree of social activity becomes less essential for satisfaction at the higher levels of gerotranscendence. All this leads us to the conclusion that the concept of gerotranscendence is clearly different from both the old concepts of disengagement and social breakdown syndrome.

The concept of gerotranscendence is more closely related to Gutman's previously mentioned concept of "passive and magical mastery." Gutman, however, regards this shift toward passive and magical mastery to be an adaptation by the individual, made necessary by individual and social changes in the aging process whereby the changes described become effects of the impact of social aging. Strained to a fine point, the changes toward passive and magical mastery become, for Gutman, defense mechanisms. In this respect, the theory of gerotranscendence is very different, both from the pure theoretical perspective and from the empirical one.

To conclude, then, we find it evident that the concept of gerotranscendence is a new concept, different from other well known theoretical concepts in gerontology. According to the response patterns, it is seemingly also relevant for the personal experiences of some older people. Furthermore, it may prove to be a theoretically fruitful concept since it focuses on new types of developmental patterns and combinations, for example, the combination of high degrees of gerotranscendence, social activity, multicoping and life satisfaction. Where in earlier theorizing such concepts have been formulated in terms of *either/or*, the theory of gerotranscendence offers *both/and*.

GEROTRANSCENDENCE
FROM A CROSS-SECTIONAL PERSPECTIVE

In the 1990 Danish study described earlier, the changes implied in the theory of gerotranscendence were measured by a series of retrospective statements. The overall impression was that a large proportion of the respondents recognized, in themselves, the changes expressed by the various statements. A closer analysis of the previous quantitative study showed, among other things, that:

- Individuals with a high degree of gerotranscendence have a higher degree of life satisfaction.

- Life crises accelerate the development toward gerotranscendence.

- Individuals with a high degree of gerotranscendence have a higher degree of self-initiated social activity than individuals with a low degree of gerotranscendence.

• The signs of gerotranscendence cannot be explained away as symptoms of disease, depression, or the consumption of psychiatric drugs.

All these findings, however, are based on data focusing exclusively on elderly persons. This provokes some important questions, on which the following analysis is intended to shed some light:

1. What would the results be if corresponding questions were asked to individuals of all ages? Would we find age differences suggesting an increase in gerotranscendence?

2. If there is a process of gerotranscendence, when does it start? Is it continuous or more like a sudden shift at some point in life?

3. Do men and women have the same or different developmental characteristics in terms of gerotranscendence?

4. How do life circumstances affect the process of gerotranscendence?

5. Is gerotranscendence unconditionally related to higher satisfaction with life and less fear of death?

In order to answer these questions we mailed a survey in 1995 to a random sample of 3000 Swedish men and women between the ages of 20 and 85.[27]

Measures in the Swedish 1995 Cross-Sectional Study

Drawing on the previous qualitative and quantitative studies, a series of questions and statements were framed in accordance with the previously described dimensions of gerotranscendence. Statements were worded in order to tap the *status* of these dimensions—not the retrospective change as in the 1990 Danish study. Each respondent was asked to rate how poorly or well each statement agreed with his or her own experience and feelings on a fixed four-point scale. So, while the previous Danish study had its focus on retrospective descriptions of change, the Swedish 1995 study aimed at snapshot presentations of the gerotranscendence level in various parts of the population.

---

[27]The response rate was 67% (2002 Ss) and the respondent group was, in terms of age and sex distribution, statistically representative of the whole Swedish population within the corresponding age span (tested by Chi^2 for goodness of fit).

The answers to the statements were analyzed by an explorative principal component factor analysis which produced the dimensions in Table 4.3.[28]

The main factor, *the cosmic dimension*, captures quite well what was also the "main factor" in the previous studies—the transcendence of time, space, and objects. We refer to this as *cosmic transcendence*. The *coherence dimension* in the factor analysis corresponding to the "ego-integrity" under the "self" dimension in the previous qualitative analysis and the *solitude dimension* corresponds to the "changed meaning and importance of relations" under the social and individual relations dimension. For each of the factors, a standardized additive index was constructed.[29]

Additive indices have also been constructed for the measurement of diseases and life crises. Respondents were asked to read a list of common diseases and mark the diseases they suffered from. The number of diseases

TABLE 4.3   Dimensions of Gerotranscendence

Cosmic dimension	Factor load
I feel connected with the entire universe	.78
I feel that I am a part of everything alive	.71
I can feel a strong presence of people who are elsewhere	.60
Sometimes I feel like I live in the past and present simultaneously	.44
I feel a strong connection with earlier generations	.41
Coherence dimension	**Factor load**
My life feels chaotic and disrupted	−.74
The life I have lived has coherence and meaning	.70
Solitude dimension	**Factor load**
I like to be by myself better than being with others	.78
I like meetings with new people	−.59
Being at peace and philosophizing by myself is important for my well-being.	.58

[28]Two restrictions were put on factors to be further analyzed: First, factors should be interpretable. Second, none of the statements in a factor should have factor loads above .40 in factors other than the ones that are presented in Table 4.3. These restrictions caused a reduction of an originally larger set of statements (reported in Tornstam, 1997 a) to the statements presented in Table 4.3.

[29]According to the rules given by Galtung (1969).

were added to create a simple index. In the same vein, the respondents were asked if they, during the last two years, had experienced something they regarded as a life crisis. The respondents could mark a number of predefined crises as well as add other types of crises. A simple additive index, showing the number of crises each respondent had reported, was constructed.

In addition to these indices, several single-item measures have been used in the analysis. Overall life satisfaction is an example of such a single-item measure, where the respondents were asked to rate how satisfied they were with their present life on a fixed five-point scale.

The Cosmic Dimension

The research questions for the cross-sectional study focus on how gerotranscendence might be related to age, gender, life circumstances, and life crises. Table 4.4 shows the relevant correlations. The eta values in the table refer to simple bivariate correlations, while beta values are the "pure" correlation when the other variables are controlled for.[30]

In the previously described Danish retrospective study, we did not find the expected age difference in gerotranscendence, which was suggested to be a result of the retrospective character of the study and of the compressed age distribution of the sample. In the cross-sectional study, however, with its wider age scope, the expected correlation appears. The degree of cosmic transcendence is higher in the higher age categories.

TABLE 4.4 ANOVA-MCA Analysis of the Correlates to the Cosmic Dimension, Cosmic Transcendence as Dependent Variable

	Eta	Beta	R^2
Gender	.13	.12	
Age	.16	.16	
Profession	.11	.11	
Crises	.15	.12	
Diseases	.14	.06	
			.07

---

[30]In an ANOVA-MCAanalysis, an analysis of variance with a Multiple Classification Analysis design that allows categorical variables as dependents.

The correlation is not overwhelming even though it is, statistically speaking, highly significant.[31]

Table 4.4 also shows a correlation with gender. Women scored higher on cosmic transcendence. Also, respondents who have (or had) self-governed professions or are students, scored higher on cosmic transcendence. Finally, respondents who, during the two years previous to the study, had experienced one or more life crises, also scored higher on cosmic transcendence.

All of the above-mentioned variables have remaining explanatory power (beta values) when we control for the others.[32] When the above-mentioned variables are entered into an CHAID[33] analysis, the subgroup with the highest value on cosmic transcendence is identified by age alone. On a five-point scale of cosmic transcendence, 31 percent of the oldest respondents (75–85) have the highest value. We might call them "transcenders." The subgroup with the lowest degree of cosmic transcendence is, according to the CHAID analysis, identified by age, gender, and crises: Men, between 20 and 44 years of age, who have not experienced any crisis during the two years previous to the study, are the least likely to have experienced cosmic transcendence. In this group only 7 percent are "transcenders."

In Figure 4.1a the degree of cosmic transcendence is shown in relation to age and gender. Four characteristics in this graph should be noted: *First*, the general pattern shows a gradually increasing degree of cosmic transcendence with increasing age. There is no sudden increase between any specific age groups. *Second*, women score higher on cosmic transcendence than men. *Third*, the difference between women and men decreases with age up to the age category 65–75. *Fourth*, in the last age category there is a split between men and women. The women continue the increase while the men drop.[34] (Figure 4.1b is commented on later.)

An interesting observation concerning this gender difference is that it disappears when we compare men and women who are not cohabiting

---

[31](eta = .16, p < .001)

[32]In an ANOVA-MCAanalysis. The total explanatory power is, however, low ($R^2 = .07$)

[33]CHAID (Chi-squared Automatic Interaction Detection) is an algorithm with which a data set is broken down into subcategories according to the explanatory power a set of predictors has on a dependent variable (AnswerTree, 1998; Kass, 1980).

[34]This difference is statistically significant (eta = .17, p < .05) even if the number of men (78) and women (79) in this age category is low.

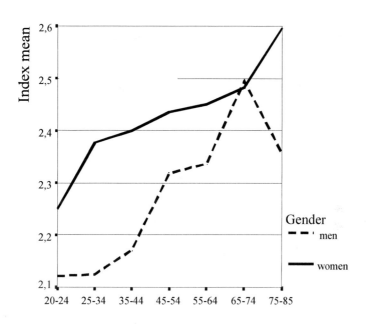

FIGURE 4.1a   Cosmic transcendence.

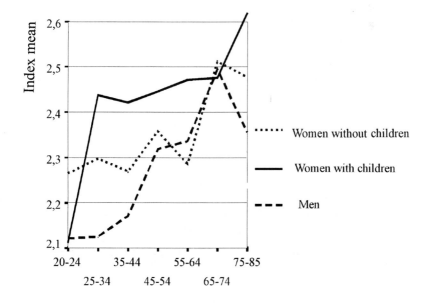

Age

FIGURE 4.1b   Cosmic transcendence—women with and without children compared with men.

(widowed, divorced, or never married). The difference remains with increased strength[35] when the comparison is made between cohabiting (married) men and women age 75–85. The cohabiting women, as described in connection with the CHAID analysis above, score considerably higher on cosmic transcendence than the cohabiting men.

According to the theory in question and in correspondence with the findings from the previous Danish 1990 quantitative study, we would expect that "transcenders" report higher life satisfaction and less fear of death. These assumptions are, however, not supported by the Swedish 1995 cross-sectional study. We shall return to this finding later in this section, and still later see how the expected correlation reappear in the 2001 study (65+) with focus on the upper end of the age scale.

The Coherence Dimension

Table 4.5 shows the correlates to the coherence dimension. The analysis reveals a rather strong correlation with age. The higher the age, the higher the degree of coherence. It should be noted that this correlation also remains when we control for all the other correlates.

Aside from the age variable, the analysis shows that women have slightly higher coherence values than men. Unmarried and divorced respondents had lower values than widows/widowers and married or cohabiting respondents. Individuals with higher incomes had higher coherence

TABLE 4.5   ANOVA-MCA Analysis of the Correlates to the Coherence Dimension, Coherence as Dependent Variable

	Eta	Beta	R^2
Gender	.05	.11	
Age	.20	.21	
Civil Status	.20	.13	
Income	.12	.13	
Crises	.23	.18	
Diseases	.13	.15	
			.15

[35](eta = .30, p < .01)

values, while individuals who had experienced crises or diseases had lower coherence values.

In Figure 4.2 the degree of coherence is shown in relation to age and gender. The general observation should be that the degree of coherence increases with age for both men and women. For women, the increase is more or less continuous. Among the men, there is a drop in coherence in the age category 35–44, and a recovery in the subsequent category. In the age category 35–44, the difference in coherence level between men and women is statistically significant,[36] while the corresponding difference in the very last age category is not.

The coherence scale correlates strongly with life satisfaction[37] and moderately with fear of death.[38] The higher the degree of coherence, the

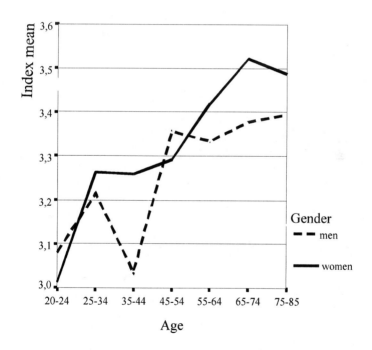

FIGURE 4.2   Coherence.

---

[36](eta = .17, p < .01)
[37](eta = .52, p < .001)
[38](eta = −.19, p < .001)

higher the life satisfaction and the lower the fear of death. These correlations are, with some small variations, found in each separate age category. The coherence dimension correlates weakly, but is statistically significantly with the cosmic dimension.[39]

The Solitude Dimension

When it comes to the solitude dimension, we have found, as shown in Table 4.6, only two independent variables worth mentioning. These variables are age and disease. Regardless of age, respondents with one or several diseases report a greater need for solitude. But controlling for health also, age alone explains just as much of the need for solitude.

Figure 4.3 shows in more detail what the general age-solitude pattern looks like among men and women. None of the differences between the slopes for men and women are statistically significant, so we should rather focus on an "average." In this case, we notice that there is not a continuous increase in the need for solitude with age. The need for solitude increases up to the age category of 35–44 and remains quite stable after that. We are, then, disregarding and averaging the statistically insignificant divergent tendencies among men and women in the oldest age categories.

The need for solitude correlates negatively with life satisfaction.[40] The less the satisfaction with life, the higher the need for solitude. The solitude dimension also correlates negatively with the coherence dimension.[41] Even if these negative correlations are small, they are theoretically

TABLE 4.6 ANOVA-MCA Analysis of the Correlates to the Solitude Dimension, Solitude as Dependent Variable

	Eta	Beta	R^2
Gender	.01	.02	
Age	.14	.11	
Crises	.08	.06	
Diseases	.14	.11	
			.04

[39](r = .09, p < .001)
[40](eta = −.16, p < .001)
[41](r = −.16, p < .001)

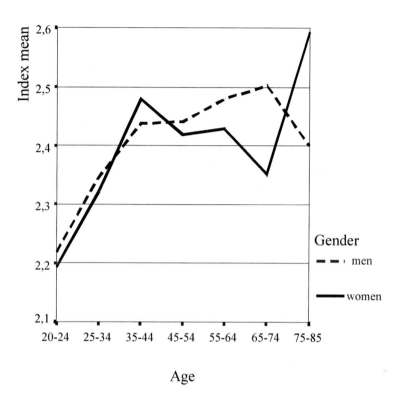

FIGURE 4.3   Need for solitude.

problematic. They indicate that solitude is not, which goes for cosmic transcendence and coherence, predominantly positive when it comes to satisfaction with life. Even if the correlation with the cosmic dimension is weakly positive,[42] the total outcome is a negative correlation with life satisfaction. The need for solitude might be a coin with both a positive and a negative side—a question to which we will return later.

Discussion of the Cross Sectional Findings

The main purpose of the Swedish 1995 cross-sectional study was to address the following question: Would it be possible, in a study including

---

[42](r = .10, p < .001)

people from a wide age range, to find age differences of the same kind as implied in the previous qualitative and retrospective quantitative studies of exclusively older people?

A special problem in this regard is that it was impossible to use the same measures. This is obvious when comparisons with the previous qualitative study are considered. We also have the same type of problem when it comes to comparisons between the two quantitative studies. In the previous quantitative Danish 1990 study, all statements were formulated retrospectively since all the respondents were at the same end of the age scale (74–100). The respondents were asked to compare their situation at age 50 with their situation at the time of the survey. In the Swedish cross-sectional 1995 study, the statements had to be designed in order to tap the present situation only. Thus, by comparing age categories, it should be possible to make some cautious conclusions about developmental patterns. So, derived from the results of the previous studies, the statements for the 1995 cross-sectional 1995 study were worded with the aim of capturing static, snapshot values of what, in the previous studies, were descriptions of processes. This methodological difference should be kept in mind when interpreting the empirical findings.

Another thing to be observed when interpreting the findings, is the limitations of the cross-sectional design. Any difference between age categories could, in theory at least, be an unknown mix of cohort effects and individual developments. With these pointers in mind we can proceed with a further discussion of the cross sectional findings.

Drawing on the outcome of the analyses of the dimensions given by the factor analysis, and again operating under the assumption that our cross-sectional data can be interpreted from a developmental perspective, we are able to suggest that both the general *cosmic* and the general *coherence* aspects of gerotranscendence develop in principally continuous ways. The general *solitude* aspect, on the other hand, develops in another way, with an early increase in the need for solitude and thereafter a steady state. We must, however, again make the reservation that our present data set is limited in several ways, culturally, temporally, and in age span. It ends with individuals at age 85. The outcome of an analysis based on a data set including even older individuals from other cultures and other cohorts might alter the above conclusions. However, as we are going to see, a later replication of this study conducted on a sample including older respondents (65–104) will confirm and elucidate the findings described above.

Modifiers

Even if some aspects or dimensions of gerotranscendence are referred to as general in the sense that they show a statistically significant correlation with age, some circumstances do modify these correlations. Gender, crises, and life circumstances have been found to be such modifiers. We refer to such modifiers as *social-matrix factors* and *incidence-impact factors*.

The outcome given by the factor analyses show that women score higher than men on *cosmic transcendence*, even though there is a tendency towards reduction of this difference, at least up to the age category 64–75. This finding parallels the perspective of generally diminishing gender personality differences with age (Huyck, 1990). In our case, the men, especially from the age category 35–44, rapidly catch up with the women. This might suggest that before this age men are too trapped by gender-role success activities to be open to this kind of development. If the "mid-life crisis" comes, this might pave the way for the further development of cosmic transcendence. The women's higher levels of cosmic transcendence, especially in the age interval 25–44, might be partly connected with childbirth. A closer analysis has shown that the difference between men and women in terms of cosmic transcendence is smaller, but not absent, when comparing women without children with men. For the men it doesn't matter if they have children or not. The age slope of cosmic transcendence is just about the same. For that reason the undivided men category can be compared with women who have children and women don't.

Figure 4.1b shows that, among women with children, the degree of cosmic transcendence increases significantly already in the age category 25–34 and continues to increase all the way up to the highest age category. It might be that, for many women, giving birth to a child represents such a developmental crisis when definitions of life are reconstructed.

We also have the drop among cohabiting men 75–85 years of age to consider. At this point, we can only speculate on this empirical finding. The result could also be, even if this statistical probability is low, a product of sampling error. If we accept the empirical finding as a fact, one explanation could be that the men in this cohort and in this culture carry with them some particular experiences in life that might explain their divergence. We will return to this issue later on.

The rapid increase in *cosmic* transcendence among men from age category 34–44 through 45–54 also has its correspondence when it concerns *coherence*. The degree of coherence drops to a minimum in the age category 35–44 and increases rapidly after that (Figure 4.2). An explanation for this might be found along the same lines as above. If we stick to the statistical rules of the game, this study shows no gender difference in the solitude dimension of gerotranscendence (Figure 4.3).

Having experienced a crisis in life is, according to our analysis, connected with higher degrees of *cosmic* transcendence, but lower degrees of *coherence*. The previous 1990 Danish retrospective study showed that individuals who, during the year previous to the survey, experienced the death of a person close to them had higher values on the cosmic gerotranscendence dimension. In the Swedish 1995 cross-sectional study, the crisis measure was wider, including anything that the respondent perceived as a crisis in life, but the result is the same. With crises come higher levels of cosmic transcendence. But, this does not hold true for the coherence dimension. What we find is the somewhat contradictory pattern that crises affect one dimension of gerotranscendence positively and another one negatively. This finding paves the way for a discussion of the possible "causal" and temporal interrelations between the dimensions of gerotranscendence. Might a crisis-induced decrease in coherence after some time be "repaired" by the simultaneous crisis induced increase in cosmic transcendence? This is yet another question to be answered in future research. In a following chapter we are going to take a closer look at various crises in old age, and their connection with gerotranscendence.

Illness has, according to the analyses, a modifying effect similar in part to other crises. As far as the *cosmic* dimension concerns, illness shows a positive simple bivariate correlation with *cosmic* transcendence. But, when we control for the experience of crises (Table 4.4), the effect of illness disappears. A possible interpretation of this is that illness creates an increase in the cosmic transcendence only to the degree to which it is experienced as a crisis. Illness has, on the other hand, remaining effects on both the solitude and the coherence dimensions (Tables 4.5 and 4. 6).

Both the *cosmic* transcendence and the *coherence* dimension are, according to the analysis, affected by life circumstances. Respondents with self-governed professions and students score higher on cosmic transcendence. Maybe a life with higher degrees of autonomy contributes to a liberation from restrictive, mainstream rules and values which might otherwise have reduced the possibility for development of cosmic transcendence.

Regarding the *coherence* dimension, both civil status and income have, as described, modifying effects. From the aforementioned findings we can draw the general conclusion that aspects of gerotranscendence are seemingly evoked and modified not only by aging, per se, but by other circumstances as well.

Gerotranscendence, Life Satisfaction, and Fear of Death

Working from the results of the previous qualitative study, we assumed that individuals with higher degrees of gerotranscendence would score higher on life satisfaction. That was in fact demonstrated in the previous 1990 Danish retrospective study where we found a statistically significant correlation between the measure of cosmic transcendence and life satisfaction.[43] In the Swedish 1995 cross-sectional study we did not find the corresponding correlation. This fact can be understood in several ways, for example: While the previous 1990 Danish retrospective study focused on experienced *changes* in aspects of gerotranscendence, the Swedish 1995 cross-sectional study taps the *static* value of these aspects. Having a "high" value in this snapshot perspective might be very different from having experienced a change. It might be the experience of a developmental change, rather than having a high or low value on cosmic transcendence, that induces or is connected with high life satisfaction.

Another explanation might be provided by referring to the differences in the age ranges used in the studies. We shall later see how the correlation reappears when we address an older group of respondents. Remember that the previous 1990 Danish retrospective study had a sample in the age range 74–100 years, while the Swedish 1995 cross-sectional study has the age range 20–85 years. This explanation might also be applicable when trying to understand why, in the Swedish 1995 cross-sectional study, we did not find any correlation between cosmic transcendence and fear of death, as was hypothesized on the basis of the previous qualitative study. When later we examine a sample including respondents 65–104 years of age, the correlation between cosmic transcendence and life satisfaction will reappear, suggesting that increased life satisfaction is a fruit of gerotranscendence that is reserved for old age.

The coherence dimension shows a very strong and positive correlation with our measure of life satisfaction, and a modest but statistically

---

[43](eta = .16, p < .001)

highly significant negative correlation with fear of death. So, if simple explanations are sought, the experience of coherence is very beneficial for life satisfaction and absence of fear of death. But, on the other hand, the concepts of coherence and life satisfaction are too close to be viewed in a causal perspective.

Conclusions Thus Far

In the Swedish 1995 cross-sectional study, which was yet a further small step towards the empirical exploration of the theory of gerotranscendence, we have found cross-sectional age differences which we cautiously, yet venturesomely, interpret in a developmental way. We do so because the main purpose of this empirical step was to see whether the results from earlier research using retrospective developmental perspectives could be replicated in a cross-sectional study.

Drawing, then, on the response patterns of the statements we have used and the scales we have constructed, we find patterns of the kind found in previous qualitative and quantitative studies of exclusively elderly people. *We have found cross sectional age patterns of increasing cosmic transcendence, coherence, and need for solitude. Our data suggest that the development of cosmic transcendence and coherence are continuous processes which start already during the first half of the adult life and gradually develop to their maximum in later life. The need for solitude also reaches its maximum in late life, but develops most rapidly during the first half of adult life. We have found that women score higher than men on cosmic transcendence, but that this difference decreases with increasing age.* We also have discovered, however, a gender difference not found in the previous 1990 Danish retrospective study—the male drop in cosmic transcendence in the age category 75–85. We will return to this surprising finding in a later section of this book.

Not only age, but also *social-matrix factors* and *incidence-impact factors* have been shown to correlate with gerotranscendence. Life crises seemingly affect the dimensions of gerotranscendence, as do profession and income. A possible interpretation of the latter is that an autonomous life contributes to a liberation from rules and values which might otherwise have reduced the possibility for the development of transcendence.

Theoretically, the results from the Swedish 1995 cross-sectional study suggest, in line with the previous studies, that there is a process of gerotranscendence, but also that this process may appear different depending on cohort affiliation, gender, and life circumstances. It is not unlikely that a comparative study would show the process of gerotranscendence to be somewhat different in different cultures. As with, for example, Jung's archetypes, the core concept (e.g., the archetype of the "wise man") is general, but its expressions are culturally dependent (in some places the "wise man" is a woman[44]).

In fact, Ahmadi (1998, 2000a, 2000b, 2001) has elaborated on this, and found that cultural elements surely are to be regarded as modifiers to the development of gerotranscendence. While Chinen (1986) pointed to supportive folk tales in certain cultures, Ahmadi points to the more fundamental ways of thinking—of constructing reality—which differ among cultures. If the culture, for example, entails elements of Sufism, individuals have been shown to develop gerotranscendence more easily.

FOCUSING THE 65+

The studies on gerotranscendence described above have suggested a pattern of developmental changes in cosmic transcendence, coherence, and the need for solitude. The study of 1,771 Swedish respondents 65–104 years of age described below, the *2001 Study (65+)*, confirms earlier findings while furthering the theory in general as well as our knowledge of gerotranscendental development at the upper end of the age scale, in particular. This new study furthers how the pure *age development* of gerotranscendence is affected by *social-matrix factors* and *incident-impact factors*.

Summing up and Moving on with Focus on the 65+

Based on the previous qualitative and quantitative studies, the dimensions of gerotranscendence were described as ontological changes in: a) the cosmic, b) the self, c) social and individual relationships. In the Swedish 1995 cross-sectional study of 2002 Swedish men and women between the ages of 20 and 85, the three dimensions of gerotranscendence were approximated with three measures: *cosmic transcendence, coherence,* and *need*

---

[44]If he were living today, Jung would most probably have exemplified the "wise man" with Gandalf in Tolkien's tale, The Lord of The Rings—a traditional kind of wise man and magician. He also might have added that the Oracle of Delphi in ancient Greece—a woman—was also in line with the archetype of the "wise man," but in the guise of a woman.

for solitude. The cross-sectional age patterns of the three measures have previously been described in Figures 4.1, 4.2, and 4.3.

The basic finding, supporting the theory of gerotranscendence, showed that the measures of gerotranscendence increase with age. We found cross-sectional age differences, which we cautiously, yet venture-somely, interpreted in a developmental way.

We registered patterns of increasing cosmic transcendence, coherence, and need for solitude. Our data suggested that cosmic transcendence and coherence are principally continuous developmental processes that begin during the first half of adult life and gradually develop to their maximum in later life. The need for solitude also has its maximum in late life, but develops most rapidly during the first half of adult life. Looking back on the earlier studies, we find that three types of factors seem to influence or explain the degree of gerotranscendence that a respondent reports: 1) pure *age development,* 2) *social-matrix factors* (e.g., gender, marital status, occupation), and 3) *incident-impact factors* (e.g., illnesses, crises).

We found, for example, that women score higher than men on cosmic transcendence, but that this difference decreases with increasing age. Yet, we also discovered a puzzling gender difference—a drop in male cosmic transcendence in the age category 75–85—which was one of the things that prompted us to take a closer look, with a new sample, at the upper end of the age scale. Whereas the Swedish 1995 cross-sectional study included the whole age range from 20 to 85, only 190 Ss (9.5% of the sample) fell into the age category 75–85. Also, no respondents above the age of 85 were included in the Swedish 1995 cross-sectional study. The study reported below, referred to as the *2001 Study (65+),* focuses entirely on the 65+ age category, with no upper age limit on the sampling procedure, which resulted in a number of respondents within the 65–104 age range.

Further Questions

The general purpose of the 2001 Study was to obtain a better understanding of the gerotranscendence patterns when the unlimited age span 65+ is studied in detail. More precisely, we wished to scrutinize each of the gerotranscendence measures in order to reveal the possible developmental patterns in the upper end of the age scale, to take a closer look at the aforementioned explanatory factors for gerotranscendence, and to discover who the transcenders and the nontranscenders in old age were. In order to do so, we asked the following questions:

- For each of the gerotranscendence measures, how can the possible development from "young" old age to "old" old age be characterized—continuous increase, leveling out, or decrease?

- What does this new empirical focus on the 65+ group add to our knowledge of gerotranscendence from earlier studies focused on ages 20–85?

- What are the explanatory factors and who are the transcenders and the nontranscenders in this 65+ sample?

- How can we understand the drop in cosmic transcendence among the "old" old men?

- Are there relationships between gerotranscendence, social activity, and life satisfaction among Ss 65+?

Method and Measures

For this survey, carried out in 2001, we mailed questions to a sample of 2,800 Swedish men and women, age 65+.[45] The total number of respondents was 1,771, the oldest respondent being 104 years.

As in the previous Swedish 1995 cross-sectional study, a series of questions and statements were framed in accordance with the aforementioned dimensions of gerotranscendence. Statements were worded so as to elicit a snapshot status of these dimensions. Table 4.7 shows all of the statements as well as the dimensions of gerotranscendence they are supposed to tap. Each respondent was asked to rate, on a fixed four-point scale, how poorly or well each statement agreed with his/her own experiences and feelings.

The statement ratings were analyzed by a factor analysis[46] that produced the dimensions in Table 4.7. In Table 4.7, the results of the Swedish 1995 cross-sectional study are compared with the analysis on the present data. The 2001 (65+) data reproduce the very same dimensions as in 1995, with similar, but not identical, factor loadings.

---

[45]The sample was age stratified, with 200 men and 200 women randomly sampled within each of the age categories 65–69, 70–74, 75–79, 80–84, 85–89, 90–94, and 95+. The response rate declined with age from 76 percent in the lowest age category to 53 percent in the highest. The overall response rate was 66 percent.
[46]A varimax rotated principal component analysis.

TABLE 4.7 Dimensions of Gerotranscendence in the Swedish 1995 Cross-Sectional Study and the 2001 Study (65+)[1]

	Factor load	
	1995	2001
Cosmic transcendence		
I feel connected with the entire universe	.78	.69
I feel that I am a part of everything alive	.71	.61
I can feel a strong presence of people who are elsewhere	.60	.75
Sometimes I feel like I live in the past and present simultaneously	.44	.68
I feel a strong connection with earlier generations	.41	.64
Coherence		
My life feels chaotic and disrupted	−.74	−.77
The life I have lived has coherence and meaning	.70	.67
Solitude		
I like to be by myself better than being with others	.78	.89
I like meetings with new people	−.59	−.71
Being at peace and philosophizing by myself is important for my well-being	.58	.51

[1]The Swedish 1995 cross-sectional study includes respondents age 20–85; the 2001 study (65+) includes respondents age 65–104.

For each of the factors, a standardized additive index was constructed.[47] Additive indices were also constructed for the measurement of diseases and life crises. Respondents were asked to read a list of common diseases and mark the diseases they suffered from. The number of diseases was calculated to create a simple additive index. In the same vein, the respondents were asked if they had experienced something they regarded as a life crisis during the past two years. The respondents could mark a number of predefined crises as well as add other types of crises. A simple additive index was constructed showing the number of crises each respondent had reported.

[47]According to the rules given by Galtung (1969). The alpha value, which is a scalability test, is .73 for the cosmic transcendence factor, .60 for the solitude factor, and .57 for the coherence factor. The latter two are below the rule-of-thumb threshold (.70), but expectedly and acceptably so, since the alpha value is highly dependent on the number of items in the scale.

Crises were of course included since the earlier Swedish 1995 cross-sectional study showed that subjectively experienced life crises are related to the dimensions of gerotranscendence. Particularly in women, subjectively experienced life crises were shown to contribute to the development of cosmic transcendence, but the impact decreased with age.

Furthermore, we used an additive activity index, where the respondents were asked how often they a) participate in activities outside the home (organizational activities, church, cinema, theatre, etc.), b) receive visitors at home (friends, neighbors, children, other relatives), and c) themselves visit friends, neighbors, children, or other relatives. Response alternatives included daily, weekly, monthly, every six months, and less often. This index resulted in a five-point activity scale.

In addition to these indices, several single-item measures were used in the analysis. Overall life satisfaction is an example of such a single-item measure where respondents were asked to rate, on a fixed five-point scale, how satisfied they were with their present existence.

RESULTS FROM THE 2001 (65+) STUDY

Cosmic Transcendence

As seen in Figure 4.4, the 2001 data focusing on ages 65+ replicate the Swedish 1995 cross-sectional study by showing a statistically significant final increase in cosmic transcendence for women,[48] but not for men. The arch-shaped slope for men is not statistically significant. Nor is the split between men and women from age 85+. Thus, the present study replicates this split, but not with statistical significance.[49] Since the split appears later in the age categorization in the 2001 study (65+) as compared with the Swedish 1995 cross-sectional study, it might be that we are dealing with a cohort difference. For some reason, it might be the men born between 1910–1920 that deviate from the otherwise consistent pattern of increasing cosmic transcendence.

The Swedish 1995 cross-sectional study however suggested that the aforementioned gender split could be related to social-matrix factors such as marital or cohabiting status. The final drop among men was, in the Swedish 1995 cross-sectional study, found particularly among cohabiting men.

---

[48](eta = .11, p < .05)
[49](eta = .09, p = .268 at age 95+)

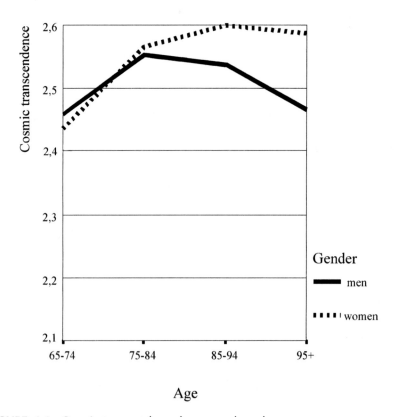

FIGURE 4.4   Cosmic transcendence by age and gender.

In the 2001 (65+) study, we tested whether social-matrix factors such as marital and cohabiting status or having children play a role, but they do not. Controlling for these factors does not produce a statistically significant split between men and women.

However, in the 2001 (65+) data, the split becomes larger and statistically significant in the age category 95+ if respondents who have experienced a crisis during the past two years are considered. Men who had experienced a crisis during the previous two years show a considerable drop in the age category 95+, while women show a continuous age development in cosmic transcendence regardless of whether they had experienced crises or not.[50] Could it be that, for some reason, the men born around

---

[50]The difference in cosmic transcendence between men and women who had experienced a crisis within the past two years corresponds, in the age category 95+, to eta = .27, p < .05.

1910–1920 have had cohort-specific experiences that made them sensitive or vulnerable to crises later in life? These men were small children during World War I and were soldiers themselves during World War II.

In the Swedish 1995 cross-sectional study, it was also demonstrated that the degree of cosmic transcendence correlated with a number of variables besides age and gender. Respondents who had at the time (or previously had, if retired) self-governed professions or were students scored higher on cosmic transcendence. Further, respondents who, during the two years previous to the study, had experienced one or more life crises also scored higher on cosmic transcendence, as did those who had experienced diseases. None of these variables correlate with cosmic transcendence in the 2001 (65+) study.

In the 2001 study we did, however, find other variables[51] that correlate with cosmic transcendence: first, the activity index,[52] again showing that cosmic transcendence is related to activity and not to disengagement; second, satisfaction with present life.[53] The latter correlation is statistically significant and about equally strong in each of the age categories 65–74, 75–84, 85–94 and 95+. We will return to this observation later on.

Who Are the Cosmic Transcenders?

In order to discover who the cosmic transcenders and the nontranscenders are, we have conducted a CHAID analysis,[54] with cosmic transcendence as the dependent variable and a series of other variables as possible predictors.[55] The CHAID analysis in Figure 4.5 identifies the transcenders and the nontranscenders in terms of age, activity, and place of residence. None of the other variables appear as significant predictors of cosmic transcendence.

Among the 560 respondents who are 75+ and at the same time at the upper half of the activity scale, 24 percent belong to the high-

---

[51]The variables checked for correlations are: age, gender, country of birth, having children, civil status, having a friend of the opposite sex, residence, former profession, education, income, parent alive, sibling alive, child alive, crises, diseases, loneliness, satisfaction with present life, activity index.

[52](eta = .08, p < .05)

[53](eta = .16, p < .001)

[54]CHAID (Chi-squared Automatic Interaction Detection) is an algorithm with which a dataset is broken down into subcategories according to the explanatory power a set of predictors has with regard to a dependent variable (Kass, 1980; AnswerTree, 1998).

[55]Age, gender, country of birth, having children, civil status, having a friend of opposite sex, residence, former profession, education, income, parent alive, sibling alive, child alive, crises, diseases, activity index.

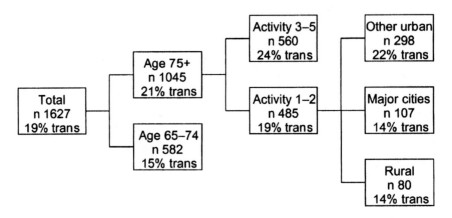

FIGURE 4.5 CHAID-analysis of cosmic transcendence.

Transcenders = individuals belonging to the 20 percent highest on the cosmic transcendence scale

transcendence group. If a cosmic transcendence index is set to 100 in the starting node (the whole sample), the index value in the aforementioned group is 123. When the analysis is set to focus on the lowest fifth of the transcendence values (not shown), the nontranscendence group is identified as 75+, low activity, rural respondents.

Even if the CHAID algorithm only produces statistically significant splits,[56] the percentage differences presented in Figure 4.5 are not overwhelming. The difference between minimum and maximum values is just 10 percentage points (14–24%).

When looking at the data from the Swedish 1995 cross-sectional study and the 2001 (65+) study at the same time, we can draw the following statistically safe conclusions:

- For both men and women, there is an increase in cosmic transcendence with age, beginning already in early adulthood.

- In the age categories from 20 to 64, the men score lower on cosmic transcendence, but from 75+ they have caught up with the women.

- During young adulthood and middle age, life crises and social-matrix factors positively contribute to the development of cosmic transcen-

---

[56]With p < .05.

dence for both men and women. In old age, social-matrix factors and crises have, with the exceptions cited below, lost their impact.

• Men 95+ who have experienced a crisis within the past two years show a moderately decreased level of cosmic transcendence. This might however be a specific cohort effect.

• Cosmic transcendence goes with higher levels of activity—not with withdrawal from activities. This signals that gerotranscendence is different from disengagement.

Coherence

In the Swedish 1995 cross-sectional study, as previously reproduced in Figure 4.2, we found significant correlations between age and coherence, for both men and women.[57] The increase started already at age 20–24 and had its maximum in the age category 75–85, with women being slightly, but not by a statistically significantly margin, above the men. Statistically significant, however, was the gender difference in the age category 35–44, where the men had a pronounced dip in the otherwise positive developmental pattern. Since the main focus here is on the upper end of the age scale, we shall leave this otherwise interesting finding behind.

In the 2001 (65+) study, as shown in Figure 4.6 (which has the same scale as Figure 4.2), there is also a very small, but statistically insignificant difference between men and women in the age category 65–74. There is also, for both men and women, a drop from 85–94, which corresponds to a very small but statistically significant correlation[58] if the age categories 65–94 are collapsed into one and compared with the 95+ category. If the whole age range is considered, there is, within the age span in focus (65–104), no statistically significant correlation between coherence and age.

In the Swedish 1995 cross-sectional study, it was demonstrated that coherence correlated with several other variables besides the aforementioned age and gender. Unmarried and divorced respondents had lower values than did widows/widowers and married or cohabiting respondents. Individuals with higher incomes had higher coherence values, while indi-

---

[57]Eta's around .23 with p < . 001.
[58](eta = .07, p < .01)

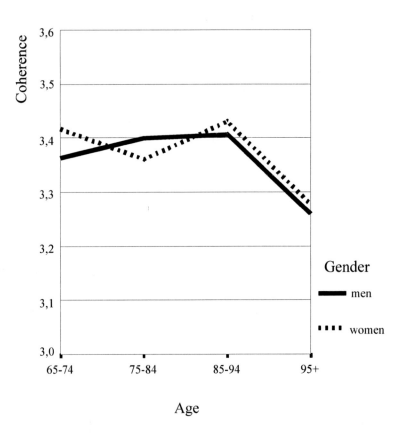

FIGURE 4.6 Coherence by age and gender.

viduals who had experienced crises or diseases had lower coherence values. Also in the 2001 (65+) study, which focus on the upper end of the age scale, these types of variables still correlate with coherence in the same way—though this is not the case with respect to cosmic transcendence. Table 4.8 shows the correlations in the 2001 (65+) study.[59] These correlations again demonstrate that the measures of gerotranscendence are not only dependent on pure *age development*, but also are affected by *social-matrix factors* and *incident-impact factors*.

---

[59]In an ANOVA-MCA analysis—an analysis of variance with a Multiple Classification Analysis design which allows categorical variables as dependents—eta values refer to simple bivariate correlations, while beta values are the "pure" correlations when the other variables are controlled.

TABLE 4.8   ANOVA-MCA Analysis of the Correlates to the Coherence Dimension, Coherence as Dependent Variable

	Eta	Beta	R^2
Age	.06	.18	
Gender	.04	.07	
Civil Status	.17	.14	
Housing	.15	.08	
Former Profession	.16	.12	
Children	.09	.06	
Crises	.18	.12	
Diseases	.12	.06	
Activity	.24	.21	
			.14

It is noteworthy that the initially insignificant correlation with age turns into a significant positive correlation when other variables are controlled for. *If the negative impacts of other factors such as widowhood, crises, and inactivity are controlled for, coherence seemingly tends to increase slightly with age, even at the very top of the age scale.*

As in the Swedish 1995 cross-sectional study, it is the unmarried and divorced respondents who have lower values on the coherence scale compared with widows/widowers and married or cohabiting respondents. Also the experience of crises indicator shows the same association. Those who have experienced crises exhibit lower degrees of coherence. Having had diseases, however, reveals a slightly different pattern. When other factors are controlled for, the diseases factor loses its explanatory power.

What is new in the 2001 (65+) study are the correlations with housing, former profession, and activity. Before controlling for other variables, there is a significant difference in coherence between respondents in different types of housing. The highest degrees of coherence are found among respondents living in their own houses, followed by respondents living in flats and lastly those living in service flats. As seen in Table 4.8, this correlation is reduced when other variables are controlled for.

The coherence among respondents with different former professions follows a professional hierarchy wherein the more skilled professions exhibit higher degrees of coherence. This finding recalls the 1990 Danish retrospective study, where another aspect of gerotranscendence, the cosmic transcendence, was shown to be higher among respondents from higher social classes and those who have had white-collar work or were metropolitan entrepreneurs.

The activity measure has a substantial and remaining correlation with coherence. This correlation is, with some small variations, found for all age groups from 65 to 95+. The higher the activity, the higher the degree of coherence. This of course indicates that "activity theory" and gerotranscendence cannot be regarded as mutually exclusive, but rather as complementary.

Another factor not introduced in the ANOVA analysis, since it is a conceptually related variable rather than a predictor, we again found a very strong correlation between coherence and life satisfaction[60]. This replicates the finding in the Swedish 1995 cross-sectional study where, for the whole sample 20–85, the corresponding correlation was of the same magnitude. This strong correlation, with some small variation, is found in each of the age categories from 65 to 95+.

Who Experiences High Coherence?

In order to discover who the respondents reporting high versus low degrees of coherence are, we conducted a CHAID analysis, with coherence as the dependent variable and a series of other variables as possible predictors (Figure 4.7).[61]

The node with the largest proportion of coherence is defined in terms of noncrises, high activity, and skilled former profession. Among the 193 respondents who had experienced no crises during the past two years, and had had some qualified profession, as well as high activity, 40 percent belong to the high-coherence group. If a coherence index is set to 100 in the starting node (the whole sample), the index value in the high-coherence group is 152. When the analysis is set to focus on the lowest coherence values (not shown), the noncoherence group is identified as having experienced crises, being single and low in activity.

When combining the Swedish 1995 cross-sectional study and the 2001 (65+) study, we can draw the following statistically safe conclusions:

- There is, for both men and women, an increase in coherence with age, beginning already in early adulthood.

---

[60](eta = .50, p < .001)

[61]In this case, we introduced gender, age, civil status, housing, former profession, having living children, activity, crises and diseases as predictors. For simplification, we also forced the CHAID algorithm to produce dichotomous splits only.

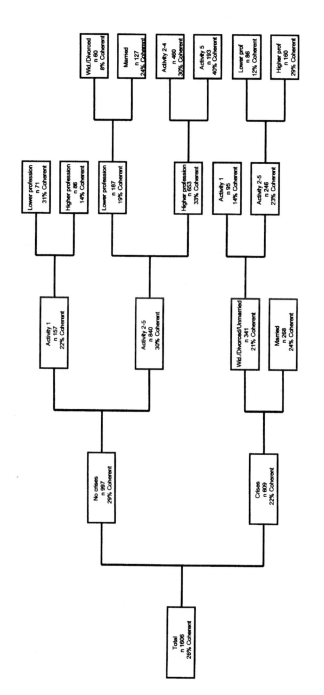

FIGURE 4.7 CHAID-analysis of coherence.

Coherent = individuals belonging to the 26% highest on the coherence scale

119

- For men this increase seems to be interrupted by a temporary drop in the age category 35–44.

- The coherence reaches a maximum in the age category 65–74 and basically flattens out thereafter.

- From age 95, there is a very modest drop compared with the age category 65–94.

- There is no difference in coherence between men and women from age 65+.

- Unlike the cosmic dimension, the coherence dimension has, even at the upper end of the age scale, several rather strong social-matrix and incident-impact predictors, of which the experiences of no crises, high activity, being married, and former qualified profession are the most important.

Need for Solitude

According to the Swedish 1995 cross-sectional study, with data for respondents between 20 and 85 years of age, the need for solitude was shown to start to increase early. The need for solitude increases up to the age category of 35–44 and principally remains stable afterward (Figure 4.3). We are, then, disregarding the statistically nonsignificant divergent tendencies among men and women in the age category 75–85.

Also, in the Swedish 1995 cross-sectional study, the need for solitude correlated negatively with life satisfaction. The less there is satisfaction with life, the higher the need for solitude. This correlation was statistically significant but rather weak.[62]

From Figure 4.8 we can see that the focus on the upper end of the age scale reveals a continued increase in the need for solitude from age 65+ and upward for women.[63] Also for men, the basic pattern is an increase in the need for solitude, with a possible, but statistically insignificant, flattening out at the end.

If, for both men and women, we define the pronounced "solitude seekers" as occupying the approximately upper fifth of the solitude scale,

[62](eta = .16, p < .001)
[63](eta = .12, p < .01)

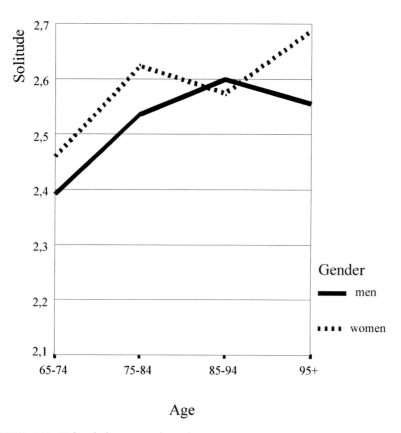

FIGURE 4.8 Solitude by age and gender.

the proportion of "solitude seekers" almost doubles from 12 percent in the age category 65–74 to 23 percent in the category 95+.

As in the Swedish 1995 cross-sectional study of the age range from 20 to 85, the 2001 study (65+) focused on the upper end of the age scale reveals a weak negative correlation between the need for solitude and life satisfaction.[64] This correlation, however, fluctuates between age groups and is insignificant in the highest 95+ category.

Among the predictor variables, the Swedish 1995 cross-sectional study showed, besides age and gender, correlations between the need for

---

[64](eta = .12, p < .001)

solitude and diseases/crises. In the 2001 study, focused on the population 65+, there are very few correlates to the need for solitude. Among a set of 18 possible predictors[65] only three show statistically significant correlations of at least 0.10. These are age, civil status, and diseases. As mentioned above, with advanced age comes an increased need for solitude.[66] Also, the respondents who are widowed, unmarried, or divorced are slightly more solitude-seeking than are the married/cohabiting ones.[67] Furthermore, respondents with diseases have a slightly higher need for solitude in comparison with the healthy ones.[68] Also, understandably, the respondents who have a higher need for solitude report less social activity. They are lower on the activity index.[69]

When the predictor variables age, civil status, and diseases are introduced in an ANOVA-MCA analysis, the explanatory power of each predictor drops considerably. The interpretation here is that the predictors are intertwined, but that none of them has major explanatory power over the others. Age, civil status, and diseases each have some limited explanatory power with respect to the need for solitude. It should be remembered, however, that we are now talking about explanations that apply within the limited age span 65–104 (the 2001 study (65+). When the larger age span 20+ is considered (the Swedish 1995 cross-sectional study and the 2001 study (65+) taken together), there is a distinct and consistent increase in the need for solitude with age. There seems to be a growing need for solitude that is dependent solely on age, i.e., a developmental factor, which can be altered by social-matrix factors, such as civil status, and incident-impact factors, such as burdens of diseases and crises.

When the seekers of solitude are sought for in an CHAID analysis[70] (Figure 4.9), we find that the largest proportion are among the 130 respondents who are 75+, have experienced a crisis during the past two years, and report four or more diseases at present. Within this group, 26 percent are pronounced solitude seekers as compared with 16 percent in

---

[65]Age, gender, country of birth, civil status, having a friend of the opposite sex, residence, housing, former profession, education, income, parent alive, sibling alive, child alive, crises, diseases, loneliness, satisfaction with present life.
[66](eta = .13, p < .001)
[67](eta = .12, p < .001)
[68](eta = .10, p < .001)
[69](eta = .23, p < .001)
[70]Age, gender, civil status, diseases, and crises used as predictors.

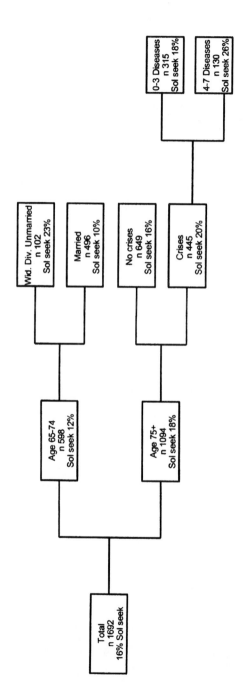

FIGURE 4.9 CHAID-analysis of solitude need.

Solitude seekers = individuals belonging to the 16% highest on the solitude scale the whole sample. If this is set as index value 100, the index value in the above-described group is 167.

The lowest proportion of solitude seekers is found among the 496 respondents in the "young old" age category 65–74 who are married/cohabiting. In this category, 10 percent are solitude seekers, as compared with 16 percent in the whole sample.

Thus, when combining the Swedish 1995 cross-sectional study and the 2001 study (65+), we can draw the following statistically safe conclusion:

• There is a continuous increase in the need for solitude, from early adulthood up to very old age.

• There seem to be two quite different causes of solitude seeking. One cause seems solely related to age developmental change per se.[71] The other cause is reactions to incident-impact factors like diseases and crises.

Transcendence and Life Satisfaction

The theory presumes that an increase in gerotranscendence, particularly cosmic transcendence, is accompanied by an increase in life satisfaction. This assumption was based on the previously reported qualitative interviews underlying the theory. In one of our quantitative studies, the 1990 Danish retrospective study, the assumption was confirmed by an expected positive correlation, but the Swedish 1995 cross-sectional study (ages 20–85) study showed no such correlation. In the 2001 (65+) study of the upper end of the age scale, we again obtained statistically significant correlations between satisfaction with life and cosmic transcendence[72] and coherence,[73] but a negative correlation with the need for solitude.[74]

Figure 4.10 shows, in the 2001 study (65+), how the percentage of respondents who are *very satisfied with present life* varies with the aforementioned dimensions. The proportion of those very satisfied with present life increases from 8 percent to 50 percent as we move from the lowest value of coherence to the highest. The corresponding change regarding

---

[71]It should be recalled that this conclusion is drawn from cross-sectional studies and needs to be confirmed by longitudinal data.

[72](eta = .16, p< .001)

[73](eta = .44, p <.001)

[74](eta = .12, p < .01)

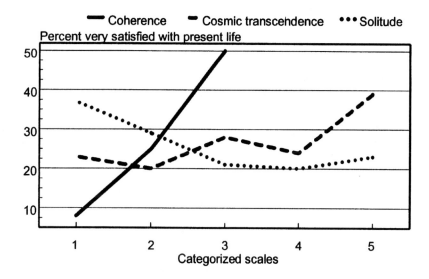

FIGURE 4.10   Dimensions of gerotranscendence and satisfaction with life.
Scales collapsed into five classes.
Coherence into three classes due to positively very skewed distribution

cosmic transcendence is from 23 percent to 39 percent. With respect to the need for solitude, there is a decrease in the very satisfied with life from 37 percent to 23 percent as we move from the lowest to the highest value of this measure.

In order to identify and disentangle the correlations with life satisfaction, we performed an ANOVA analysis with the life satisfaction as dependent variable and the transcendence measures plus the strongest correlates as predictors.

From Table 4.9 we can conclude that the coherence measure of gerotranscendence is the top predictor of satisfaction with present life, even after the introduction of other predictors.

The next category, with about half or less of the explanatory power of coherence, includes activity, crises, health, and cosmic transcendence. All four of these variables drop considerably in explanatory power when the other predictors are introduced,[75] but they still have some individual residual explanatory power after the introduction of the other predictors.

---

[75]Beta-values considerably lower than eta-values

TABLE 4.9 ANOVA-MCA Analysis of the Satisfaction With Present Life

	Eta	Beta	R^2
High Coherence	.44	.34	
High Activity Index	.29	.14	
No Crises	.23	.11	
Good Health	.21	.11	
High Cosmic Transcendence	.14	.10	
Self-Sustained Housing	.21	.09	
Married/Cohabiting	.16	.04	
Skilled Former Profession	.16	.07	
Age: Young Old	.13	.07	
Low Need for Solitude	.13	.04	
			.29

For plainness the variable values connected with high degree of satisfaction with present life are given in the predictor column.

The last group of predictors, including civil status, former profession, age, and need for solitude, initially showed significant correlations with life satisfaction, but these are more or less swept away when other, more crucial and co-varying predictors are introduced. Age is an example of this. The initial correlation between age and satisfaction is a weak, but statistically a significantly negative one. With higher age comes a slight decrease in satisfaction with present life. When other predictors are introduced, however, this significant correlation is practically swept away, showing that the small decrease in satisfaction with life has little to do with age *per se*, but is related to other correlates of age.[76]

As regards the gerotranscendence measures, we can conclude that cosmic transcendence and surely coherence are positively correlated with satisfaction with present life, even when controlling for other probable predictors. The need for solitude, however, shows a weak initial negative correlation with satisfaction with present life. This negative correlation is washed away when we account for other predictors.

In conclusion:

[76]It should be noticed that the R^2 value in Table 4.10 is considerable. No less than 29 percent of the variance in satisfaction with present life is explained by the 10 predictors in the table. If the bottom five predictors are removed, the R^2 value still remains as high as 27.

- The coherence measure of gerotranscendence has very robust positive explanatory power as regards satisfaction with present life, even when other probable predictors are controlled for.

- The cosmic measure of gerotranscendence shows modest, but significantly positive explanatory power as regards satisfaction with present life, even when other probable predictors are controlled for.

- The need for solitude measure seems to be unrelated to satisfaction with present life when other probable predictors are controlled for.

- Age *per se* is unrelated to satisfaction with life when other variables are controlled for.

Summing Up

In our search for explanatory factors concerning the development of gerotranscendence, we have found three types of explanatory factors when looking at data from both the Swedish 1995 cross-sectional study (ages 20–85) and the 2001 study (65+): *age-developmental factors*, *social-matrix factors*, and *incident-impact factors*. Gerotranscendence can be understood as a developmental process, sometimes modified by social-matrix factors, such as gender and profession, and by incident-impact factors, such as diseases and crises.

We can suggest that, during the major part of adult life, there seems to be a developmental pattern of increased *cosmic transcendence*. This increase levels out at the high end of the age scale. In the younger age categories, the degree of gerotranscendence is also modified by social-matrix factors and incident-impact factors, but these factors seem to have lost their importance when old age is reached.

At the outset of the 2001 (65+) study, our intention was to shed some light on a puzzling gender difference in cosmic transcendence found in the Swedish 1995 cross-sectional study (ages 20–85), which showed a continuous development with age for women, but a final age drop for men. In the 2001 study (65+), this pattern was replicated, but with a time lag, hinting at a possible cohort phenomenon.

The pattern from the Swedish 1995 cross-sectional study, showing married/cohabiting men to have a lower degree of cosmic transcendence in comparison with married/cohabiting women, was not replicated in the 2001 study (65+). Instead, this study indicates that the experience of crises seems to affect old men and women differently. For women 65+, the experience of crises seems to have lost its effect on the level of cosmic transcendence. Also for men 65–94, the experience of crises seems to have lost its effect, while the effect appears to become negative for the oldest men, those 95+. This brings to mind the old Chinese saying that crises carry the potential of both threat and opportunity. To gain a deeper understanding of this, we will probably have to use other qualitative methods.

The *coherence dimension* of gerotranscendence is different from the cosmic dimension in that both social-matrix factors and incident-impact factors still play a role in old age. In old age, the developmental factor, the social-matrix factors, and the incident-impact factors seem to be independently and equally important.

The *solitude dimension* also shows a similar pattern. There seems to be a clear developmental age factor, still prevalent in old age, supplemented with some social-matrix factors and incident-impact factors. There seems to be an age-dependent and growing need for solitude, a developmental factor, which can be affected by factors such as widowhood, divorce, and diseases.

Finally, returning to the positive correlation between cosmic transcendence and *satisfaction with present* life in the 2001 (65+) study, we presume that cosmic transcendence is positively related to life satisfaction in old age, but not among younger subjects. In two different empirical studies, both focusing on older respondents (the 1990 Danish retrospective study, and the 2001 study (65+)), we have found this positive correlation between cosmic transcendence and satisfaction with life, while the Swedish 1995 cross-sectional study focusing on ages 20–85, showed no significant correlation. Thus, the combination of cosmic transcendence and satisfaction with present life would seem to be a fruit especially reserved for old age.

LIFE CRISES AND GEROTRANSCENDENCE

The theory of gerotranscendence suggests that life crises, as incidence-impact factors, may sometimes accelerate development toward gerotranscendence. This suggestion was originally based on the previously described qualitative study in which respondents related to crises as having had such effects. In agreement with this, the 1990 Danish retrospective study of 912 representative men and women between 74 and 100 years of age showed that individuals who had experienced the death of a loved one during the last year before the survey scored higher on the cosmic dimension of gerotranscendence. The Swedish cross-sectional 1995 study also produced correlations between the experiences of crises and the dimensions of gerotranscendence.

Now we are going to look more closely at life crises and their possible connection with the development of gerotranscendence. The database for this is primarily the Swedish 1995 cross-sectional study with 2002 representative men and women, ages 20–85.

In particular we shall focus on the following topics:

- What are the life crises that respondents have experienced in various age groups?

- Does the number of life crises experienced, the *crisis load*, increase with age?

- Do men and women have different *crisis patterns*?

- How can life crises be shown to be related to gerotranscendence?

We should remember that, as described previously, three aspects of gerotranscendence have been operationalized in the Swedish 1995 cross-sectional study. The core aspect is the *cosmic transcendence* measure.

The distinguishing qualities of *cosmic transcendence* are the respondents' feelings of connection with the whole of the universe, of being part of everything alive, the tendency to feel the strong presence of persons who are elsewhere, a tendency to feel as if they are living in the past and present simultaneously, and a strong feeling of connection with earlier generations.

The *coherence in life* measure is part of the major "self" dimension and corresponds roughly to Erikson's (1950, 1982) "ego integrity" stage in his developmental model. Respondents who score high on this measure report strong feelings of coherence and meaning in life.

The *solitude* measure is part of the "social and individual relations" dimension. Respondents who score high on this measure report a dislike for meeting new people and a strong need for positive solitude, i.e., filled with peace and philosophizing.

The *life crises* measure was a subjective item combining fixed response alternatives and open response. The item was subjective in the sense that only stressors defined by the respondents themselves as life crises were asked for. In terms of stress theory, the measure combines a stressor and an appraisal perspective as described by Lazarus and Folkman (1984). It takes into account not only what incidents (stressors) to consider but also the subjective experience of the incidents (appraisal).

The respondents were asked the following question: Have you, during the last two years, experienced something you regard as a crisis in life? The respondents could mark a "No" alternative or one or several of the following: own disease, another's disease, death, separation, other (specify).

Age and Gender Distribution of Crises

Table 4.10 shows the proportions of respondents in specified age and gender categories who have experienced various types of life crises during the last two years. The table should be read in the following way: Among the men 20–24 years of age, 5 percent stated that during the last two years they had experienced a life crisis in connection with their own disease (top left figure in Table 4.10). This percentage increases with age

TABLE 4.10   Percentages, Within Age/Gender Categories, Who Within the Last Two Years Have Experienced a Crisis in Life in Connection with . . .

Age	Own disease		Others' disease		Death		Separation		Other	
	men	women	men	women	men	women	men	women	men	women
20–24	5	9	6	5	3	10	12	8	5	3
25–34	4	7	5	5	8	11	8	10	8	13
35–44	7	10	7	8	9	11	7	8	7	11
45–54	8	14	6	7	9	10	5	7	8	10
55–64	16	11	2	9	8	12	1	3	4	4
65–74	17	11	4	9	6	10	1	2	3	1
75–85	23	20	9	10	10	17	1	0	1	2
Age eta	.20***	.12*	.06^{ns}	.07^{ns}	.07^{ns}	.07^{ns}	.16***	.14**	.11^{ns}	.17***
Total pct.	11	12	6	7	8	11	5	6	6	7

***p < .001
**p < .01
*p < .05
^{ns}not significant

and is 23 percent among men 70–85 years of age. This increase corresponds to a statistically highly significant correlation.[77]

Some characteristics in Table 4.10 should be noted. First, as mentioned and expected, the proportion of respondents who had experienced a crisis in life in connection with their own disease increases with age for both men and women. The increase is more pronounced for men.

Second, and quite contrary to what might be expected from a misery perspective of aging, the proportion of respondents who had experienced a crisis in life in connection with another person's disease did *not* increase with age. There is no statistically significant correlation between this type of crisis and age. This is also the case for crises in connection with another person's death. We shall return to these seemingly strange findings below.

Third, crises related to partner separations decrease with age and, fourth, other types of crises also decrease with age. The most frequent "other" types of crises reported by the respondents were crises related to unemployment (25 respondents), family conflicts (21), problems at work (18), and the economy (18). In exceptional cases, crises concerning the war in Europe, accidents, drug problems, and abortion were mentioned. One single respondent reported a life crisis in connection with "becoming old" and another single respondent mentioned "early retirement" as having caused a crisis. None of the respondents mentioned ordinary retirement as a crisis in life. (Approximately 100 of the respondents may have retired within two years before the measurement.)

Crisis Load in Various Age Groups

The respondents could, at least in theory, have experienced several different crises during the period. In reality, however, this was very rare. Our data showed that the majority of the respondents, 68 percent, had not experienced any life crises at all during the previous two years; 27 percent of the respondents had experienced only one crisis. Four percent had experienced two crises, and only one percent (19 respondents) had experienced three different crises. Since this distribution is extremely skewed, the following analyses are based on a dichotomized measure of crises— respondents who had not experienced any crises and respondents who had experienced one or more crises during the last two years.

---

[77](eta = .20, p < .001)

Table 4.11 shows a constancy in the crises load from age 20 to 74 for both men and women, and an increase in the last age category, 75–85. None of the age/crises patterns in Table 4.11 are, however, statistically significant. Even if the age variable is dichotomized in two age groups, 20–74 and 75–85, the difference between these two age groups is very small, and statistically significant only among the women.[78] Among the "younger" (20–74) women, 35 percent had experienced one or more crises during the previous two years, as compared with 45 percent of the older (75–85) women. Basically the same pattern is found when the 2001 (65+) data is considered and the age range expanded to 104 years.

Table 4.11 also shows a recurrent difference in crises load between men and women. In each age category, women reported more life crises than men. This difference is most pronounced in the age category 25–34. However, a closer analysis revealed that this gender difference is statistically significant only among respondents who are not married or cohabiting (separated, widowed, never married). Among the male respondents in this group, 35 percent had experienced a crisis in life during the previous two years. Among the female respondents in the same category, the corresponding percentage is 45.[79] An even greater gender difference is

TABLE 4.11 Percentage of Respondents Who Have Experienced One or More Crises During the Last Two Years

	Percent[1]			n
Age	Men	Women	Total	
20–24	27%	32%	30%	165
25–34	26%	36%	31%	362
35–44	32%	38%	35%	325
45–54	28%	37%	33%	416
55–64	31%	32%	32%	274
65–74	25%	30%	27%	270
75–85	37%	45%	41%	190
Total	29%	36%	32%	2002

[1]Differences between age groups are not significant.

[78](eta = .06, p < .05)
[79](eta = .11, p < .01)

found if the analysis is restricted to the age category 35–64, where 51 percent of the noncohabiting women reported a crisis in life during the previous two years, compared with 38 percent among the men.[80]

Crises and Cosmic Transcendence

Table 4.12 shows a statistically highly significant total correlation[81] between the crisis measure and the measure of cosmic transcendence. Respondents who had experienced one or more crises during the previous two years scored higher on cosmic transcendence. Table 4.12 also shows that this correlation is higher for women. But, the table also reveals that these correlations are primarily focused on the first four age categories embracing the age span 20–54. Data from the 2001 (65+) study further support this observation. In this later study, there is no correlation between the experiences of crises and cosmic transcendence. *The conclusion seem to be that during young adulthood and middle age, life crises contribute positively to the development of cosmic transcendence for both men and women. In old age, however, crises seem to lose their impact in this respect.*

TABLE 4.12 Correlations Between the Experience of Crises and Cosmic Transcendence

Age	Men	Women	Total
20–24	.10^{ns}	.20^{ns}	.16*
25–34	.17*	.20*	.20***
35–44	.12^{ns}	.18*	.16**
45–54	.08^{ns}	.27***	.19***
55–64	.04^{ns}	.07^{ns}	.06^{ns}
65–74	.16^{ns}	.10^{ns}	.13*
75–85	.06^{ns}	.04^{ns}	.07^{ns}
Total	**.10***	**.17***	**.14***

^{ns}not significant
*p < .05
**p < .01
***p < .001

[80](eta = .14, p < .05)
[81](eta = .14, p < .001)

In Figure 4.11 this correlation pattern is shown in another way. In order to make the figure easy to interpret, we have inserted age-related trend lines for the level of cosmic transcendence for those who had experienced one or more crises in life during the previous two years, and those who had not.

Four characteristics of Figure 4.11 should be noted. First, the cosmic transcendence for those who had experienced crises is, for each age group, above the trend line for those who had not experienced any crises. This corresponds to the correlation between the measure of crises and cosmic transcendence.

Second, both trend lines are positive: Irrespective of having experienced crises or not, the degree of cosmic transcendence increases with age. This corresponds to a positive correlation between age and cosmic transcendence.

Third, the trend line for those who had not experienced any crises is somewhat steeper. The correlation between age and cosmic transcendence is higher and statistically significant in this group.

Fourth, the two trend lines converge, which means that with increasing age, having or not having experienced a crisis becomes less important for the degree of cosmic transcendence.

The combined effects of age and crises on the degree of cosmic transcendence are further illuminated in Figure 4.12, where the data from

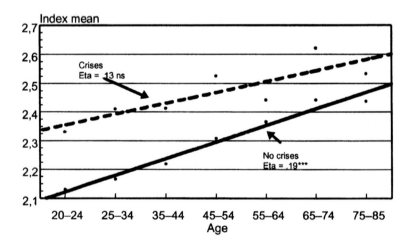

FIGURE 4.11 Cosmic transcendence by age, controlling for crises.

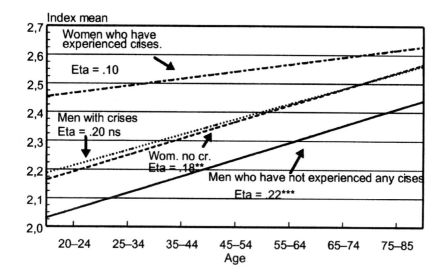

FIGURE 4.12   Cosmic transcendence by age, controlling for crises and gender.

men and women, with and without crises, are separated. Figure 4.12 shows that among women who had experienced crises, age is rather unimportant for the degree of cosmic transcendence. The other extreme is the group of men who had not experienced any crises. In this group, age shows quite a strong correlation with the degree of cosmic transcendence.

Figure 4.12 also shows that the trend line for men who had experienced crises is practically identical to the trend line for women who *had not* experienced any crises. The greatest difference in the degree of cosmic transcendence is found between the young women who had experienced crises and the young men who had not.

In order to further disentangle the relationships between the experience of crises, age, and cosmic transcendence, for men and women, respectively, the two ANOVA-MCA[82] analyses summarized in Table 4.13 were done.

The analyses reveal that, among men, the age variable has twice as much explanatory power as the crises variable in terms of explaining the

[82]Analysis of variance with a Multiple Classification Analysis design, which allows categorical variables as dependents.

TABLE 4.13 ANOVA-MCA Analysis of Cosmic Transcendence With Age and Crises as Independents

	Men		Women	
	eta	beta	eta	beta
Age	.21	.21	.14	.14
Crises	.10	.11	.17	.16
R^2		.05		.05

impact on the dependent variable, cosmic transcendence. For women, age and crises have approximately the same amount of explanatory power.

Crises and Coherence in Life

The simple bivariate correlation between *life crises* measures and *coherence in life* measures is a substantial negative one.[83] Respondents who, during the previous two years, had experienced a crisis in life reported less coherence in life.

Figure 4.13, however, reveals a rather interesting modification of this finding. In order to illustrate this, the slopes in Figure 4.13 have been calculated as linear trend lines. First, as an expression of the above mentioned correlation, Figure 4.13 shows a difference between the trend lines for the respondents who had and who had not experienced crises during the previous two years. Second, this difference decreases with age. While the difference in reported coherence between those who had and those who had not experienced crises is considerable among respondents 20–24 years of age,[84] this difference is, statistically speaking, almost nonexistent among the respondents 75–85 years of age.[85] In the 2001 (65+) study, this trend is not fully followed. In this later study the correlation between the experience of crises and the degree of coherence is life is somewhat higher,[86] but still quite below the corresponding correlation for the respondents 20–24 years old in the Swedish 1995 cross-sectional study.

[83](eta = .22, p < .001)
[84](eta = .31, p < .001)
[85](eta = .09, p > .05)
[86](eta = .19, p< .001)

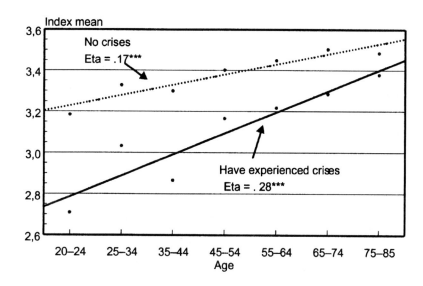

FIGURE 4.13 Coherence in life by age, controlling for crises.

Third, among both the respondents who had experienced a crisis during the last two years and among those who had not, the age slope for coherence in life is positive. The higher the age is, the higher the degree of coherence. But, since the slope for those who had experienced crises is steeper, we can say that *aging seems to buffer against the loss in coherence created by a crisis. Having experienced a crisis in old age has less impact on the feeling of coherence in life, in comparison with the impact at a younger age.*

Crises in Life and the Need for Solitude

As described previously, the general pattern of the relationship between cross-sectional age and the need for solitude is an increase up to the age category 35–44 years and thereafter a "steady state."

In Figure 4.14 this pattern is also shown for those *having* and *not having* experienced a crisis in life during the last two years. Respondents who had experienced a crisis in life systematically reported a higher need for solitude in comparison to respondents who had not experienced any crises. This systematic difference is, however, rather small. Only for two

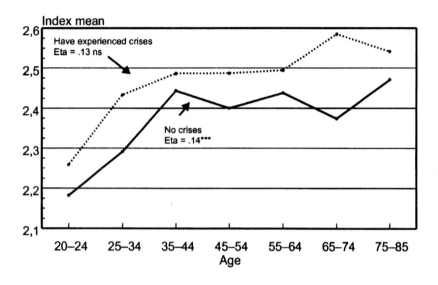

FIGURE 4.14   Need for solitude by age, controlling for crises.

age categories did this difference reach statistical significance: ages 25–34[87] and ages 65–74.[88] In both cases the difference was caused by men who had experienced crises. They deviated with higher need for solitude. In the 2001 (65+) study there was no correlation at all between the experience of crises during the previous two years and the need for solitude.

Summing Up the Crisis Perspective

Before returning to the main focus, how crises relate to gerotranscendence, it may be interesting to note that from the "misery perspective" of aging, it has almost been taken for granted that old age is connected with stress and crises (Rodin, 1986). Several empirical findings seem, however, to contradict this assumption. Paykel (1983) found, for example, that younger people report more stress and crises than the elderly. Several explanations to these paradoxical findings have been suggested. Aldwin, Sutton, Chiara and Spiri (1996) discuss a series of such explanations, ranging from measurement errors to developmental changes in appraisal

[87](eta = .12, p < .05)
[88](eta = .16, p < .05)

and coping. We can see this, as described in a previous chapter, as an example of how we tend to explain away findings that do not fit our favorite theories. Here we will only briefly refer to some of these explanations since our aim is not to test them *per se*. Our main objective is to find out if crises in life are related to the dimensions of gerotranscendence.

We have defined life crises as *those events which people themselves define as crises*. No life event, regardless of how stressful it might appear to an outsider, has been defined as a crisis in life unless it has been characterized in that way by the respondent. Given the above definition of life crises, several observations should be noted.

The *composition of life crises* differs between age groups. Each age has its own types of crises. The frequency of certain types of life crises increases with age, while the frequency of others decreases with age. The Swedish 1995 cross-sectional study showed that crises in life related to a person's own disease increased with age, while crises connected with separation or other circumstances decreased. Noteworthy is the fact that subjectively defined life crises in connection with other peoples' diseases or death showed no correlation with age. There might be a very simple explanation for this lack of correlation: It is easy to assume that old people must experience more unavoidable diseases and deaths of loved ones, but we forget that it is equally unavoidable that parents fall ill and die away from young people, who thereby are exposed to the possibility of experiencing a crisis in connection with another persons death.

But, given the assumption that we objectively experience more disease and death with increasing age, this lack of correlation can be understood in terms of age-related changes in appraisal and coping, as mentioned above. A related explanation can be found in Neugarten's (1977) concept of *timing*. There is a schedule for events in life which, by its very existence, prepares us for these events, provided they happen on schedule. This schedule of life events teaches us, for example, that disease and widowhood are unlikely events in our younger years, but likely in old age. In line with this, Blau (1973) found that elderly widows experienced less stress than young widows. The widowhood of the elderly women was on schedule, while the widowhood of young women was off schedule. Regardless of theoretical explanations, the fact itself should be remembered: When using a subjective definition of life crises, there is no correlation between respondent's age and the experience of a crisis in life in connection with other people's diseases or death in particular.

The above-mentioned concept of *timing* can also explain why none of the respondents connected ordinary retirement with a life crisis. This is by now a recurrent pattern in social gerontological research findings. The trauma expected by many scholars in connection with retirement does not materialize in empirical research. Aldwin (1990) has shown that retirement generally has a very low stress value. It is at the very bottom of a long list of possible stressors in old age. (For a general discussion of these findings see Robinson, Coberly, & Paul, 1985.)

Regarding *the total load of subjectively experienced crises* in life there is no statistically significant difference between the age groups up to age 74. Note that even if we compare the oldest respondents with the youngest, we find nothing but minor differences in the total crisis load. The most straightforward explanation to this finding is probably, as above mentioned, the simple fact that each age has its own types of crises. Regardless of which explanations we propose, the finding could be regarded as another piece of evidence against the notion of old age as an abyss of stress and crises, particularly if we allow people themselves to determine if an event has been a crisis or not.

A *gender difference* is that women systematically report more crises in life than men. This parallels other similar findings. For example, in most studies where respondents are asked directly if they feel lonely, female respondents report more loneliness than male respondents (Borys & Perlman, 1985). In an attempt to explain this difference, Tornstam (1992b) empirically tested several possible hypotheses ranging from omission errors among men to women's reduced self-esteem and unfulfilled expectations of marriage. None of these hypotheses were confirmed. The study could only confirm that women report more loneliness then men, with the interesting qualification that this difference only existed among married or cohabiting men and women. In the case of crises in life, we have found the opposite pattern. The gender difference is only found among respondents who are separated, widowed, or never married. Among respondents who are married or cohabiting there is no gender difference in reported life crises.

These findings may seem contradictory but could be comprehensible theoretically with the hypothesis that women, by nature or due to a socially constructed gender role, are more vulnerable both in marriage or cohabitation, and outside these settings. If we focus on gender differences in vulnerability rather than civil status, it would make sense that this higher female vulnerability expresses itself differently in different settings. Within marriage or cohabitation, as loneliness, and outside these settings, as crises in life.

When it comes to the gerotranscendence-crisis relationship, a main result of our analysis is that there certainly is a connection between crises in life and *cosmic transcendence*. Interpreted in a causal developmental way, the data support the assumption that crises in life may induce higher degrees of cosmic transcendence. This is, of course, not a conclusion to be drawn on the basis of cross-sectional data only, but since the result of the above analysis parallels what was found in the earlier qualitative and quantitative studies, this interpretation bears more weight. Drawing on the parallels between earlier results and the present data, we allow ourselves some tentative interpretations, which, in reality, go far beyond what can be inferred from a cross-sectional analysis.

As mentioned, a correlation exists between crises and cosmic transcendence, but this correlation decreases with age, as shown in both Table 4.12 and Figures 4.11 and 4.12. A possible interpretation is that, with increasing age, crises have less power to induce cosmic transcendence. This is so because among respondents who had not experienced any crises, the degree of cosmic transcendence increased more rapidly with age. Another way of interpreting this pattern is that aging per se reduces or buffers against the impact of crises on cosmic transcendence. Aging itself becomes more important for the development of cosmic transcendence.

There is, however, an important gender difference in this regard. Among women who had experienced crises, aging as such seems less important, especially in comparison with men who had not experienced any crises. Although it is an oversimplification, we might say that, *for women, crises are relatively more important for the development of cosmic transcendence while aging is more important for men.*

The analysis has also revealed a connection between the experience of crises and *coherence in life*. Also in this case, aging seems to reduce the impact of crises. When young, a crisis in life reduces the feeling of coherence considerably. When old, a crisis in life doesn't seem to reduce the feeling of coherence to the same degree. Also, in the end, individuals who had experienced crises reported almost the same feeling of coherence as those who had not. We suggest that they do so because their developmental pattern is faster. The experience of crises reduces the feeling of coherence in life at the same time as it accelerates the developmental process towards coherence.

The *need for solitude* also shows a pattern in which aging seems to reduce the impact of crises, at least among men. If we regard the "development" at the end of the age scale (Figure 4.14), we see again that the need for solitude is almost the same regardless of whether the respondent has experienced a crisis or not.

Summing Up

The pattern of subjectively defined crises in life differs partly between age groups. Some crises are life cycle defined, e.g., divorce and a person's own disease, while others cut across the whole age span, e.g., another person's disease or death. This contributes to the fact that the total load of subjectively experienced life crises is almost the same regardless of age. However, widowed, separated, or never married women of all ages, reported more crises than men in the same situation.

Subjectively experienced crises in life seem to contribute to the development of cosmic transcendence, especially among women. With increasing age the impact of crises is weakened. Among men, aging per se, relatively speaking, has a more powerful impact on cosmic transcendence.

The feeling of coherence and the need for solitude are negatively affected by the experience of life crises. But, with a developmental perspective, these negative impacts seem to subside with age. The result seems to be that, in the end, the experience of coherence in life and the need for solitude are on the same level regardless of whether the individual has experienced crises or not.

THE FUNCTIONS OF REMINISCENCE ON GEROTRANSCENDENCE

Drawing on the Erikson developmental theory, reminiscence—looking back at the life lived—can be understood as a way of integrating the elements of the past in order to restore and stabilize the identity. In fact, reminiscence, from such a perspective, is a backward process which aims at creating a sense of coherence in the life lived—within the same old construction on the world as before. The theory of gerotranscendence, on the other hand, opens the possibility that reminiscence might contribute to reorganization and change of the identity. In the following we will take a closer look at the functions of reminiscence. In particular we are interested to see if reminiscence has functions other than that of stabilizing and already developed identity. Could it perhaps sometimes play an instrumental role in a developmental change and reconstruction of not only the identity, but also the way we distinguish reality—a function in line with the theory of gerotranscendence?

The Reminiscence Perspective in Gerontology

Ever since Butler (1963) introduced the *life review* concept in gerontology, there has been a growing interest in its offspring: *reminiscence theory* and *reminiscence therapy*. Considerable effort has been made to classify, organize, and theoretically explain what reminiscence is, and there is an ongoing debate as to whether or not reminiscence has anything to do with aging (Cohen & Taylor, 1998). As suggested by Webster (1995), the occurrence of reminiscence might be determined by gender and personality rather than by age.

Despite this uncertainty, reminiscence therapy for the elderly has become very popular and is also considered to be quite successful (Comana & Brown, 1998; Puentes, 1998). In terms of theoretical orientation, most of the contemporary writings on the topic, as described by Parker (1995), are based on a continuity perspective. The assumption is that reminiscence therapy is successful because it helps to maintain and stabilize the identity. For example, according to Parker (1995), when reminiscence occurs in times of stress and strain its function is to stabilize the identity. Thus, in this perspective, the occurrence of increased reminiscence in times of stress is an indication of the continuity function of reminiscence.

In summary, then, we find that underlying many of the approaches to the question of reminiscence is the assumption that it serves to stabilize the identity for people in need. These people are sometimes, but not necessarily, elderly.

We would, however, like to suggest another possible theoretical perspective on this issue. The success of reminiscence might not always be related to continuity, but instead to just the opposite. Reminiscence might sometimes contribute to the change and reconstruction not only of the identity, but also of the very way in which we understand reality. It might be part of a process of reorganization and reconstruction—a process focused on change rather than stability. It might even be the case that the function of reminiscence changes during the life course—from identity stabilization in the early years, to the change and reconstruction of how we define reality later in life.

When Erikson's developmental theory is used as the basis for under-standing reminiscence (Carlson, 1984; Castelnuovo-Tedesco, 1978; Taft & Nehrke, 1990), the process of remembering might in a limited way be understood in the perspective of change and reconstruction. The Erikson approach, however, basically refers to a possible change of the perception of the self, within the same old ontology, cosmology or "metaworld" as before. The entire definition of reality is not changed, only the definition of elements of the past life.

As we have argued, the theory of gerotranscendence goes further—by suggesting a developmental process including ontological changes in the comprehension of the world and the self and by describing human devel-opment towards maturity and wisdom. Understanding the functions of reminiscence in this perspective allows us to relate reminiscence not only to identity and life course reconstruction, but also to more extensive changes in the ontological definitions of existence.

Reminiscence from the Perspective of Gerotranscendence

Simply put, gerotranscendence implies a transcendental shift in metaper-spective. This shift seems to be gradual, starting in early adulthood and normally reaching its peak in old age. Under certain conditions, however, even young individuals can reach a high level of gerotranscendence. We have in a previous section shown that life crises can, particularly for younger individuals, function as catalysts in this respect.

According to the initial qualitative study previously described in this book, the gerotranscendent individual typically experiences a new understanding of fundamental existential questions—often a feeling of cosmic communion with the spirit of the universe, a redefinition of time, space, life, and death, and a redefinition of the self and relationships to others. The individual becomes, for example, less preoccupied with self and at the same time more selective in his/her choice of social and other activities. There is an increased feeling of affinity with past generations, a decreased interest in superfluous social interaction and the positive solitude becomes more important.

From such a perspective, reminiscence could be understood as part of a reconstruction process, rather than as an instrument used to stabilize old conceptions of identity and the world. In this way, the theory of gerotranscendence certainly differs from Erikson's (1950, 1982) model of personal development. In both cases, aging is regarded as a developmental process that, at very best, ends with a higher state of maturity. Also, in both cases, the mature state includes a new form of contentment and a new feeling of affinity with past generations. However, according to Erikson's theory, ego-integration primarily refers to the integration and possible reconstruction of elements from the life that has passed. The individual reaches a fundamental acceptance of the life lived, regardless of how it might be viewed from the outside. In this way, the ego-integrity described by Erikson is more a process of backward integration taking place within the same world view, whereas the process of gerotranscendence implies a more forward or outwardly directed process, including a redefinition of reality. Thus, from the perspective of gerotranscendence, reminiscence might become part of a much larger reorganization and reconstruction process than is implied by Erikson's developmental theory.

The previously described empirical studies have shown that such developmental changes seem to take place and are associated not only with aging as such, but are also affected by social-matrix factors and incident-impact factors like gender and experienced crises in life. But what about the real role of reminiscence in this process?

The primary aim of this section is to empirically elaborate the question of whether or not the functions of reminiscence are related to the gerotranscendental process. This is accomplished by empirically relating certain operationalized functions of reminiscence to a measure of gerotranscendence and its determinants, of which age, crisis experiences, and gender are the most important.

We also want to contribute to the discussion of whether reminiscence should be solely understood within a continuity-oriented theoretical perspective, or opened up for a possible function connected with developmental change.

Methods and Measures

The subsequent analysis is based on the Swedish 1995 cross-sectional study of 2002 representative Swedish men and women. As described earlier, scales approximating specific dimensions of *gerotranscendence* were constructed. The core dimension is the cosmic dimension, here referred to as *cosmic transcendence*, which is defined as the core dimension for two reasons. First, its content is very close to the theoretical assumptions in the theory and second, its measure is empirically the most salient one.[89]

---

[89]The factor analysis produced a factor with an Eigenvalue of 3.22

The distinguishing qualities of *cosmic transcendence* are the respondents' a) feelings of being connected with the whole of the universe, b) feelings of being part of everything alive, c) tendency to feel a strong presence of persons who are elsewhere, d) tendency to feel as if they are living in the past and present simultaneously, and e) strong feelings of connection with earlier generations.

Inspired by the work of Webster (1993, 1997), we have constructed a condensed, three-dimensional *reminiscence functions scale*.[90] The statements used in our condensed *reminiscence functions scales* appear in Table 4.14.

For each "function" the respondents were asked to rate, on a four-point scale, how often they talk about the past for this particular reason. Response alternatives were *never, seldom, sometimes,* and *often*. Observe that we have not tried to quantify the occurrence of reminiscence, but focused on the functions of or reasons for reminiscing, operating under the assumption that everybody thinks and talks about the past. The answers to

TABLE 4.14   Functions of Reminiscence

Unity of Existence	*Factor load*
Remember somebody who has passed away	.82
Tell younger family members/people how it was when I was young/how it was to live in the old days	.60
Help me to accept death	.58
Relive happy moments in life	.54
Identity	*Factor load*
Understand myself better	.81
Help me solve problems	.78
Get an overview of my life	.69
Relive bitter memories	.52
Conversation	*Factor load*
I am expected to	.74
Gives me something to do	.63
Others do	.60
Others ask me to	.60

---

[90]When constructing our scales we have utilized a selection of items from Webster's scales and added some of our own. In selecting items from Webster's scales, we have chosen the item with the highest factor load from each of Webster's dimensions.

the statements were analyzed with a factor analysis,[91] which produced the factors in Table 4.14.

Our factor analysis produced three dimensions that we have named *unity of existence function, identity function* and *conversation function.* For each of the dimensions, a standardized additive index was constructed.[92]

The first dimension includes statements that unite the dead with the living, the past with the present, and present life with approaching death. We have chosen to refer to this reminiscence function as the *unity of existence function.* The second dimension includes statements that are more limited in scope. They all refer to the self and the individual life. We have chosen to label this dimension the *identity function.* The third dimension includes only statements that are directly related to the *conversation function* of reminiscence.

Additive indices have also been used for the measurement of *diseases* and *life crises.* Here we remind that the respondents were asked to read a list of common diseases and mark the diseases they were suffering from at the moment. The number of diseases were added to create a simple index. In the same vein, the respondents were asked if, during the last two years, they had experienced something they regarded as a life crisis. The respondents could mark a number of predefined crises as well as add other types of crises. A simple additive index, showing the number of crises each respondent had reported, was constructed.

In addition to these indices, several single-item measures have been used in the below analysis. Overall *life satisfaction* is an example of such a single-item measure, where respondents were asked to rate, on a fixed five-point scale, how satisfied they are with their present existence.

Reminiscence Functions and Age

If we disregard the theoretical possibility that the age differences in Figure 4.15 are cohort effects and permit ourselves to take the risk of making developmental interpretations, we do find a clear pattern in which the *unity of existence function* of reminiscence increases linearly with age. Thus,

---

[91]An orthogonal principal component factor analysis with a varimax rotation Three restrictions were put on the analysis: 1) Factors should have a minimum of 1.0 as eigenvalue; 2) Minimum item loading should be equal to or greater than .50; 3) No item should load higher than .45 in other factors.
[92]According to the rules given by Galtung (1969).

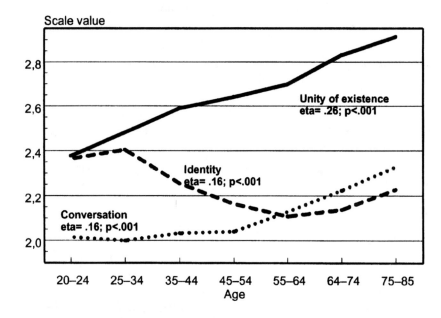

FIGURE 4.15   Reasons for reminiscence.

the *unity of existence function* of reminiscence becomes increasingly important as we age, whereas the *identity function* of reminiscence principally decreases after the age category 25–34 years. This is very much in line with our assumption that the function of reminiscence changes during the course of life.

Figure 4.15 also shows that the *conversation function* of reminiscence is more or less the same up to the age category 45–54, after which it starts a moderate increase from the age category 55+.

Gender Differences

Regarding the *unity of existence function* of reminiscence, the age slopes for men and women parallel each other, with women being constantly higher. In all age categories, women score higher on the *unity of existence function* of reminiscence than do men.[93] In one way this parallels the

[93](eta = .17; p < .001).

observation described earlier that women score higher on cosmic transcendence in most of the age categories.

At the extreme ends of the age continuum, men and woman also differ in terms of how they score on the *identity function* of reminiscence. Younger and older women (20–34 years, 75–85 years) score higher on this function than do men in corresponding age categories.[94] In the age categories 35–74 years, there is no gender difference in this respect. The scores on the *conversation function* of reminiscence does not differ between men and women in any age category.

Gerotranscendence and Reminiscence

As mentioned, the distinguishing qualities of *cosmic transcendence* are respondents' feelings of connection with the whole of the universe, feelings of being part of everything alive, the tendency to feel a strong presence of persons who are elsewhere, the tendency to feel as if they were living in the past and present simultaneously, and a strong feeling of connection with earlier generations. Our thesis is that reminiscence might be part of the gerotranscendental change, and might therefore play an instrumental role in this process. In the case of *cosmic transcendence*, this implies a change in the very way in which we understand our whole being. But what is the specific role of reminiscence in gerotranscendence? There are three alternatives. First, reminiscence might be regarded as promoter or "cause" of gerotranscendence. Second, gerotranscendence might be regarded as the "cause" of changes in reminiscence functions. Third, both reminiscence and gerotranscendence might be part of the same entity.

Table 4.15 summarizes an ANOVA-MCA analysis in which cosmic transcendence is regarded as the dependent variable. This analysis shows that the *unity* and *identity* reminiscence functions are the two variables that, together with pure age, are able to predict cosmic transcendence better than others. Each one of these two variables has a substantial positive explanatory power even when other variables are controlled for.[95] The conversation reminiscence, however, which initially has a significant positive correlation with cosmic transcendence, loses its explanatory power when the other variables are controlled for.

---

[94](eta = .18; p < .001; eta = .17; p < .001).
[95]It should be noted that with more identity reminiscence comes more cosmic transcendence, in spite of the fact that identity reminiscence has a negative correlation with age. Even if identity reminiscence fades a little bit with age, it is still important for cosmic transcendence.

TABLE 4.15 ANOVA-MCA Analysis of Cosmic Transcendence With Dimensions of Reminiscence and Other Variables as Independents

Independents	Cosmic Transcendence	
	eta	beta
Age	.17	.13***
Gender	.13	.06***
Crises	.15	.07***
Illness	.15	.05^{ns}
Life satisfaction	.03	.06^{ns}
Unity reminiscence	.37	.19***
Identity reminiscence	.33	.23***
Conversation reminiscence	.25	.07^{ns}
R^2		.21

***$p < .001$
^{ns} not significant

If we accept the assumption of the causal order where reminiscence precedes cosmic transcendence, we can conclude that *unity reminiscence* and *identity reminiscence* seem to positively affect the degree of cosmic transcendence, while *conversation reminiscence* does not.[96]

However, the second assumption of the causal order between cosmic transcendence and reminiscence is the one where cosmic transcendence precedes reminiscence. Table 4.16 summarizes the outcome of three ANOVA-MCA analyses, one for each of the reminiscence dimensions. In these analyses, reminiscence is regarded as the dependent variable.

As possible independent variables related to the alternative reasons for reminiscence, we have introduced the experience of cosmic transcendence together with age, gender, the experience of crises, illness, and life satisfaction. The latter variables have previously been shown to be empirically related to the experience of cosmic transcendence and, thus, have to be included in the analysis.

---

[96]The original correlation between conversation reminiscence and cosmic transcendence (eta = .25) can be understood as a by-product of the intercorrelations between the reminiscence functions. With identity reminiscence and unity reminiscence comes also conversation reminiscence, which, as such, is unimportant for cosmic transcendence.

TABLE 4.16   ANOVA-MCA Analyses of Reminiscence Dimensions

Independents	Unity		Identity		Conversation	
	eta	beta	eta	beta	eta	beta
Age	.26	.18***	.16	.20***	.16	.13***
Gender	.17	.13***	.08	.04***	.02	.00^{ns}
Crises	.14	.09***	.20	.14***	.10	.05***
Illness	.18	.07**	.05	.03^{ns}	.10	.02^{ns}
Life satisfaction	.07	.07*	.11	.08^{ns}	.06	.05^{ns}
Cosmic transcendence	.35	.28***	.32	.32***	.25	.22***
R^2		.20		.17		.09

***$p < .001$
**$p < .01$
*$p < .05$
^{ns}not significant

As can be seen from Table 4.16 (and from Table 4.15), the bivariate correlations (eta values) between the cosmic transcendence scale and the reminiscence dimensions are quite strong. They are, in fact, the strongest of all the possible independent variables. Moreover, these strong correlations remain (as beta values) after the introduction of the other independent variables. The explanatory power of crises, illness, and life satisfaction are, on the other hand, generally much lower, especially after the introduction of other independent variables. The exception is the explanatory power of experience of crises, which still has a remaining explanatory power on the *identity function* of reminiscence. This is still, however, less than half the explanatory power of cosmic transcendence.

Without going into details, Table 4.16 could be summarized as follows: First, that cosmic transcendence appears to be related to reminiscence, even when variables like age, gender, crises, etc., are controlled for. Second, age, even when other independent variables are controlled for, also explains a good deal of the variation in reasons for reminiscence. Gender explains some of the variance in the *unity function*, but little or none of the variation in the *identity* or *conversation* functions. Third, the "stress variables" are more or less washed out as explanatory variables when the other independent variables are introduced into the analysis. This contradicts the suggestion by Parker (1995) that reminiscence should be understood primarily as a stabilizing reaction in times of stress and strain. To support this latter interpretation of reminiscence, we should have obtained the highest beta values for crises and illness, while the beta values for cosmic transcendence and age would have been minimal.

Another way of using Table 4.16 is to ask which variables should be used if we want to predict who will use reminiscence for purposes of *unity, identity* or *conversation*. A person who uses reminiscence for the purpose of creating *unity of existence* is, then, likely to be a transcendent elderly woman. The person who uses reminiscence for *identity* purposes is likely to be a transcendent younger individual who has experienced life crises during the last year. The user of reminiscence for *conversation* purposes is likely to be a transcendent older person. These category descriptions have been confirmed by CHAID analyses; thus, precisely the above mentioned categories were produced by the CHAID algorithm.

The third interpretation of the correlations between the cosmic dimension of gerotranscendence and the dimensions of reminiscence is that they are part of the same entity, rather than existing in a cause-effect relationship. In order to test this hypothesis, we have done a factor analysis with all the items of cosmic transcendence and all the items of the three dimensions of reminiscence in one and the same explorative factor analysis. If the concept of cosmic transcendence and the dimensions of reminiscence were part of the same entity, we would expect the items from the cosmic gerotranscendence dimension and the items from the reminiscence dimensions to mix. However, they do not. The analysis simply reproduces the three functional dimensions of reminiscence and a separate dimension of cosmic transcendence. Thus, we have support for the assumption that the concepts represent different entities involved in some kind of causal relationship. In Table 4.15, we made the assumption that the different aspects of reminiscence are supportive to the development of cosmic transcendence. The reverse assumption is in theory, however, also reasonable, as presumed in Table 4.16.

Conclusions about Reminiscence

In this section, we have theoretically connected the functions of reminiscence with the theory of gerotranscendence. This also made it empirically possible to say something about the functions of reminiscence in a developmental perspective. Our data suggest that the functions of reminiscence change with age such that, roughly speaking, the *unity of existence function* becomes more important with age. Therefore, our results both deviate from and agree with what has been summarized by Cohen and Taylor (1998). They report that reminiscence studies normally do not show any age differences unless we consider specific life-stage-related tasks or problems. The function of "boredom reduction" is, for example, considered to be more prevalent among young people, whereas "death preparation" is considered to be more prevalent among the old.

Our analysis, however, shows that the *unity of existence function* grows continuously with age, suggesting that this is related to a developmental identity process, rather than to any stage-dependent tasks. The almost linear age slope indicates this.

The *identity function* of reminiscence, on the other hand, seems to be more stage-specific. It peaks at age category 25–34, drops to a low at age category 55–64 and thereafter increases marginally again. The *identity function* of reminiscence however seems to be most important during young age.

One question about reminiscence, treated in the introduction, is whether it should be regarded as instrumental for change or for continuity. Parker (1995) suggested that evidence of increased reminiscence in times of stress would be indicative of its continuity function.

Even if our data do provide some very weak evidence that situations of stress (life crises in particular) might stimulate the *identity function* of reminiscence, this can not be taken as support for the continuity hypothesis. Since the crisis-induced *identity function* of reminiscence appears in connection with cosmic transcendence[97]—which implies change and reorganization—it must be interpreted in the same way, in terms of change and reorganization. In other words, our data indicate that *the reminiscence induced by a crisis is more likely to contribute to identity reorganization and reconstruction than to identity preservation.* Last, but not least, the phenomena of gerotranscendence and reminiscence are, according to our analyses, intertwined. The concepts are separate, but they appear together.

If these conclusions are correct, then they have implications for practical reminiscence work. One such implication is that, since the *unity of existence* function of reminiscence becomes more important with age, reminiscence work with the elderly should focus more on that dimension. Another implication is that, since the functions of reminiscence seem

---

[97]The explanatory power of crises is also nearly washed out in a multivariate analysis together with cosmic transcendence.

related to the changes and reconstructions described in the theory of gerotranscendence, reminiscence work should be carried out with a possible outcome of such gerotranscendental changes and reconstructions in mind.

CHAPTER 5

Gerotranscendence
in Practice[98]

NURSING STAFF'S INTERPRETATIONS OF
GEROTRANSCENDENCE-RELATED BEHAVIOR

The theory of gerotranscendence identifies a number of "signs" of gerotranscendence, accounted for in detail in the chapter on the qualitative
content of gerotranscendence. These signs include, for example, changes
in the definitions of time and space, body-transcendence, ego-integrity,
and emancipated innocence. These signs are evident in certain behaviors
and attitudes that might be observable by, for example, nursing staff.

In order to find out if staff members working with the elderly notice
such behaviors and how they interpret them, we have, in a special study,
presented a number of care givers with descriptions of specific behaviors
and asked if they have noticed these behaviors among the old people they
care for. When such behaviors were recognized, we asked for the staff
members' interpretations of these behaviors and deconstructed the interpretations. As we will show in this section, a common denominator in
the interpretations of "gerotranscendental behaviors" is that they are
constructed within the scope of the theories the nursing staff are familiar
with. This means that the pathology perspective is most frequent and the
behaviors are understood as symptoms of, for example, dementia.

Possible Ways to Interpret Gerotranscendental Behavior

In the 1990 Danish retrospective study described earlier, one hypothesis
was that "gerotranscendental behaviors" could, in fact, be symptoms of

---

[98]This chapter builds, with permission, in part on what previously was published in Tornstam,
L., 1996b, Caring for Elderly: Introducing the Theory of Gerotranscendence as a Supplementary

155

dementia, depression, or drug use, rather than part of a positive development towards wisdom and maturation. Even if this might have been the case in specific instances, the study disproved this hypothesis on a general level. "Gerotranscendental behavior" is most common in elderly people without dementia, depression, or drug use. This very hypothesis, together with its disproof, highlights the fact that identical behaviors can be interpreted in very different ways, ranging from positive development to pathology.

Drawing on theories offered by social gerontology, it is our hypothesis that what we term "gerotranscendental behavior" could, aside from the theory of gerotranscendence, be understood from any of the previously mentioned perspectives, and possibly others, such as:

- The *pathological* perspective, which more or less equates aging with disease, and interprets various behaviors in old age as manifestations of physical or mental pathology.

- The *activity* perspective, which assumes that all kinds of physical and social activity is beneficial for the aging individual, and that lack of activity can result in maladjustment.

- The *disengagement* perspective, which assumes an inherent and natural drive to disengage mentally and socially when growing old.

- The *continuity* perspective, which assumes a positive and natural urge to prolong the mid-life lifestyle and identity into old age.

- The *developmental* perspective, which assumes a positive developmental change of identity as one moves into old age.

- The *mask of aging* perspective, which assumes an increasing distance between the real inner self and the betraying, aging body.

- The *masquerade perspective*, where a masquerade in old age becomes part of a coping strategy to maintain identity as a means of keeping one's options open.

- The *SOC perspective*, where the behavior is understood as ways to cope with the difficulties in old age by means of selection, optimization and compensation.

Frame of Reference for the Care of Elderly, *Scandinavian Journal of Caring Sciences*, *10*:144–150; Tornstam, L. & Tornqvist, M., 2000, Nursing staff's interpretations of "Gerotranscendental Behavior" in the Elderly, *Journal of Aging and Identity*, *5*(1):15–29.

The question, thus, is which perspective we take, consciously or unconsciously, when we are confronted with behaviors that we here call "gerotranscendental." This is an even more interesting question as regards the perspectives taken by nursing staff, since different perspectives also imply different ways of reacting to these behaviors. When we interpret a certain behavior as pathological, we react differently than when we interpret the same behavior as a development towards wisdom and maturity. The interactive identity-shaping process might, thus, take very different paths depending on whether "gerotranscendental behaviors" are regarded as signs of pathology or signs of a positive developmental process.

Staff Interpretations

The interviewees in a first study (1998) on how staff members interpret gerotranscendental behavior were some nurses and care aides[99] working in a Swedish service house for the elderly. Staff members in these categories have the most frequent contact with the service house residents. This particular Swedish service house is for relatively healthy elderly people who are, nevertheless, in need of access to daily care due to their frailty. This house is formally classified as independent living, but there are common facilities like a restaurant, therapy, and 24-hour staff. The residents are, however, encouraged to live as independently as possible.

Each of the staff members was interviewed using a semistructured qualitative approach. They were asked if they had noticed in the residents a series of behaviors, which we had derived from the theory of gerotranscendence. In cases of an affirmative response, they were then asked to interpret these behaviors. All of the interviews were tape recorded, reviewed several times, and analyzed. The basic principle in the analysis was to deconstruct the interviews in order to decide whether or not the answers could be related to any of the interpretative perspectives outlined above.

As can be seen from Table 5.1, there are variations in the degree to which the staff members noticed the different "gerotranscendental behaviors" in the residents, ranging from all staff members to just a couple of them. The following presentation begins with the behaviors that were noticed by all of the staff members and continues with the less well-

---

[99] 9 nurses and 5 care aides.

TABLE 5.1 Number of Staff Members Who Have Noticed Specific "Behaviors" in the Residents and the Cardinal Interpretation of the Behavior

Behaviour	Noticed by	Cardinal interpretation
Transcendence of time	14	Negative, pathological
Increasing need for solitude	14	Negative, pathological
Rejoicing in small events	14	Negative, pathological or activity loss
Rediscovery of the child within	14	Positive, developmental
Connection to earlier generations	14	Positive, activity perspective
Ego-integrity	14	Positive, developmental
Modern ascetism	10	Negative, activity perspective
Self-transcendence	6	Negative, activity perspective or Positive, continuity theory perspective
Disappearing fear of death	5	Positive, developmental or Negative, pathological
Self-confrontation	4	Neutral, continuity theory perspective
Body transcendence	3	Neutral, continuity theory perspective
Everyday wisdom	2	–

recognized behaviors. The fact that we have made a frequency distribution of the qualitative categories does not imply that we have used a traditional quantitative approach. It is still the qualitative aspect of the statements that are in focus, but we want to present as lucid a picture of the data as possible.

Transcendence of Time

One of the "behaviors" described in the theory of gerotranscendence is transcendence of the time borders between past and present. All of the interviewees confirmed that the elderly sometimes act as if the border between past and present was erased. They discussed residents who talk about school days as if it were yesterday and about long-deceased relatives as if they were alive. As regards this "behavior," most interviewees interpreted it as a result of some pathological condition, as evidenced by the following comments:

> *The beginning of dementia*
> *It can be caused by some disease*

It depends on their physical age. More of them have become senile and demented with age.

Confusion.

In a few interviews, this "behavior" was attributed to defense mechanisms triggered by lost security, inactivity, or just aging decline. In short, all of the interviewees noticed the transcendence of time borders, and the cardinal qualitative interpretation of this was within the framework of a negative pathological perspective. Of course this phenomenon can be, and sometimes is, a symptom of a beginning dementia, but from our analyses we know that perfectly healthy individuals also experience this transcendence of time. If you do not know that this phenomenon in at least some instances can be understood within a healthy developmental perspective, you are of course left with the pathological interpretations with which you are familiar.

In a replication of our study, Wadensten and Carlsson (2001) reach the same result with a sample of 34 nursing staff, including nursing assistants, registered nurses, and occupational therapists. The transcendence of time was, without exception, interpreted as dementia, incipient dementia, or as a state of confusion. The most common response was to try to bring these individuals back into the present.

Increased Need for Solitude

According to the theory of gerotranscendence, the individual redefines the importance of social relationships in such a way that he/she becomes more selective, prefers one-on-one communication to more superficial contacts with many, and experiences an increased need for solitude. All of the interviewees in our study confirmed that they have noticed a decreased need for social interaction and an increased need for solitude in their patients. They also valued this negatively and their spontaneous ideas about its causes are reflected in the following comments:

Maybe they don't have the energy to get together . . . Physically or maybe mentally too . . . No, it must be more physical.

I don't think it's good when they can't . . . Maybe they've lost their spark and don't have the strength to seek out people like when they were young. People get lonely and isolated.

The more friends that die, the more funerals you attend, the more you withdraw, withdraw into yourself. Old people don't want new contacts,

don't want them or don't dare to make them like when they were
younger. It's so sad, they don't build up a new network, new interfaces.

All but one of the interviewees gave the decreased need for social interaction and the increased need for solitude some kind of negative interpretation. Depression, illness, loneliness, and isolation were mentioned in this connection. The only interviewee who did not make this kind of interpretation stated that the behavior in question is quite a natural part of aging.

The interviewees were also specifically asked if the elderly sometimes refuse to be activated. The answers to this question were very much along the same line, but here every other interviewee also criticized the therapy programs offered, as expressed in these comments:

Everybody doesn't think Rev. Jansson and the accordion are so great.
All people can't fit into the same mold.

For example, some think it's ridiculous to go down to the physiotherapist
and throw balls like little kids.

To sum up, all of the interviewees had noticed the decreased need for social interaction and the increased need for solitude and tended to interpret this negatively. A withdrawal from social interaction was interpreted as a sign of loneliness and isolation, or as a sign of different pathological conditions. Withdrawing into solitude was regarded as a problem. Being socially active and participating in various social activities were described as desirable. Activity was regarded as very important for the well-being of the elderly. The underlying, activity theory perspective, was obvious. Also regarding the interpretation of the increasing need for solitude, the Wadensten and Carlsson (2001) study reached a similar result. The staff that they interviewed interpreted the increased need for solitude as a kind of defense reaction to losses of friends and close relatives, together with lack of energy to find new friends.

Rejoicing in Small Events

As earlier described as part of the qualitative content of gerotranscendence, transcendent individuals often change their view of what gives joy in life, from spectacular events to small and commonplace things, often events and experiences in nature. All of the interviewees reported noticing that the elderly tend to express increased pleasure in simpler things such as:

Changes in nature.

. . . that today is different from yesterday.

Sewing on a button. . . .

. . . a little pat or hug.

The last quote is an examples of sources of pleasure that are related to relationships. Some of the interviewees mentioned elderly people's unfulfilled need for social and interpersonal contact. These interviewees understood this shift in causes of joy—from the great to the small—as something problematic, as a sign of unintentional loneliness and isolation. In these statements we find explanations such as:

. . . because they are very isolated.

Their lives are often so meager that any type of change is perceived as positive . . .

In addition to the interpretations above, the interviews contains explanations more directly focused on pathology:

But when they reach a certain limit, they're dependent on the help of others, they're sick and mentally weak and they can't take care of themselves. They can't manage by themselves so the smallest thing can be a great joy.

. . . of course it can be illness that does it, the eyes aren't working, hearing is bad, and so on.

The ones that are a little bit depressed. . . .

Another category of interpretations was also found. This category is similar to the last in that elderly people's tendencies to express pleasure in small as opposed to great events were interpreted as reflecting their resignation. We have, however, chosen to include these statements in a separate category, as this is more a question of social withdrawal than of a pathological condition such as depression. The interviewees related how the elderly often withdraw into themselves in a negative way:

. . . they're inside themselves, in their own world.

It's a kind of resignation, like they've just given up. . . .

In summary, all of the interviewees reported noticing that the elderly tend to appreciate and express pleasure in simpler events and experiences. However, this behavior pattern is interpreted in various ways. In some statements, it is seen as a sign of different pathological states, in others as a sign of loneliness and isolation. We can imagine that behind these statements lies an activity-oriented theoretical perspective. Such a perspective can even be discerned in those statements in which elderly people's tendency to shift their sources of pleasure is understood as a sign of resignation. This tendency was interpreted as a negative consequence of their social withdrawal. The interviewees felt that the way in which the elderly withdraw from social contact and spend more of their time alone constitutes a problem. The Wadensten and Carlsson (2001) study also showed that elderly people's rejoicing in small events was interpreted negatively by the staff they interviewed.

Return to Childhood

One characteristic of a development towards gerotranscendence is returning to and reinterpreting childhood in terms of the collected experiences of a life lived. All of the interviewees affirmed that the elderly they cared for are glad to talk about their childhood, as revealed by these typical comments:

> Poverty, siblings, experiences. They can tell you about both the positive and the negative sides.

> They're really happy when they get to talk about childhood. You can just see how they come to life.

One of the interviewees noted how elderly people often return to a certain childhood event that they willingly talk about. In this statement, returning to and working through childhood events were interpreted by the interviewee as being both positive and necessary. The interviewee further stressed the importance of being able to "put your life in order," to accept the past in order to avoid embitterment.

In addition, a couple of the interviewees reported that elderly people tend to embellish certain childhood events. These interviewees interpreted willingness to talk about childhood either as way to express acceptance of childhood events or as a sign that the elderly person in question has mostly positive childhood memories. Some of the interviewees thought that the very act of telling about childhood and childhood events could be a source of pleasure for the elderly, thus explaining their willingness to talk.

Several interviewees reported that elderly people often want to talk about difficulties connected with their childhood. Again, we see that the importance of accepting the life lived is stressed when interpretations of this behavior are made. The interviewees point out repeatedly that an acceptance of the past is necessary if people are to avoid becoming embittered.

In summary, all of the interviewees noted that the elderly tend to talk about their childhood. This behavior was essentially interpreted as being positive in that it is part of a "healthy" developmental process in which the life lived is put in order and reconciled with. The interpretations are largely in line with Erikson's theory of psychosocial development, which is taught in the curriculum of Swedish nurses and is therefore well-known. Again, the above pattern was replicated in the Wadensten and Carlsson (2001) study, where the staff interpreted talk about childhood as a positive and necessary thing to bring life to completion.

Connection to Earlier Generations

An increased feeling of affinity primarily with earlier, but also with future, generations is one of the characteristics of gerotranscendental development. All of the staff members had observed this tendency. The primary interpretation of this behavior was positive and seemed to be related to activity theory:

> It helps them make contact . . . because they still want some kind of contact, they can talk about their lives outside the service home, cleaning, and . . . the fact that there's also something else.

> It's good that they care about what society is like today or in the past.

For those elderly who do not talk about earlier and future generations, the interpretation was that the *lack* of such topics was a negative sign, indicating withdrawal, isolation, loneliness, and illness. In the Wadensten and Carlsson (2001) study the interpretation made by their respondents was also positive, with the addendum that old people had better and closer contacts with their parents than people of today and that they had considerable time to think about their older relatives.

Ego-Integrity

As in Erikson's developmental theory, the theory of gerotranscendence also includes an assumption that we have, especially late in life, a need to create coherence in the life lived. This may be revealed as an increased need for reminiscence—to think and talk about our life in an attempt to arrange its elements into a coherent whole. All of the interviewees confirmed that this is a common phenomenon, and the main interpretation of this behavior is very much in line with Erikson's theory. Telling the life story, according to the staff, is a sign of having accepted the life lived in a positive way:

> It's about coming so far that you can say okay, I've done that, a bunch of stupid things, but so what? Most old people have succeeded. . . .
>
> They think life has been really good. They even seem to accept the things that weren't good, they don't need everything to be so perfect.
>
> It seems like they've accepted things mostly, maybe because they understand that they can't change anything.
>
> They accept what's happened, some know things weren't great but they still dared to keep going, they went through what they went through, and did what they could. . . .

Some of the interviewees also explicitly linked the *inability* to accept life to feelings of bitterness in old age. As an exception, one of the interviewees interpreted story telling as an expression of the individual's dissatisfaction with a present situation that is characterized by isolation, loneliness, and dependency.

In the Wadensten and Carlsson (2001) study also, the staff noticed old people talking about their lives, and regarded that as natural. At the same time they noticed that none of the staff reported to have observed that older people looking back upon their lives claimed to understand events and episodes in a new light or as reaching a new, mature state of coherence. This latter finding can of course be due to the fact that none of the old people these staff have met, had talked about their lives in this reconstructive manner. It could also be due to the staff's lack of preparation to observe this kind of reconstructive approach to storytelling.

Modern Asceticism

Most of the interviewees reported that many elderly people show a decreased interest in material objects, precisely as described in the theory of gerotranscendence:

. . . it seems like they think there's no use in getting things 'cause maybe they'll die tomorrow, but you can't think like that. Even young people die. Lots of them think like that.

In this statement, as in others, "modern asceticism" was understood negatively as being a result of elderly people's withdrawal from the outside world, that is, their withdrawal into themselves and their decreased social contacts. Here we might suspect the indirect or direct influence of underlying assumptions from activity theory.

Although these negative interpretations, presumably originating from activity theory, dominate the material, there are also examples of other bases of interpretation. In some statements, elderly people's decreased interest in material things is described in terms of priorities: The elderly place more value on the nonmaterial. In a couple of statements, this was interpreted as a result of aging, i.e., from a developmental perspective. In an additional two statements, a theory of continuity could be discerned in the interpretations, i.e., such nonmaterialistic values are determined and secured earlier in life. The cardinal interpretation was, however, labeled as negative, with roots in activity theory.

In the Wadensten and Carlsson (2001) study, however, the cardinal interpretation was labeled as "normal" signs of a positive adaptation to, and satisfaction with, what the old people had, and as a possible generational phenomenon.

Self-Transcendence

Only a few of the staff members reported ever noticing any altruistic self-transcendence in the elderly. On the contrary, the most common answer was that most elderly behaved quite selfishly, and, as in the following comment, notions of pathology seemed to underlie these interpretations of selfish behavior:

It's also a matter of their mental health. Maybe they're mentally disturbed.

However, in the few cases where altruistic self-transcendence was observed, the interpretations were characterized by two different theoretical perspectives. In certain statements, a more unselfish approach to oneself and others was interpreted as a sign of resignation. Thus, loneliness and inactivity were thought to contribute to this undesirable shift in perspective among the elderly:

> *... mostly they're pretty passive and idle. They're not as demanding when they get older. They're afraid of becoming a problem.*
>
> *Maybe some resignation, maybe. That's not good, they should ... almost everybody should stand up and yell, "Here I am!*

The negative interpretations discussed above stem from the perspective of activity theory, while the interpretations below belong to a more positive, continuity-oriented theoretical perspective:

> *... I think it has to do with people's personality, what they were like when they were young, for example.*
>
> *... it depends on how family life has been, and all, what that was like. It probably depends on early life experiences.*

The results from the Wadensten and Carlsson (2001) study replicates the above findings almost identically. The modal answer from their respondents was that self-transcendence was not present, but that increased egoism was the rule. In the few cases where self-transcendence was observed, the explanation was either that it was the continuity of a personality trait from earlier in life, or part of an adaptive acceptance to the strains of growing old.

Disappearing Fear of Death

Based on the theory of gerotranscendence, as well as results from other studies (see Kastenbaum, 1996), it was expected that staff members would report many cases of elderly who do not fear death. Only a few staff members in our study, however, reported that the elderly tend to be unafraid of death, and in these cases the main interpretation was based on a positive developmental perspective as reflected in comments like the following:

> *... they accept it. That that they're going to die. It comes with age.*
>
> *They are somehow complete and secure.*

Some staff members, on the other hand, gave interpretations more related to assumptions about depression and defense mechanisms:

> *When they reach a difficult period of serious illness and pain they can't manage, then they definitely think about death.*

When I go to them, they seem like they want to die because they know that's what will happen anyway.

In the Wadensten and Carlsson (2001) study the absence of fear of death appears to be more commonplace, with similar interpretations as above. In addition, there was the possibility that this specific generation could rely on a Christian belief and that their generation had lived closer to death in a more natural manner than succeeding generations. In that study it was also reported that even when an older person obviously was not afraid of death, and wanted to talk about these matters, the usual procedure was to change topics.

Self-Confrontation

According to the theory of gerotranscendence, self-confrontation, discovering new sides of oneself, may be part of a gerotranscendental development. The modal observation by the staff, however, was that most elderly displayed rigidity rather than any developmental self-confrontation. The minority of staff members who reported observing self-confrontation among the elderly interpreted this behavior in two different ways. The first type of interpretation referred to a flexible personality type established earlier in life and continued into old age, i.e., it reflected the continuity perspective, for example:

Like how you are as a person or how you've been raised, maybe

I think you're born with it, being positive and such until you get old. It's in the genes.

The other interpretation, put forth by only one staff member, was in line with a developmental perspective in which self-confrontation is attributed to aging as such. In the Wadensten and Carlsson (2001) study self-confrontation belonged to the "invisible" group of signs and none of the staff had observed anything resembling it.

Body Transcendence

Only few of the staff members reported noting any body transcendence in the elderly and, on the contrary, most of them observed a dominant pattern of body obsession. Those who did observe a pattern of body transcendence interpreted this in terms of continuity theory by referring to the personality and its continuation into old age:

. . . it depends on how life has been. What you think about yourself, if you're satisfied with yourself, if you have a strong opinion of yourself.

It is notable that none of the staff members interpreted body transcendence from a developmental perspective.

In the Wadensten and Carlsson (2001) study body transcendence, when it was observed, was categorized among the signs of gerotranscendence described as "normal" by the interviewed staff members. Here the interpretations focused on coping processes. The old people were said to have adapted to their bodily changes and accepted the fact that one changes. It was also argued that those who have led good lives may find it easier to accept difficulties (like bodily changes). So, the "normality" here was not a normality in any developmental perspective, but rather the normality of having the capacity to cope with stress and strain.

Everyday Wisdom

According to the theory of gerotranscendence, having everyday wisdom may be part of a gerotranscendental development. Everyday wisdom was defined as the tendency to be broadminded as opposed to condemning in one's attitudes. The common attitude among the staff members was that most elderly people are more condemning than broadminded, but some staff members did describe cases of "everyday wisdom." Their interpretations, however, could not be placed within any of the theoretical perspectives mentioned above. Wadensten and Carlsson (2001) also reported on the invisibility of everyday wisdom and of stubbornness and self-confidence as being the norm. In the few cases where their informants could recall old people showing signs of everyday wisdom, these old people were thought to be insecure and lacking in self-confidence.

What Do These Studies on Staff Members' Interpretations Reveal?

The question was whether staff members have observed approaches and behaviors in line with the theory of gerotranscendence and, if so, how they interpret them. Our assumption was that these interpretations and discourses can be related—explicitly or implicitly—to certain theoretical perspectives which might be familiar to the staff. In particular, a) the pathology perspective, b) activity theory, c) disengagement theory, e) continuity theory, and d) developmental theory.

A general observation is that there are certain behaviors that the staff members hardly noticed at all. An example of this is "everyday wisdom," which most of the interviewees did not observe in the elderly they cared for. Of course, this could mean that the interviewees have not met with this phenomenon in their everyday reality, but another just as likely explanation is that the nursing staff's frames of reference cannot accommodate these types of observations. The everyday discourse of these care givers is constructed using specific theoretical building blocks. This simultaneously creates keen-sightedness in certain directions and blindness in others. This can help us understand why some gerotranscendendental behaviors were hardly observed at all by the staff. In addition to everyday wisdom, this also means blindness to self-transcendence, self-confrontation, body transcendence, and, in one of the studies, the disappearing fear of death. Instead of stating that these behaviors just were not there, we suggest they possibly might have been, but that staff had no preparation to observe them. But, to be sure, gerotranscendence is not reached by everyone, so the presence of some signs may actually be rare. At the same time, having cared for old people for many years would likely have enabled the staff members to observe gerotranscendental behaviors in at least some individuals.

In cases where the interviewees did notice gerotranscendental behaviors, the results clearly reveal the diversity of perceptions as defined in terms of recognized theories, i.e., the same behavior is interpreted differently by different people. The least common denominator, however, is that a majority of the interpretations—whether direct or indirect—were made within the perspective of activity theory or in pathology-oriented terms. This would seem to indicate that nursing staff members' perceptual fields are largely distinguished and limited by pathology-oriented and activity-oriented theoretical points of departure. This does not, of course, place any blame on staff members. It is, instead, an example of how reality is constructed and defined in terms of the frames of reference at hand.

In those interpretations that seem to reflect an underlying activity-oriented theoretical understanding of aging, the various behaviors were associated with both negative and positive meanings. In the case of positive meanings, the behavior in question was interpreted as a positive expression of an active and outgoing life. In the case of more negative interpretations, the "problem behaviors" were interpreted as signs or causes of loneliness, inactivity, isolation, passivity, or various pathological conditions. Overall, gerotranscendental behaviors tended to be understood as the undesirable consequences of loneliness and inactivity.

Frames of reference other than activity theory were also clearly displayed in staff members' interpretations of the behaviors they observed. A recurring theme was understanding based on continuity theory. The behaviors in question are, thus, described as being dependent on the personality and lifestyle characteristics of a continuous, lifelong pattern.

Additional interpretations of observed behavior are informed by more intuitive, developmentally oriented reasoning. Interpretations within this frame of reference are marked by the fact that they are not focused on problems; on the contrary, the behaviors are associated with positive meanings. As regards those behaviors we have called return to childhood, ego-integrity, and disappearing fear of death, it has been possible to refer to Erikson's developmental model, which is well-known to most people working with the elderly. In keeping with Erikson, the interviewees have been able to associate the behaviors in question with positive meanings. On the other hand, as regards behaviors categorized as transcendence of time, increasing need for solitude, and rejoicing in small events, no "positive" frames of reference have been available. Interpretations of these behaviors have, thereby, fallen into the more "negative" and pathology-oriented frames of references that the staff members have at hand.

Since we maintain that gerotranscendence describes something that is, at least for some people, a positive development, the above studies would seem to indicate that care givers working with the elderly need more theoretical knowledge about alternative frames of reference. If care givers were more aware of the existence of different theories, a broader understanding of how different individuals can age in a positive way would be facilitated. This, in turn, would lead to an increase in the quality of the care currently offered to elderly people.

THE IMPACT OF THE THEORY ON NURSING STAFF

In the previous section studies were presented where staff members were shown to know nothing about gerotranscendence and, in fact, often were prone to classify gerotranscendendental behavior as pathological, since this followed from the theoretical frameworks that were familiar to them— consciously or unconsciously. But what happens if nursing staff come to know about gerotranscendence?

This section describes an attempt to introduce the theory of gerotranscendence to nursing staff. The venture included two steps: 1) the introduction of the theory, and 2) six months later, an impact evaluation. As will be described below, the impact evaluation showed that almost half of the staff came to a new understanding of specific care recipients after learning about the theory of gerotranscendence, and that a third of the staff also changed their attitude towards caring for specific individuals. The introduction of the new theory also reduced staff members' feelings of guilt about insufficiency at work.

The Intervention Group and the Intervention

The intervention took place in the small Swedish rural municipality, Essunga. In this municipality, the total nursing staff working with the elderly in various institutional settings consisted of approximately 100 women, which allowed a nearly full-scale intervention. The intervention was primarily aimed at staff working at institutions for the elderly, but a few staff from the open community service also wished to participate and were included in the intervention.[100]

The introduction of the theory included some creative participation on the part of the staff. Instead of presenting them with a ready-made care model, the idea was to build on staff members' experiences. In choosing this approach, we diverged from a classic experimental design, where the manipulation is totally controlled by the researcher.

The introduction phase took place during the period October 1993 to March 1994 and started with a half-day seminar. During this seminar, ways of understanding and caring for the elderly were presented and discussed. Along with the more or less familiar perspectives offered by activity theory, continuity theory, and ordinary developmental theory, the theory of gerotranscendence was introduced to the staff and discussed in small subgroups where each subgroup included staff of different professions and from different settings. The discussions aimed at promoting

---

[100]Nine of the 90 staff members present at the first presentation of the theory later dropped out due to sick leave or pregnancy leave. Out of the remaining 81 staff members, 74 responded to the impact survey, giving a response rate of 91 percent. Of the 74 staff members constituting the respondents to the impact survey, there were 11 registered nurses, 30 enrolled nurses, 27 aides or home service aides and 10 "others," including single individuals from among the ranks of district nurses, physical therapists, occupational therapists, and managers of the community home service. The age span of the staff was 22–62.

sensitivity to possible gerotranscendental developments and to make the staff members aware of their own ways of thinking and acting upon this.

Following the first introduction and discussions, the staff later participated in another two rounds of self-managed group discussions at their work sites. The reported outcome from these discussions helped to *formulate the topical questions* to be empirically assessed in the impact survey.

As noted, the research strategy can expose us to some criticism. Since the staff in the "experimental group" has, at least to some extent, helped to define the impact dimensions, the manipulation is not clean. If, however, we understand that this study is not a classical experiment, but rather an inventive process in which the staff has participated, it makes sense to study the outcome of this process. This type of study would, in fact, be impossible to carry out within the methodological frame of the classical experiment. What would we measure, for example, in a control group?

The Impact Survey

Six months after the concluding round of group discussions, a mail survey consisting of an *impact measurement* was sent to the participants.[101] We believed that a six-month period was long enough that any exaggerated post-intervention enthusiasm would have faded away, and that the answers we got would be thoughtful and serious.

The survey targeted the topics below using easy-to-answer questions with fixed response alternatives. In order to counterbalance biases to "agree" with the theory, rejection-response alternatives always appeared first. Respondents were prompted to add qualitative explanations and

---

[101]A technical remark about the data analysis is appropriate at this point. As a full-scale intervention, principally including all staff, the intervention might be regarded as rather extensive. However, when it comes to the analysis of the quantitative data from the impact survey, the data set is very small—in fact, much too small for the more elaborate analyses we would like to do. Thus, we must make the interpretations with caution. On the other hand, since the data reflect a full-scale intervention, there has been no statistical sampling procedure and an orthodox interpretation of the statistical rules of the game would say that we have no reason to make any probability calculations. Despite this, we have supplied probability calculations in the analyses to follow. We did this under the assumption that some readers might wish to regard the intervention group as a sample from a larger population, e.g., defined as "Swedish municipal staff working with the elderly?. The probability measures are all based on Chi-square. The coefficients of association are Eta correlations, allowing nominal data. Regarding the circumstances, however, the reader is advised to pay more attention to the magnitude of the Eta measures than to the probability calculations.

examples at any point and, specifically, when effects of the theory were an issue. The impact survey produced the results discussed below.

Most of the Staff Members Understood the Theory

According to the reports given in the impact survey, 73 percent of the participants reported that they, to a "certain" or "high" degree, understood the point of the theory (Table 5.2).

Reported understanding of the theory was lower among staff working in nursing homes (55 percent) as compared with staff working in old age homes and group dwellings (82 percent), or in the open community service (80 percent). Reported understanding of the theory also varied according to professional status. The degree of understanding was highest (100 percent) among the registered nurses, followed by the aides (78 percent), and the enrolled nurses (57 percent).

Most of the Staff Members Agreed That the Theory Corresponded with Reality

Out of all the staff, 72 percent thought the theory corresponded to a "certain" or "high" degree (see Table 5.2) to the reality they knew. The hypothesis was that this belief would correlate with both personal and professional experiences. Table 5.3 shows that this hypothesis was partly confirmed.

Recognition of a gerotranscendental process in oneself correlated, in the predicted way, with the opinion that the theory corresponded to reality. We also found correlations with professional status and institutional setting. It was the registered nurses who rated the theory as most

TABLE 5.2 Impact of the Theory of Gerotranscendence

	No	Possibly	Yes	Total	n
Understands theory?	5	23	73	101%	73
Corresponds with reality?	5	24	72	101%	68
Affected outlook on own old age?	26	42	22	100%	73
New understanding of care receiver?	57	–	43	100%	73
Changed behavior?	36	30	33	99%	69
Guilt reduction?	34	22	45	101%	65

TABLE 5.3 Correlates of the Impact of the Theory of Gerotranscendence

	Theory corresponds with reality	Affected own aging	Understood care-receiver	Increased listening and permissiveness	Satisfaction with tasks	Satisfaction with workplace	Guilt reduction	General impact index
Age	$.23^{ns}$	$.35^{*}$	$.03^{ns}$	$.13^{ns}$	$.40^{**}$	$.12^{ns}$	$.30^{*}$	$.13^{ns}$
Profession	$.34^{*}$	$.27^{ns}$	$.34^{*}$	$.25^{ns}$	$.37^{*}$	$.04^{ns}$	$.30^{*}$	$.34^{ns}$
Time in profession	$.08^{ns}$	$.22^{ns}$	$.30^{*}$	$.22^{ns}$	$.22^{ns}$	$.10^{ns}$	$.25^{ns}$	$.24^{ns}$
Setting (nursing home, etc.)	$.24^{*}$	$.45^{**}$	$.32^{ns}$	$.43^{**}$	$.39^{**}$	$.25^{ns}$	$.44^{**}$	$.47^{***}$
Understands theory	$.45^{***}$	$.29^{*}$	$.34^{***}$	$.27^{*}$	$.19^{ns}$	$.06^{ns}$	$.30^{*}$	$.48^{***}$
Recognizes own development	$.28^{*}$	$.27^{*}$	$.17^{ns}$	$.29^{*}$	$.17^{ns}$	$.03^{ns}$	$.03^{ns}$	$.27^{*}$

$*p < .05$
$**p < .01$
$***p < .001$
^{ns}not significant

realistic, and the staff working at nursing homes who rated the theory as least realistic.

For Some of the Staff Members the Theory Had an Impact on Their Attitude Toward Their Own Old Age

It is often said that one of the obstacles in caring for the elderly is the staff's own fear of aging and death. Does the theory of gerotranscendence have the potential to create in staff members a more positive outlook towards their own old age? Table 5.2 shows that this effect was restricted to 22 percent of the respondents who, to a "certain" or "high" degree, reported that the theory had positively affected their outlook on their own aging and old age.

When describing this effect in qualitative terms, the respondents used two types of descriptions—cognitive and emotional. The cognitive descriptions were of the following type:

I now see these types of changes as normal.

Thus, instead of viewing coherence and continuity as absolute criteria of "normality" in aging, change and discontinuity were also seen as normal. The emotional descriptions were of the following type:

Aging feels simpler.

My perspective is more hopeful now.

As can be seen from Table 5.3, the theory's effect on staff members' outlook on their own aging and old age correlated with their ages. The older the staff member was, the greater the impact.

The correlations with type of setting and professional status were similar to those seen above. The respondents who reported the least effect on their outlook on their own aging and old age were found among the staff at nursing homes. Among the professions, the registered nurses reported the greatest effect.

The Theory Helped Many Staff Members to See Care Recipients in a New Light and to Understand Them Better

An important aim of the venture was to see whether the theory of gerotranscendence could help staff members understand specific care recipients in a new way. Theoretically, care recipient behavior previously interpreted as negative withdrawal, signs of depression, or just unintelligible behavior, might acquire new, more positive meanings in the light of the theory. The staff members were asked if there were specific care recipients whom they understood in a new way in light of the theory.

Table 5.2 shows that 43 percent of the staff reported that they had gained new insights into one or more specific care recipients after presentation of the theory. Qualitatively speaking, this new understanding was described as:

> *Understanding and acceptance of their need for solitude.*
>
> *Understanding the difference between my own and the care recipients' value systems.*
>
> *Understanding their reluctance about activation.*

The correlations with type of setting and professional status were, again, similar to those seen earlier. Registered nurses reported most frequently that they had come to understand one or several care recipients in a new light. With regard to settings, the staff at nursing homes reported this change the least frequently.

A Third of the Staff Members Became More Permissive and Better Listeners

Another important impact of the intervention would certainly be changes in staff behavior and methods in accordance with the theory. Table 5.2 shows that 33 percent of the staff reported that, to a "certain" or "high" degree, they changed their behavior in relation to the care recipients. Qualitatively, these changes were described with phrases like:

> *Less nagging about activities*
>
> *Listening more to care recipients' wishes than before*
>
> *Thinking more about care recipients' integrity*
>
> *Allowing care recipients to be by themselves*
>
> *Not imposing my own needs on care recipients*

Clearly, these statements suggest an increased attention to the desires of care recipients over those of the staff. We might call this *increased*

listening and *permissiveness*. During the introductory phase of the intervention, one suggestion was that staff could discuss developmental issues
related to the theory of gerotranscendence with the care recipients in
order to get their opinions and perhaps trigger new processes of development. The survey revealed that 88 percent of the respondents did nothing
of that sort. Thus, changed practices in terms of increased listening and
permissiveness were not uncommon,[102] but the introduction of new topics
of conversation and new developmental stimuli were very rare, next to
nonexistent.

Familiarity with the Theory Seemed to Reduce
Feelings of Insufficiency at Work

During the group discussions, members of the staff suggested that the
theory of gerotranscendence might help to reduce feelings of insufficiency
at work by, among other things, presenting an intelligible view of care
recipients' increased need for solitude.

A question related to this suggestion is: What proportion of the staff
reports such feelings of insufficiency at work and to what extent are these
feelings related to general job dissatisfaction and/or particular environ-
mental factors? In relation to this question, staff members were asked
whether they liked their work tasks, place of work, and colleagues, and
if they had feelings of guilt or insufficiency at work.

Overall, the staff were quite satisfied with both their tasks and their
places of work and colleagues. Of the total, 87 percent were "rather" or
"very" satisfied with their tasks. No less than 94 percent were "rather"
or "very" satisfied with their place of work and colleagues.

There were, however, some variations that should be mentioned.
Behind the correlation between age and satisfaction with tasks shown in
Table 5.3, was the pattern that satisfaction was somewhat higher among
the middle-aged staff members as compared with younger and older ones.
Satisfaction with tasks also differed as a function of professional status.
Aides were more satisfied than registered nurses, who were more satisfied
than enrolled nurses. Also, satisfaction with tasks differed as a function
of work setting. Staff working in the community home service were most

---

[102]The data show that increased listening and permissiveness, were more common in settings
outside nursing homes. Table 5.3 shows a correlation of .43 between institutional setting and
increased listening and permissiveness.

satisfied, followed by staff working in old age homes, home care, and nursing homes. This pattern might reflect an underlying care burden dimension. It is usually regarded as more laborious to work with the frail elderly at nursing homes.

Even if the staff in this study reported a high degree of satisfaction with their jobs, there was, as expected, one important indicator signaling a special problem. No less then 81 percent of the respondents stated that they, to a high or certain degree, have feelings of insufficiency at work and/or guilt about being insufficient. In this case we found no differences between subgroups of different ages, or from different professions or work settings. Also, regardless of how many years the respondents had been working, the feelings of insufficiency remained the same. The feelings of guilt about insufficiency cut through all the professional categories in the study. Since it is most likely that these categories are subject to different workloads and care burdens, the workload hypothesis is probably not a good explanation of the high proportions of staff suffering from feelings of guilt and/or insufficiency. A possible explanation is that these feelings of insufficiency are based on something different, i.e., that they are based on approaches to care that are rooted in inaccurate and inefficient theories about the aging process. In short, the feelings of guilt and insufficiency might be due to not having the proper tools in the theoretical toolbox. Might this be solved by the introduction of a new frame of reference as offered by the theory of gerotranscendence—that is, by adding a new theoretical tool to the tool box? Table 5.2 reveals that 45 percent of the staff reported that the theory of gerotranscendence helped, to a "certain" or "high" degree, to reduce feelings of guilt about insufficiency.

Table 5.3 shows that respondents' ages correlated with the degree of guilt reduction. Thus, the older the respondent, the more the theory was reported to have reduced guilt. We also found a strong correlation between work setting and guilt reduction. The correlation of .44 shown in Table 5.3 results from the deviant reports from staff at nursing homes, where the guilt reduction was reported to be significantly lower in comparison with reports from staff in other settings.

The Overall Impact

In order to shed some light on when and where, generally speaking, the intervention worked when the staff described it as applicable or not applicable, we constructed a general-impact index. The index is simple.

For each respondent, we counted the number of times the respondent reported that the theory of gerotranscendence had an impact, to a "certain" or "high" degree, in the following five areas: *1) Did the staff think the theory had any basis in reality? 2) Did the theory have an impact on the staff's outlook on their own old age? 3) Did the theory help the staff to understand care recipients in a new light? 4) Did the theory change staff's approach to care giving? 5) Did the theory help to reduce any feelings of insufficiency or guilt at work?*

From the construction of the index, it follows that its range is between zero and five. The mean number of "impacts" was 2.03, which simply means that, on average, the respondents reported 2.03 areas in which the theory had an impact.

From Table 5.3 we can see that the deviations from this average, expressed by the correlation coefficients, are apparent. Most obvious, but hardly surprising, was the strong correlation between the general-impact index and the level of understanding of the theory. The better the theory was understood, the stronger the impact.

More interesting was the equally strong correlation between the general-impact index and the work setting. Behind the correlation of .47 is the pattern we have earlier observed. The impact was at its lowest among staff at nursing homes, who reported an average of 1.2 areas of impact. Staff at old age homes reported 2.3 areas of impact, and staff at group dwellings, 2.5 areas of impact. Staff in the community home service, finally, reported an average of 3.4 areas of impact. Furthermore, regarding professional status, the pattern is by now well-known: registered nurses reported the highest number of impact areas (3.3), and enrolled nurses the lowest (1.6).

Conclusions About Educating Staff in Gerotranscendence

After a six-month latency period the theory of gerotranscendence was recognized as a theory describing relevant parts of the reality staff members meet in their work with certain elderly care recipients. High proportions of the staff not only understood the theory, but also held the opinion that it corresponded to the reality they knew as professional care givers. Also, nearly half of the staff reported that they gained new insights into specific care recipients in light of the theory.

Underlying this result, we have found recurrent patterns of correlation particularly involving setting and professional status. Registered nurses reported understanding of the theory and cases which fit the theory more frequently while, among settings, staff working in nursing homes reported less impact and applicability of the intervention. They had, for example, more difficulties understanding the theory and recognizing gerotranscendent care recipients. There can be several explanations for this finding. One of them is that the environment in a nursing home is rather hospital-like and may be inappropriate for the application of the theory of gerotranscendence; physical rather than spiritual well-being is the primary focus. Another explanation might be that in nursing homes several of the patients may be suffering from true dementia and thus are outside the scope of the theory's applicability.

Two comments can be made on this, one trivial and one important. The trivial comment is that if there are no gerotranscendent individuals present, you cannot recognize any. *The important comment is that gerotranscendent individuals are probably not totally absent from nursing homes, they are probably just fewer in number. At the same time, the nursing home environment and existing evaluative frameworks make it more difficult for them to be seen.*

If gaining new understanding of care recipients was relatively common based on our interviews, the logically subsequent changes in caring practices were more unusual. One third of the staff became better listeners and more permissive, while almost none introduced new developmental stimuli. *It is quite obvious that the intervention must be more powerful if we want to reach the ultimate goal of modification of care practices.* Even if the desired behavioral changes were hardly reached with this intervention, the outcome was unexpectedly positive in many respects. One positive finding was the guilt-reducing capacity of the theory.

The reduction in guilt, however, highlighted yet another problem. There was a minority (10 percent) of the respondents who, to a "certain" or "high" degree, saw an ethical problem connected with the theory. Qualitatively, the ethical problem was described as follows: "Who decides what to do, I and the care recipient or the relatives?" Prior to this intervention, the staff had a problem—relatives often wanted more activation and more active care than care recipients themselves desired. Application of the new theory would seem to magnify this problem. The feeling of guilt about insufficiency in relation to the care recipient seems to be reduced, but perhaps substituted by the problem with the relatives of the care recipients. It may be that staff members are not the only ones who need to know about gerotranscendence, but relatives as well.

PRACTICAL GUIDELINES FOR STAFF MEMBERS

In the previous section it was emphasized that while staff members acquired an increased listening and permissiveness after learning about the
theory of transcendence, the introduction of new topics of conversation
or new developmental stimuli was very rare, or nearly nonexistent. In
order to reach more substantial changes in the behavior of staff members,
other efforts are needed.

Such efforts have been undertaken by Wadensten and Carlsson (2002)
who, as a first step, have derived theory-driven guidelines for the practical
care of older people based on the theory of gerotranscendence. With the
help of focus groups they have arrived at a series of guidelines focusing
on three levels: 1) what the individual staff member can do in meetings
with the care recipient, 2) new types of activities to arrange, and 3)
measures on the organizational level.

Wadensten and Carlsson relied on three different focus groups in
this endeavor. One group consisted of individuals without experiences in
care giving, a second group consisted of staff with care giving experience,
but not in geriatric care. A third group was made up of staff with experience
in care giving for old people in a nursing home setting. Each focus group
attended a lecture on the theory of gerotranscendence, after which they
participated in a group discussion aiming at finding which kind of actions
and components of care could promote development towards gerotranscendence or what might constitute good care for people already approaching gerotranscendence. The participants in the focus groups also
were asked for procedures, activities, or behaviors to omit in order not
to counteract the processes of gerotranscendence. Each "sign" of gerotranscendence was discussed in the focus groups in order to reach practical
guidelines for recognizing all the aspects and behaviors characteristic of
gerotranscendence. The suggestions from the focus groups resulted in
the following two sets of guidelines, summarized here as "what to do"
and "what to avoid":

✓ Do accept signs of gerotranscendence as possibly normal signs in the
   aging process.
✓ Do choose a topic of conversation not focusing on health and physical
   limitations.
   Link to theory: This is in accordance with the development of body transcen-
   dence proposed in the theory.

✓ Do respect the fact that that older people can have a different perception of time, such that the boundaries between past, present and future are transcended.
  Link to theory: This is related to the cosmic level—changes in the definition of time and space.

✓ Do ask the person to talk about their "adventures" in the past.
  Link to theory: This is related to the cosmic level—changes in the definition of time and space.

✓ Do listen when someone talks about death, let them speak, ask questions, stimulate further thoughts.
  Link to theory: This is related to the cosmic level; the fear of death disappears and a new comprehension of life and death results. The fear of death generally decreases with age, thus it becomes more natural to talk about death.

✓ Do inform residents if someone among them has died, and allow them to talk about it.
  Link to theory: As above.

✓ Do ask in the morning what the older person dreamed about instead of asking how they feel. If they did dream, ask questions about the dream and what it might mean.
  Link to theory: Analyzing dreams is, according to Jung, a pathway to the archetypes in the collective unconscious.

✓ Do encourage the older person to recall and talk about childhood and old times, and how they have developed during life.
  Link to theory: This is stimulating the process of transfiguring childhood and reaching ego integrity.

✓ Do let older people decide for themselves whether they want to be alone or participate in "activities."
  Link to theory: The need for positive solitude may have increased and should be respected.

✓ Do discuss in a group or in individual conversations the topic of growing old, and introduce older people to the theory of gerotranscendence as a possible and positive process of aging.
  Link to theory: The developmental path of gerotranscendence may be either unknown or experienced, but connected with shame.

✓ Do start reminiscence therapy as a way of "working" with one's own life history. This can be done in different ways, such as writing down the life history, talking about life history with staff, or talking about life history in a group of other older people.

Link to theory: Certain aspects of reminiscence are related to gero-transcendence.

✓ Do arrange a meditation course. Meditation may be a way to get in touch with inherited mental structures, as suggested by Jung.
Link to theory: Meditation is also regarded by Jung as a pathway to the transcendent connection with the eternal questions of life, captured in the archetypes.

✓ Do remember to plan and organize for quiet moments of rest and also to respect people's wishes to be alone in their room.
Link to theory: The need for positive solitude may have increased and should be respected.

✓ Do organize so that older persons can have meals in their own room if desired.
Link to theory: As above.

✖ Do not regard signs of gerotranscendence as undesirable and incorrect.
Link to theory: Studies have shown that gerotranscendent behaviors are frequently misinterpreted as pathological signs.

✖ Do not always try to correct older people with signs of gerotranscendence or change aspects of their behavior.
Link to theory: As above.

✖ Do not routinely ask the residents how they feel.
Link to theory: This is in accordance with the development of body transcendence proposed in the theory.

✖ Do not routinely correct older people about the time when, for example. they seem to be in the past.
Link to theory: This is related to the cosmic level, changes in the definition of time and space.

✖ Do not always try to bring them back to the present.
Link to theory: As above.

✖ Do not lead the conversation away from death to other topics.
Link to theory: This is related to the cosmic level; the fear of death disappears and a new comprehension of life and death results. The fear of death generally decreases with age, thus it becomes more natural to talk about death.

✖ Do not assume that participating in arranged activities is always the best alternative.
Link to theory: The need for positive solitude may have increased and should be respected.

✖ Do not, without reason, nag a person to participate in arranged activities.
Link to theory: As above.

✖ Do not, without reason, question the person or see the fact that some want to spend a great deal of time alone as a problem.
Link to theory: As above.

✖ Do not organize a large number of activities in the main rooms or have the television or radio on in the dayroom the whole day.
Link to theory: As above.

The above guidelines were produced after an analysis of existing nursing theories in which Wadensten and Carlsson (2002, 2003a) made the following observation that nursing theories offer no practical guidelines when it comes to the care of older people:

> *Nursing theorists take individuality in care into consideration and mention the importance of structuring nursing on the basis of each individual's needs. This is a basic assumption, regarding individuals as people with unique wishes. However, these theories might also appear to be too general, because they do not discuss specific needs of older people; instead they seem to be age-blind. The present guidelines, in contrast, focus on older people, the aging process and ideas about how to support older people's individual development, which is something that nursing theorists have not taken into consideration. Many have adopted a relatively clear developmental perspective in their theories, but have not provided practical guidelines for care of older people. Therefore, the present guidelines serve to fill a gap, and show what might be of special interest in the care of older people. (Wadensten & Carlsson, 2002, p. 469)*

Wadensten and Carlsson (2002) came to the conclusion that if staff members are to adopt guidelines like those described above, the first prerequisite is knowledge about the theory and the guidelines. It is also necessary to work with a supporting organization. Finally, there is need for training to achieve the guidelines in practical work. The mere knowledge of the theory and the guidelines is not enough for adherence. A guided and promoted intervention is needed and has been undertaken by Wadensten and Carlsson (2003b) in a "software innovation" based on the theory of gerotranscendence.

INTRODUCING GUIDELINES IN A NURSING HOME ENVIRONMENT

With their innovative "software," Wadensten and Carlsson (2003b) introduced the above guidelines to the staff in two experimental nursing home wards. The staff members were introduced to the theory of gerotranscendence and were then given instructions on how to use the guidelines in relation to the residents. The aim of the experiment was to see to what extent the staff changed their interpretations of gerotranscendent behaviors in the residents, and to what extent the staff members changed their own behavior, by adopting the guidelines. The authors were also interested to see whether individual staff members could be identified as "early adopters" versus "laggards."

The intervention took place in a rather large Swedish city, at a nursing home with eight wards where two were randomly selected as experimental wards. Twenty-six residents lived on these two wards, which together had 18 staff members. After the introduction of the theory and the guidelines, the activities at the wards were followed by means of participant observation and interviews with staff and residents at several points in time.

Also in this intervention study the most distinct effect of the new "software" was increased listening and permissiveness on the part of staff members. Their post-intervention treatment of the residents included more acceptance of their behavior. When it came to the different groups of guidelines, it proved easier to adopt the guidelines that focused on individual meetings between staff members and residents. The guidelines focusing on new activities and the organization were more difficult to follow since the staff members, as they explained, lacked both the time and the experience to do so. They also explained that these latter tasks were not their duties.

Wadensten and Carlsson (2003b) also made an effort to classify the staff members in the adapter categories described by Rogers (1995) in his innovation-theoretical model. The staff members categorized as *early adopters* described many of the gerotranscendental behaviors as normal from the very beginning and started promptly to follow the guidelines. Characteristic of these staff members was that they recognized in themselves a personal development in line with the theory of gerotranscendence. They felt that they had developed and changed in connection with personal experiences, which had started developmental processes in line with the theory. Otherwise these staff members differed in age as well as in the degree of experience they had with elder care.

The staff members belonging to the category labeled *early majority* adapted the guidelines without furthering them and without being promoters. They were younger than the staff members in the *late majority* and *laggard* categories and had less experience with elder care. The *late majority* category included staff members who changed their interpretations of gerotranscendental behaviors from pathological to normal, but not their behavior. It was difficult to identify any common characteristics in this group, other than that they had a skeptical attitude. The most skeptical group, however, comprised the *laggards*. The staff members belonging to this category were not only skeptical of the theory, they impeded the intervention by avoiding participation in the lectures and group discussions. The common denominator for the staff members in this group was that they had a generally negative attitude towards their work. Their jobs were merely a livelihood rather than a profession. The distribution of the staff members over the adopter categories was close to a normal frequency distribution, with most of the staff members belonging to the *early majority* and fewer in the surrounding categories.

Wadensten and Carlsson (2003b) argue that the norms and structure of the organization are part of the success or failure of a venture like this. The above intervention focused primarily on individual staff members and not on the leadership role. The managers neither appeared to be engaged in the care nor were they involved in the promotion of the intervention process.

When venturing into an intervention like this, Wadensten and Carlsson (2003b) recommend trying to find the potential early adopters at an early phase of the project and trying to enlist their assistance. They might be able to influence other staff members, thereby facilitating the intervention process. Since the early adopters are those who from the very beginning feel aligned with the theory of gerotranscendence, it might be possible to identify them. The recommendation is also to try to identify the laggards as soon as possible, in order to possibly get them motivated to participate or, at the very least, reduce their negative influence on the rest of the group.

CHAPTER 6

Conclusions and Summary

Here we should recall that the theory of gerotranscendence was born of a dissatisfaction with the mismatch between several common assumptions and the empirical findings within social gerontology, e.g., the presumed retirement trauma and loneliness peak in old age. This led to the understanding that much of the theorizing within social gerontology has been directed by the special values held by middle-aged scholars in modern Western society, with its focus on success, productivity, effectiveness, and independence. We tend to project these values on old age as the norm, where divergences or developments away from these norms become "pathological" according to our predefined notions.

In order to reach a new understanding of the development during life and into old age, a technique was suggested whereby the thought is allowed that there is a developmental process going on, where midlife view gives way to new perspectives on life and new values.

In order reach a description of what kind of developmental changes this gerotranscendence process includes, we have listened to what those who have come far in such a development had to tell us. A qualitative study of people who themselves have experienced developmental changes in life, has formed the conceptual bases for the further quantitative studies.

In doing so we used a phenomenological approach in order to reach a "from-within" understanding of what developments come with aging. The subjective meaning given to aging has been given preference before the meaning researchers ascribe to aging.

THE DIMENSIONS AND SIGNS OF GEROTRANSCENDENCE

As an outcome of the initial qualitative study, developmental changes within three main dimensions were described as follows:

The Cosmic Dimension

- *Time and childhood.* Changes in the definitions of time and the return of childhood. The transcendence of borders between past and present occurs. Childhood comes to life—sometimes interpreted in a new reconciling way.

- *Connection to earlier generations.* Attachment increases. A change in perspective from link to chain ensues. The important thing is not the individual life (link), but rather the stream of life (chain).

- *Life and death.* The fear of death disappears and a new comprehension of life and death results.

- *Mystery in life.* The mystery dimension in life is accepted.

- *Rejoicing.* From grand events to subtle experiences. The joy of experiencing the macrocosm through the microcosm materializes, not infrequently related to experiences in nature.

The Dimension of the Self

- *Self-confrontation.* The discovery of hidden aspects of the self—both good and bad—occurs.

- *Decrease in self-centeredness.* Removal of the self from the center of one's universe may eventuate. However, if self-esteem from beginning is low, it may instead be a question of struggling to establish a level of confidence that feels appropriate.

- *Development of body-transcendence.* Taking care of the body continues, but the individual is not obsessed with it.

- *Self-transcendence.* A shift may occur from egoism to altruism. This may be a special matter for men.

- *Ego-integrity.* The individual realizes that the pieces of life's jigsaw puzzle form a wholeness. This may be a delicate state, demanding tranquility and solitude.

The Dimension of Social and Personal Relationships

- *Changed meaning and importance of relations.* One becomes more selective and less interested in superficial relations, exhibiting an increasing need for periods of solitude.

- *Role play.* An understanding of the difference between self and role takes place, sometimes with an urge to abandon roles. A new, comforting understanding of the necessity of roles in life often results.

- *Emancipated innocence.* Innocence enhances maturity. A new capacity to transcend needless social conventions.

- *Modern asceticism.* An understanding of the petrifying gravity of wealth and the freedom of "asceticism" develops, i.e., having enough for a modern definition of the necessities of life, but not more.

- *Everyday wisdom.* The reluctance to superficially separate right from wrong, thus withholding from judgments and giving advice is discerned. Transcendence of the right-wrong duality ensues, and is accompanied by an increased broad-mindedness and tolerance.

In the first quantitative study on the subject, the 1990 Danish retrospective study, it was empirically confirmed that randomly selected older (74–100 years) people report on developmental changes in line with the ones described above. Thus, it must be accepted that a substantial proportion of real people do experience developmental changes in line with the theory of gerotranscendence. In this first quantitative study it was also shown that these experiences could not be explained away with reference to conditions of psychological strain, depression, mental insufficiency, or consumption of psychotropic medications, since the influence of such confounding factors was controlled for. The only conclusion in this regard was that consumption of psychotropic medications seemed to be a hindrance to achieving gerotranscendence.

THE DEVELOPMENTAL PATTERNS

In two different quantitative cross sectional studies,[103] statements were worded in order to tap the *status* of gerotranscendence—not the retrospective change as in the 1990 Danish study. Three factors or approximations of gerotranscendence were identified empirically and further analyzed: *cosmic transcendence*, *coherence*, and *the need for solitude*.

Drawing on the outcome of the factor analysis, and again operating under the assumption that the cross sectional data can be interpreted

---

[103]The Swedish 1995 cross-sectional study and the 2001 study (age 65–104).

from a developmental perspective, our data suggest that the development of cosmic transcendence and coherence are continuous processes which start already during the first half of adult life and gradually develop to their maximum in later life. The need for solitude also increases to a maximum in late life, but seems to develop most rapidly during the first half of adult life. It was also shown that at the upper end of the age scale, with more of cosmic transcendence (and coherence) comes more satisfaction with life. It seems that the combination of cosmic transcendence and enhanced life satisfaction is a combination especially reserved for old age.

When considering the above conclusions we must again, however, make the reservation that the data on which we have built these conclusions and the ones that follow are limited in several ways, culturally, temporally, and, equally important, the fact that they are retrospective and cross-sectional, not longitudinal.

THE IMPACT OF CIRCUMSTANCES IN LIFE

Cosmic transcendence is, according to the analysis, not only affected by aging as such, but also, when young and middle-aged, by life circumstances—what we call social-matrix factors. Respondents with self-governed professions and students score higher on cosmic transcendence. Maybe a life with higher degrees of autonomy contributes to a liberation from restrictive, mainstream rules and values which might otherwise have reduced the possibility for development of cosmic transcendence.

Being male or female also makes a difference when it comes to cosmic transcendence. In the age categories from 20 to 64, men score lower than women on cosmic gerotranscendence, but from 75 upwards, they have caught up with the women. There is some empirical support for the assumption that this has something to do with what many women experience as a developmental crisis when giving birth to a child. Women without the experience of giving birth, score lower on cosmic transcendence. It is, in fact, shown that during young adulthood and middleage, life crises—which are incident-impact factors—positively contribute to the development of cosmic transcendence for both men and women. For men however, during young adulthood and middleage, age as such has twice as much explanatory power as the crises in terms of the impact on cosmic transcendence. For women, during young adulthood and middleage, age and crises have approximately the same amount of explanatory power. We could say that for women during young adulthood and middleage, developmental crises are relatively more important for the development of cosmic transcendence, while aging as such is relatively more important for men. *In late old age however, crise, as well as social-matrix factors seem to have lost their impact on the degree of cosmic transcendence for both men and women.*

Unlike cosmic transcendence, *coherence*, even at the upper end of the age scale, has several rather strong social-matrix and incident-impact predictors, of which the experiences of no crises, high activity, being married, and former qualified profession are the most important. When late old age is reached, the degree of experienced coherence seem to be equally determined by a) a pure positive age development, and b) social-matrix and incidence-impact factors, which might have either a positive or a negative impact on the degree of coherence.

When it comes to *the need for solitude*, there seem to be two quite different causes. One cause seems to be solely related to age developmental change. With increasing age comes a greater need for positive solitude. The other cause is reactions to incident-impact factors like diseases and crises. As a reaction to these strains a negative solitude seeking comes in the form of withdrawal. Solitude seeking is, then, a coin with two sides—a positive one, which we regard as part of gerotranscendence, and a negative one, which is related to traditional defense reactions like withdrawal and avoidance.

When it comes to incident impact factors—crises in life, as defined by the individual—these crises seem to produce, during young adulthood and middleage, both decreases in the experience of coherence and increased solitude seeking. In late old age however, the experience of coherence and the need for solitude seem to be the same whether the individual has experienced crises or not.

GEROTRANSCENDENCE IN PRACTICE

From two different studies we know that staff working with the elderly do recognize in old people many of the signs of gerotranscendence accounted for above. No less than 72 percent of the staff attested to the theory's correspondence with the reality they meet in their work with elderly. The theory also helped 43 percent of the staff members to understand specific care recipients in a new light, in particular care recipients who previously had been difficult to understand. Furthermore, 45 percent of the staff members felt that the theory had helped them to reduce feelings of insufficiency and/or guilt at work, probably because it added a missing tool to their theoretical tool box. The theory also produced a more favorable outlook on the personal old age of 22 percent of the staff members.

When it came to changes in the staff's approach to care giving, 33 percent of the staff members reported on such changes. These changes were, however, of a rather passive kind. The care receivers were met with increased listening and permissiveness, but the introduction of new developmental stimuli or new topics of conversation was nearly nonexistent.

In order to reach more substantial changes in practical care practice, a more forceful procedure is obviously needed. Such an implementation of the gerotranscendence theory was undertaken as a participant study by a registered nurse and doctoral student[104] in Caring Sciences. This intervention started out with a series of focus-group sessions, where a number of practical guidelines were derived from the theory of gerotranscendence. These guidelines, reported on previously, were focused on what a) the individual staff member should and should not do in the interaction with the care recipients, b) which kinds of activities should and should not be arranged, and c) how the ward should be organized in order to stimulate, or at least not counteract, the development of gerotranscendence. These guidelines were introduced to the staff in two experimental wards, where the observation was made that certain staff members more easily adopted the new approach, namely those who, disregarding age and professional experience, recognized in themselves aspects of the development described in the theory.

GEROTRANSCENDENCE IS NOT DISENGAGEMENT IN A NEW DISGUISE

Even if one of the points of departure for the development of the theory of gerotranscendence was the feeling that some unknown train of thought was washed away untried when we got rid of the disengagement theory,

---

[104]Barbro Wadensten, now PhD.

is must be emphasized that this does not imply any theoretical kinship between the two. The theory of gerotranscendence is not the disengagement theory in new disguise. Gerotranscendence seem to be a positive developmental possibility with individual variations.

Already from the first qualitative study it was obvious that gerotranscendence cannot be regarded as any uniform development which is the same for all aging individuals. It is rather a developmental possibility, which can take different forms from individual to individual. Metaphorically, it may be that "the seed of gerotranscendence" is within us all, but needs proper watering to grow. This also implies that the above "signs" of gerotranscendence not were equally pronounced among the informants. It is important, however, that the individual characteristic of gerotranscendence still form, for the individual, coherent developmental patterns, where active involvement in new mental areas, high degrees of life satisfaction, and absence of psychological strain, depression, and neurotic symptoms are parts. Quantitative studies also indicate that a high level of gerotranscendence goes with social activity and not with withdrawal and disengagement. This is particularly true when self-chosen activities are considered. Gerotranscendent individuals are shown to be more active when it comes to self-chosen activities, as compared with nongerotranscendendental individuals. They also show psychological involvement in new areas of mental activity.

As earlier accounted for, both *satisfaction with present life* and *social activity* correlate positively with cosmic transcendence. This illustrates that gerotranscendence in general, and cosmic transcendence in particular, are surely something other than a "disengaged mystic withdrawal," as is sometimes incorrectly suggested (e.g., by Jönson & Magnusson, 2001). As previously shown in the 1990 Danish retrospective study of 912 Danes between the ages of 74 and 100, cosmic transcendence correlated positively with social activity.[105] In the 2001 study (65+), we also found a small but statistically significant positive correlation between cosmic transcendence and social activity, at the same time as the correlation between cosmic transcendence and satisfaction with present life is also positive. This shows clearly that cosmic transcendence is not a condition related to any depressive or passive withdrawal. On the contrary, cosmic transcendence is positively related to higher social activity and more satisfaction with

---

[105]In the Danish study eta = .17, p < .001.

present life. From this we can conclude that gerotranscendence certainly seems to be something different from passive withdrawal as implied by the disengagement theory.

WHY GEROTRANSCENDENCE GOES BEYOND OTHER DEVELOPMENTAL MODELS

Erikson's (1950, 1982, 1986) well-known developmental model in particular, as well as Baltes's (1993) wisdom criteria, border on the concept of gerotranscendence. In both the Erikson model and the theory of gerotranscendence, the process of aging is regarded as a developmental process which, at very best, ends with a higher state of maturity—in Erikson's case ego-integrity, in ours gerotranscendence. In Erikson's theory, ego-integration primarily refers to an integration of the elements of the life that has passed. The individual reaches a fundamental acceptance of the life lived, regardless of how good or bad it might seem from the outside. In this way, the ego-integrity described by Erikson becomes more of a backwards integration process within the same definition of the world as before, while the process of gerotranscendence implies more of *a forward or outward direction, including a redefinition of reality*. In the Baltes (1993) discussion of the criteria of wisdom, these criteria also remain within the same definition of the world as before, while gerotranscendence goes further and beyond it. Significantly enough, when Joan M. Erikson, wife and coworker of Erik H. Erikson, learned about the theory of gerotranscendence, she boldly added a ninth step in the Eriksonian model, in order to include the precautionary measures necessary to reach gerotranscendence, and then published an updated book on the Erikson model.

The reconstructive quality of the gerotranscendence process, which distinguishes gerotranscendence from other abovementioned developmental models, was also suggested when we focused on the functions of reminiscence. According to our analysis,[106] the *unity of existence function* of reminiscence, which is greatly gerotranscendence related, becomes increasingly important as we age, whereas the *identity function* of reminiscence, which is related to the preservation and stabilizing the identity, decreases after the age category 25–34 years. The importance of continuity

---

[106]The Swedish 1995 cross-sectional study.

and the preservation of identity decline when growing older, while the importance of gerotranscendence-related outlook and change increases.

The theory of gerotranscendence does not, however, invalidate the importance of the identity function of reminiscence. Neither does the theory of gerotranscendence deny the importance of the ego-integrity stage in the Erikson model, nor the importance of "activity" for life satisfaction. These concepts are included in and qualified in the theory, at the same time as the theory of gerotranscendence goes further. Whereas in earlier theorizing many concepts have been formulated in terms of either/or, e.g., activity versus disengagement, or continuity versus change, the theory of gerotranscendence offers a new both/and framework.

Appendix:
Suggested Exercises
for Personal Development

In this appendix we suggest some exercises for increasing your personal awareness of possible gerotranscendental development. In doing so, we depart from how gerotranscendental individuals themselves have described the paths to gerotranscendence, which was described in the chapter on the qualitative content of gerotranscendence. The exercises suggested below are just examples of how it is possible to derive such exercises from the dimensions of gerotranscendence described earlier. You may refer to the chapter on the qualitative content of gerotranscendence to devise additional exercises suiting your personal profile.

The Time and Place Exercise

Pick out a philosopher, novelist, playwright, or composer from the past who has made an impression on you and imagine that you are living at the same time, and are present in the same room. Imagine that you have a discussion with this person. Try to transcend the feeling that this is an exercise and evoke the feeling that you really are living simultaneously. Try to find out what feelings and opinions you have in common. How does this exercise affect you?

The Generation Chain Exercise

Try to imagine that your individuality is part of something larger. You are not an isolated individual but part of a chain of human beings with much more in common than different. Try to visualize an infinite genetic chain to which you belong. Try to understand that within this genetic chain you have an eternal life. Feel the peace that comes with this insight.

Being a Flower

Go outdoors and find a beautiful flower of your liking. Concentrate on that flower and contemplate the fact that you and this flower are made of the very same basic molecular components. Try to comprehend that by this fact the flower is part of you, and you are part of the flower, at the same time as both you and the flower are parts of the universe. Try to feel how the separateness of you and the flower is transcended and substituted with a feeling of a wholeness and togetherness. You and the flower are the same. Experience the joy and pleasure of this comprehension.

Rediscover and Transfigure Important Life Events

Go back in your life and find important periods and life events from early childhood till now. In the light of the life you have lived, try to reinterpret these periods and events. Might it be that the experiences you have had as an adult changes the understanding of some childhood experiences? Might it be that what you know today adds new meaning to some memories from earlier in life. Actively try to reinterpret the memories from the past in the same way you would do if somebody else told you events from his or hers or past and you were to interpret this from the foundation of your experience in life. Contemplate on the new meanings you will attribute to earlier periods and events in your own life. Compare the new understandings of important events and periods in your life with the new ones and explain the difference to yourself.

Climbing the Mountain of Life

Imagine that living your life has been like climbing a mountain. During the climb you have been facing the mountain and have seen little but the rugged mountainside on which you have hurt your knees and elbows. When you reach the top of the mountain, however, you turn around and become aware of the beauty of the landscape below and in front of you. This is the landscape of your life! Try to imagine what new kind of coherence and beauty in your life you can see from the outlook.

Breaking Unnecessary Rules

Try to find out which unnecessary social norms or rules have hampered you earlier in life. Remember from our earlier discussion the person who was afraid of asking questions for fear of making a fool of himself, and now dares to ask all the "stupid" questions, and the woman who nowadays played with bicycling around with torn stockings, breaking the futile rule of not wearing torn stockings. Which are the unnecessary rules in your life that you may now allow yourself to play around with. Find them, play with them, and experience the freedom and joy of gerotranscendence.

References

Achenbaum, W. A., & Orwoll, L. (1991). Becoming wise: A psych-geronto-logical interpretation of the Book of Job. *International Journal of Aging and Human Development, 32*(1), 21–39.

Ahmadi, F. (1998). Sufism and gerotranscendence: The impact of the way of thinking, culture, and aging on spiritual maturity, *Journal of Aging and Identity, 3*(4), 189–211.

Ahmadi-Lewin, F. (2000a). Gerotranscendence and life satisfaction: Studies of religious and secular Iranians and Turks. *Journal of Religious Gerontology, 12*(1), 17–41.

Ahmadi, F. (2000b). Reflections on spiritual maturity and gerotranscendence: Dialogues with two sufis. *Journal of Religious Gerontology, 11*(2), 43–74.

Ahmadi-Lewin, F. (2001). Gerotranscendence and different cultural settings. *Aging and Society, 21*(4), 395–415.

Åkerman, S. (1981). *De stackars pensionärerna. Några iakttagelser utifrån en intervjuundersökning.* Arbetsrapport nr 3 från projektet Äldre i samhället—förr, nu och i framtiden, Uppsala, Sweden.

Aldwin, C. M. (1990). The Elders Life Stress Inventory: Egocentric and Nonegocentric Stress. In M. A. P. Stephens, J. H. Crowther, S. E. Hobfoll, & D. L. Tennenbaum (Eds.), *Stress and coping in later-life families.* New York: Hemisphere Publishing Corp.

Aldwin, C. M., Sutton, K. J., Chiara, G., & Spiri, A. (1996). Age differences in stress, coping, and appraisal: Findings from the Normative Aging Study. *Journal of Gerontology: Psychological Sciences, 4*, 179–188.

Angel, J. L., Buckley, C. J., & Sakamoto, A. (2001). Duration or disadvantage? Exploring nativity, ethnicity, and health in midlife. *Journal of Gerontology: Social Sciences, 56B*(5), S275–S284.

AnswerTree 1. 0 User's Guide (1998). Chicago: SPSS Inc.

Antonovsky, A. (1987). *Unraveling the mystery of health: How people manage stress and stay well.* San Francisco: Jossey-Bass.

Atchley, R. (1971). Retirement and leisure participation: Continuity or crisis? *The Gerontologist, 2*, 13–17.

Atchley, R. (1980) *The social forces of later life: An introduction to social gerontology, 3rd ed.* Belmont, CA: Wadsworth.

Atchley, R. C. (1999). *Continuity and adaptation in aging: Creating positive experiences.* Baltimore: Johns Hopkins University Press.

Atchley, R. C. (2000). *Social forces and aging: An introduction to social gerontology,* 9th ed. Belmont, CA: Wadsworth.

Babchuk, N., & Beates, A. P. (1963). The primary relations of middle-class couples: A study in male dominance. *American Sociological Review, 28,* 377–384.

Baltes, P. B. (1993). The aging mind: Potential and limits. *The Gerontologist, 33*(5), 580–594.

Baltes, P. B., & Baltes, M. M. (1990). Psychological perspectives on successful aging: A model of selective optimization with compensation. In P. B. Baltes & M. M. Baltes, (Eds.), *Successful aging: Perspectives from the behavioral sciences.* New York: Cambridge University Press.

Bengtson, V., Parrott, T., & Burgess, E. O. (1996). Progress and pitfalls in gerontological theorizing. *The Gerontologist, 36*(6), 769–772.

Bengtson, V., Burgess, O., & Parrott, T. M. (1997). Theory, explanation, and a third ceneration of theoretical development in social gerontology. *Journal of Gerontology, 52B*(2), 572–588.

Bernard, K. (1982). The first step to the cementery. *Newsweek,* Feb. 22, 15.

Biggs, S., Hendricks, J., & Lowenstein, A. (2003). The need for theory in gerontology. In S. Biggs, J. Hendricks, & J. Lowenstein (Eds.), *The need for theory: Critical approaches to social gerontology.* New York: Baywood Publishing Company.

Biggs, S. (2003). Negotiating aging identity: Surface, depth, and masquerade. In S. Biggs & J. Hendricks (Eds.), *The need for theory: Critical approaches to social gerontology.* New York: Baywood Publishing Company.

Biggs, S. (2004). Age, gender, narratives, and masquerades. *Journal of Aging Studies, 18*(1), 45–58.

Blau, P. M. (1964). *Exchange and power in social life.* New York: John Wiley & Sons.

Blau, Z. S. (1973). *Old age in a changing society.* New York: Franklin Watts.

Bohm, D., & Peat, F. D. (1987). *Science, order and creativity.* New York: Bantam Books.

Bohrnstedt, G. W., & Knoke, D. (1982). *Statistics for Social data analysis.* Itasca, IL: F. E. Peacock Publishers, Inc.

Borys, S., & Perlman, D. (1985). Gender differences in loneliness. *Personality and Social Psychology Bulletin, 11,* 63–74.

Bradford, K. (1979). Can you survive your retirement? *Harvard Business Review, 57*(6), 103–107.

Burgess, E. W. (1960). Aging in Western Culture. In E. W. Burgess (Ed.), *Aging in western societies.* Chicago: University of Chicago Press.

Butler, R. N. (1963). The life review: An interpretation of reminiscence in the aged. *Psychiatry, 26*, 65–76.

Carlson, C. M. (1984). Reminiscing: Toward achieving ego integrity in old age: Social casework. *The Journal of Contemporary Social Work, 65*, 81–89.

Castelnuovo-Tedesco, P. (1978). The mind as a stage: Some comments on reminiscence and internal objects. *International Journal of Psychoanalysis, 58*, 19–25.

Chinen, A. B. (1985). Fairy tales and transpersonal development in later life. *The Journal of Transpersonal Psychology, 17*, 99–122.

Chinen, A. B. (1986). Elder tales revisited: Forms of transcendence in later life. *The Journal of Transpersonal Psychology, 26*, 171–192.

Chinen, A. B. (1989a). From quantitative to qualitative reasoning: A developmental perspective. In E. E. Thomas, *Research on adulthood and aging: The human science approach.* City, ST: State University of New York Press.

Chinen, A. B. (1989b). *In the ever after: Fairy tales and the second half of life.* Wilmette, IL: Chiron Publications.

Clark, M., & Anderson, B. G. (1967). *Culture and aging: An anthropological study of older Americans.* Springfield, IL: Charles C. Thomas.

Cohen, G. C., & Taylor, S. (1998). Reminiscence and aging. *Aging and Society, 18*, 601–610.

Coleman, P. (1990). Adjustment in later life. In J. Bond & P. Coleman (Eds.), *Ageing in society.* London: Sage.

Comana, T., & Brown, V. (1998). The effect of reminiscence therapy on family coping. *Journal of Family Nursing, 4*(2), 182–97.

Cumming, E., Newell, D. S., Dean, L. R., & Mc Caffrey, I. (1960). Disengagement: A tentative theory of aging. *Sociometry, 23*, 23–35.

Cumming, E., & Henry, W. (1961). *Growing old: The process of disengagement.* New York: Basic Books.

Cumming, E. (1963). Further thoughts on the theory of disengagement. *UNESCO International Science Journal, 1963*, 377–393.

Desroches, H. F., & Kaiman, B. D. (1964). Stability of activity participation in an aged population. *Journal of Gerontology, 1964*, 211–214.

Ekerdt, D. J. (2001). Retirement. In G. L. Maddox, *The encyclopedia of aging*, 3rd Ed. New York: Springer.

Elliot, H. C. (1974). Similarities and Differences Between Science and Common Sense. In R. Turner (Ed.), *Ethnomethodology.* Harmondsworth: Penguin.

Erikson, E. H. (1950). *Childhood and society.* New York: W. W. Norton.

Erikson, E. H. (1982). *The life cycle completed: A review.* New York: W. W. Norton.

Erikson, E. H., Erikson, J. M., & Kivnick, H. Q. (1986). *Vital involvement in old age.* New York: W. W. Norton.

Erikson, J. M. (1995). Personal correspondence.

Erikson, J. M. (1997). Gerotranscendence. In E. H. Erikson, *The life cycle completed*. New York: W. W. Norton.

Estes, C., Binney, E., & Culbertson, R. A. (1992). The gerontological imagination: Social influences on the development of gerontology, 1945–present. *Journal of Aging and Human Development, 35*(1), 49–65.

Featherstone, M., & Hepworth, M. (1991) The mask of ageing and the postmodern life course. In M. Featherstone, M. Hepworth, & B. S. Turner (Eds.), *The body: Social process and cultural theory*. London: Sage

Fromm, E. (1960) Psychoanalysis and Zen Buddhishm. In D. T. Suzuki, E. Fromm, & R. De Martino, *Zen Buddhism and psychoanalysis*. London: Harper Colophon Books.

Galtung, J. (1969). *Theory and methods of social research*. Oslo: Universitetsforlaget.

Gamliel, T. (2001). A social version of gerotranscendence: Case study. *Journal of Aging and Identity, 2*, 105–114.

Gaunt, D. (1983) Den pensionerade jordbrukaren: Dennes egendom och familjeförhållanden sedan medeltiden: Norra och centrala europa. In B. Odén, A. Svanborg, & L. Tornstam (Eds.), *Äldre i samhället—förr, nu och i framtiden. Del 2: Probleminventeringar*. Stockholm: Liber.

Gubrium, J. F., & Wallace, J. B. (1990). Who theorises age? *Aging and Society, 10*, 131–149.

Gutman, D. (1976). Alternatives to Disengagement: The Old Men of the Highland Druze. In J. F. Gubrium (Ed.), *Time, roles and self in old age*. New York: Human Sciences Press.

Hammarström, G. (1986). *Solidaritetsmönster mellan generationer*, Arbetsrapport nr 27 från projektet Äldre i samhället—förr, nu och i framtiden. Uppsala, Sweden: Dept. of Sociology, Uppsala university.

Hansson, S. O. (1980). *Var det bättre förr?* Stockholm: Prisma.

Hareven, T. (1978). Historical Changes in the Life Course and the Family: Policy Implications for the Aged, Select Committee on Aging, U.S. House of Representatives and the Select Committee on Population, U.S. House of Representatives, May 24.

Havens, B. J. (1968). An investigation of activity patterns and adjustment in an aging population. *The Gerontologist, 8*, 201–206.

Hess, B. (1972). Friendship. In M. W. Riely, M. Johnson, & A. Foner (Eds.), *Aging and Society, volume III*. New York: Rusel Sage Foundation.

Hickey, T. (1992). The continuity of gerontological themes. *Journal of Aging and Human Development, 35*(1), 7–17.

Hill, R., et al. (1979). *Family development in three generations: A longitudinal study of changing family patterns of planning and chievement*. Cambridge, MA: Schenkman Publishing Company, Inc.

Hochschild, A. R. (1976). Disengagement Theory: A Logical, Empirical, and Phenomenological Critique. In J. F. Gubrium (Ed.), *Time, roles and self in old age*. New York: Human Sciences Press.

Holstein, B. E., Almind, G., Due, P., & Holst, E. (1990). Äldres selvrapporterede helbred og lägemiddelforbrug. Ugeskrift for l'gere, *152*(6), 386–391.

Holton, G. (1973). *Thematic origins of scientific thought*. Cambridge, MA: Harvard University Press.

Hooyman, N. R., & Asuman Kiyak, H. (1988). *Social gerontology: A multidisciplinary perspective*. Boston: Allyn and Bacon, Inc.

Huyck, M. H. (1990). Gender Differences in Aging. In J. E. Birren & K. W. Schaie (Eds.), *Handbook of the psychology of aging*. New York: Academic Press.

Jönson, H., & Magnusson, J. A. (2001). A new age of old age? Gerotranscendence and the re-enchantment of aging. *Journal of Aging Studies, 15,* 317–331.

Joravsky, D. (1970). *The Lysenko affair*. Cambridge, MA: Harvard University Press.

Jung, C. G. (1930). Die Lebenswende. *Gesammelte Werke 8*. Olten, Germany: Walter-Verlag, 1982.

Jung, C. G. (1953). *Collected works of C. G. Jung, vol 7*. New York: Pantheon.

Jung, C. G. (1984). Die Lebenswende. In Danish in F. Alt (Ed.), *Jung: Texter og tanker*. Copenhagen: Borgens Forlag.

Juul-Jensen, U. (1984). *Moralsk ansvar og menneskesyn. Om holdninger i social- og sundhedssektoren*. Copenhagen: Munksgaard.

Kapnick, P. L., et al. (1968). Political behavior in the aged: Some new data. *Journal of Gerontology, 1968,* 305–310.

Kass, G. (1980). An exploratory technique for investigating large quantities of categorical data. *Applied Statistics, 29,* 119–127.

Kastenbaum, R. (1996). Death and dying. In J. E. Birren (Ed.), *Encyclopaedia of gerontology*, vol 1. New York: Academic Press.

Kaufman, S. R. (1986). *The ageless self: Sources of meaning in late life*. Madison, WI: University of Wisconsin Press.

Kelly, J. R (1993). *Activity and aging: Staying involved in later life*. Newbury Park, CA: Sage Publications, Inc.

Kuhn, T. S. (1962). *The structure of scientific revolutions*. Chicago: The University of Chicago Press.

Kuypers, J. A., & Bengtson, V. L. (1973). Social breakdown and competence. A model of normal aging. *Human Development, 1973,* 181–201.

Laslett, P. (1976). Societal development and aging. In R. H. Binstock & E. Shanas (Eds.), *Handbook of aging and the social sciences*. New York: Van Nostrand Reinhold.

Lazarus, R. S., & Folkman, S. (1984). *Stress, appraisal and coping*. New York: Springer Publishing.

Lemaine, G., et al. (Eds.) (1976). *Perspectives on the emergence of scientific disciplines.* Chicago: Aldine.

Lowenthal, M., & Boler, E. (1965). Volontary vs. involontary social withdrawal. *Journal of Gerontology, 1965,* 363–371.

Lowenthal, M., & Haven, C. (1968). Interaction and adaptation: Intimacy as a critical variable. *American Sociological Review, 1968,* 20–30.

Lowenthal, M. F., & Robinson, B. (1976). Social Networks and Isolation. In R. H. Binstock & E. Shanas (Eds.), *Handbook of aging and the social sciences.* New York: Van Nostrand Reinhold.

Maddox, G. L. (1968). Retirement as a Social Event in the United States. In B. L. Neugarten (Ed.), *Middle age and aging.* Chicago: University of Chicago Press.

Mazur, A. (1973). Disputes between experts. *Minerva, 11,* 243–262.

Miller, S. J. (1965). The Social Dilemma of the Aging Leisure Participant. In A. M. Rose & W. A. Petersen (Eds.), *Older people and their social world.* Philadelphia: F. A. Davis.

Mulkay, M. (1979). *Science and the sociology of knowledge.* London: George Allen & Unwin.

Nelkin, D. (1975). The political impact of technical expertise. *Social Studies of Science, 5,* 35–54.

Neugarten, B. L. (1964). *Personality in middle and late life.* New York: Atherton Press.

Neugarten, B. L. (1977). Personality and aging. In J. E. Birren & K. W. Schaie (Eds.), *Handbook of the psychology of aging.* New York: Van Nostrand Reinhold.

Odén, B. (1991). Relationer meellan gererationerna: Rättsläget 1300–1900. In B. Ankarloo (Ed.), *Maktpolitik och husfrid.* Lund: Lund University Press.

Odén, B. (2002). Den gamla goda tiden: Kvinnor I äldreomsorgen förr och nu. In L. Andersson (Ed.), *Socialgerontologi.* Lund: Studentlitteratur.

Ofstad, H. (1972). *Vårt förakt för svaghet: Nazismens normer och värderingar— och våra egna.* Stockholm: Prisma.

Ogburn, W. F. (1922). *Social change with respect to culture and original nature.* New York: Viking Press.

Olsen, L. K. (1982). *The political economy of aging.* New York: Columbia University Press.

Palmore, E. B. (1968). The effects of aging on activities and attitudes. *The Gerontologist, 1968,* 259–263.

Palmore, E. G., Burchett, B., Fillenbaum, G., George, L., & Wallman, L. (1985). *Retirement: Causes and consequences.* New York: Springer Publishing.

Parker, R. G. (1995). Reminiscence: A continuity theory framework. *The Gerontologist, 35*(4), 515–525.

Parnes, H. S., & Nestel, G. (1981). The Retirement Experience. In H. S. Parnes (Ed.), *Work and retirement: A longitudinal study of men.* Cambridge, MA: The MIT Press.

Paykel, E. S. (1983). Methodological aspects of life events research. *Journal of Psychosomatic Research, 27,* 341–352.

Peck, R. (1956). Psychological Development in the Second Half of Life. In J. E. Anderson (Ed.), *Psychological aspects of aging.* Washington: American Psychological Association.

Peck, R. (1968). Psychological Developments in the Second Half of Life. In B. L. Neugarten (Ed.), *Middle age and aging. A reader in social psychology.* Chicago: The University of Chicago Press.

Puentes, W. J. (1998). Incorporating simple reminiscence techniques into acute care nursing practice. *Journal of Gerontological Nursing,* February, 15–20.

Rehn, T. (1984) *Tjänstemäns pensionering. En longitudinell studie om hälsa, livstillfredsställelse och inställning till pensioneringen,* Arbetsrapport nr 15 från projektet Äldre i samhället—förr, nu och i framtiden. Uppsala, Sweden.

Robinson, P. K., Coberly, S., & Paul, C. E. (1985). Work and Retirement. In R. H. Binstock & E. Shanas (Eds.), *Handbook of aging and the social sciences, 2nd ed.* New York: Van Nostrand Reinhold Company.

Rodin, J. (1986). Health, Control, and Aging. In M. M. Baltes & P. B. Baltes (Eds.), *The psychology of control and aging.* Hillsdale, NJ: Lawrence Erlbaum.

Rogers, E. M. (1995). *Diffusion of innovations.* New York: The Free Press.

Roos, K. (1975). *Aktiviteter och åldrande: Socialpsykologiska studier kring aktivitet och åldrande.* Uppsala, Sweden: Akademisk avhandling.

Shanas, E. (1968). Family help patterns and social class in three countries. In B. L. Neugarten (Ed.), *Middle age and aging: A reader in social psychology.* Chicago: University of Chicago Press.

Spinelli, E. (1989). *The interpreted world: An introduction to phenomenological psychology.* London: Sage.

Stevens Barnum, B. J. (1990). *Nursing theory: Analysis, application, evaluation.* Glenview, IL: Scott, Foresman/Little, Brown.

Storer, N. W. (1966). *The social system of science.* New York: Rinehart & Winston.

Streib, G. F., & Schneider, C. J. (1971). *Retirement in American society: Impact and process.* Ithaca, NY: Cornell University Press.

Taft, L. B., & Nehrke, M. F. (1990). Reminiscence, life review, and ego integrity in nursing home residents. *International Journal of Aging and Human Development, 30,* 189–196.

Teeland, L. (1978). Keeping in Touch: The Relation Between Old People and their Adult Children. Monograph 16. Gothenbourg Department of Sociology.

Thomae, H. (1969). Cross-National Participation: Problems of Interpretation. In R. J. Havighurst, et al. (Eds.), *Adjustment to retirement: A cross national study*. New York: Publisher.

Tilak, S. (1989). *Religion and aging in the indian tradition*. Albany: State University of New York Press.

Tissue, T. L. (1971). Disengagement potential: Replication and sse as an explanatory variable. *Journal of Gerontology, 1971*, 76–80.

Tornstam, L. (1973). Att åldra:; Socialgerontologiska perspektiv. Doctoral Dissertation. Uppsala Universtiy Dept. of Sociology. Uppsala, Sweden.

Tornstam, L. (1978). *Åldrandets socialpsykologi*. Stockholm: Rabén & Sjögren.

Tornstam, L. (1981). *Realiteter och föreställningar om vardagsproblem bland äldre, medelålders och yngre*. Uppsala, Sweden: Sociologiska Institutionen.

Tornstam, L., Odén, B., & Svanborg, A. (1982). Inledning. In L. Tornstam, B. Odén, & A. Svanborg (Eds.), *Äldre i samhället—förr, nu och i framtiden. Del 1: Teorier och forskningsansatser*. Stockholm: Liber.

Tornstam, L. (1983a). *Kunskaper och okunskaper om äldre*. Arbetsrapport nr 13 från projektet Äldre i samhället—förr, nu och i framtiden. Uppsala, Sweden: Dept. of Sociology, Uppsala university.

Tornstam, L. (1983b). Solidariteten mellan generationerna. In B. Odén, A. Svanborg, & L. Tornstam (Eds.), *Äldre i samhället—förr, nu och i framtiden. Del 2: Probleminventeringar*. Stockholm: Liber.

Tornstam, L. (1983c). Våra attityder till åldrandet. In B. Odén, A. Svanborg, & L. Tornstam (Eds.), *Äldre i samhället—förr, nu och i framtiden. Del 2: Probleminventeringar*. Stockholm: Liber.

Tornstam, L. (1988). *Ensamhetens ansikten. En studie av ensamhetsupplevelser hos svenskar i åldrarna 15–80 år*. Arbetsrapport nr 29 från projektet äldre i samhället—förr, nu och i framtiden, Uppsala, Sweden: Sociologiska Institutionen.

Tornstam, L. (1989). Gero-transcendence: A meta-theoretical reformulation of the disengagement theory. *Aging: Clinical and Experimental Research, 1*(1), 55–63.

Tornstam, L. (1990). Dimensions of loneliness. *Aging: Clinical and Experimental Research, 3*, 259–265.

Tornstam, L. (1992a). The Quo Vadis of Gerontology: On the Gerontological Research Paradigm. *The Gerontologist, 32*(3), 318–326.

Tornstam, L. (1992b). Loneliness in marriage. *Journal of Social and Personal Relationships, 9*, 197–217.

Tornstam, L. (1994). Gerotranscendence: A Theoretical and Empirical Exploration. In L. E. Thomas & S. A. Eisenhandler (Eds.), *Aging and the religious dimension*. Westport: Greenwood Publishing Group.

Tornstam, L. (1996). Caring for the elderly: Introducing the theory of ferotranscendence as a supplementary frame of reference for caring for the elderly. *Scandinavian Journal of Caring Sciences, 10*, 144–150.

Tornstam, L. (1996b). Gerotranscendence: A theory about maturing into old age. *Journal of Aging and Identity, 1*, 37–50.

Tornstam, L. (1997). Gerotranscendence: The contemplative dimension of aging. *Journal of Aging Studies, 11*(2), 143–154.

Tornstam, L. (1997). Gerotranscendence in a broad cross sectional perspective. *Journal of Aging and Identity, 2*(1), 17–36.

Tornstam, L. (1997). Life crises and gerotranscendence. *Journal of Aging and Identity, 2*, 117–131.

Tornstam, L. (1999). Gerotranscendence and the functions of reminiscence. *Journal of Aging and Identity, 4*(3), 155–166.

Tornstam, L. (1999). Late-life transcendence: A new developmental perspective on aging. In L. E. Thomas & S. A. Eisendandler (Eds.), *Religion, belief, and spirituality in late life*. New York: Springer Publishing.

Tornstam, L., & Tornqvist, M. (2000). Nursing staff's interpretations of "gerotranscendental behavior" in the elderly. *Journal of Aging and Identity, 5*(1), 15–29.

Tornstam, L. (2000). Transcendence in later life. *Generations, 23*(4), 10–14.

Tornstam, L. (2003). *Gerotranscendence from young old age to old old age*. Online publication of The Social Gerontology Group, Uppsala, Sweden. Available at http://www.soc.uu.se/publications/fulltext/gtransoldold.pdf

Townsend, P. (1986). Ageism and social policy. In C. Phillipson & A. Walker (Eds.), *Ageing and social policy*. Aldershot, England: Gower.

Videbeck, R., & Knox, A. B. (1965). Alternative Participatory Responses to Aging. In A. M. Rose & W. A. Peterson (Eds.), *Older people and their social world*. Philadelphia: Davis.

Wadensten, B., & Carlsson, M. (2001). A qualitative study of nursing staff members' interpretations of signs of gerotranscendence. *Journal of Advanced Nursing, 36*(5), 635–642.

Wadensten, B., & Carlsson, M. (2002). Theory-driven guidelines for practical care of older people, based on the theory of gerotranscendence. *Journal of Advanced Nursing, 41*(5), 462–470.

Wadensten, B., & Carlsson, M. (2003a). Nursing theory views on how to support the process of aging. *Journal of Advanced Nursing, 42*(2), 118–124.

Wadensten, B., & Carlsson, M. (2003b). Nursing Home Staff's Adoption of a "Software Innovation" based on the Theory of Gerotranscendence. Unpublished manuscript.

Webster, J. D. (1993). Construction and validation of the reminiscence functions scale. *Journal of Gerontology: Psychological Sciences, 48*(5), 256–262.

Webster, J. D. (1995). Adult age differences in reminiscence functions. In B. K. Haight & J. D. Webster (Eds.), *The art and science of reminiscing: Theory, research, methods and applications*. Washington, DC: Taylor and Francis.

Webster, J. D. (1997). The reminiscence functions scale: A replication. *Aging and Human Development, 44*(2), 137–148.

Young, R. M. (1973). The historiographic and ideological context of nineteenth-century debate on man's place in nature. In M. Teich & R. M. Young (Eds.), *Changing perspectives in the history of science.* London: Heinemann.

Zusman, J. (1966). Some explanations of the changing appearance of psychotic patients: Antecedents of the social breakdown syndrome concept. *The Millbank Memorial Fund Quarterly, 64,* 1–2.

Index

Activity theory, 8, 32–33, 46, 113–115, 156, 160, 163, 165–166
Age correlations, 96–100, 108, 113–116, 120–124, 130–133, 135–136, 147–148, 178
Aging, successful, concept of, overview, 3
Altruism, 62–63
Asceticism, modern, 68, 70, 74, 164–165, 189
Assets, material, attitude towards, 67–68
Atchley, Robert C., 18

Baltes' wisdom criteria, 77–78, 194
Being flower exercise, 197
Body preoccupation, 44–45
Body transcendence, 44–45, 74, 167–168, 188
Bohr, Niels, 41, 43
Breaking unnecessary rules, exercise, 197–198
Buddhism, 37–39

Changed meaning, 74, 94, 188
Childhood, 55–56, 73, 162–163, 188
Circumstances in life, impact of, 190–191
Classical antiquity, view of science in, 20
Climbing mountain of life, exercise, 197
Coherence dimension of gerotranscendence, 94, 98–100, 104–108,

115–120, 124–128, 137, 189–191. *See also* Ego-integrity
Collective unconscious, 38
Comte, Auguste, 22
Condescending pity, transformation of contempt into, 13
Confidence, increase in, 65
Confrontation with self, 60–61, 74, 167, 188
Connection to earlier generations, 163, 188
Contempt for weakness, 12–13
Our Contempt for Weakness, 13
Continuity of life patterns, 33. *See also* Continuity-oriented theoretical perspective
Continuity-oriented theoretical perspective, 9, 166
Conversation reminiscence, 150
Copernican system, 35–36
Copernicus, 21, 39
Coping patterns, 79–80, 84, 86–87
Cosmic dimension of gerotranscendence, 55–60, 73, 81, 94–98, 103–108, 111–115, 120, 127, 129, 133–136, 141, 145–146, 149–150, 188–191, 193
Crises, 9, 44–45, 71–72, 89, 112–113, 128–142
defined, 139
Critical theory, 7
Cultural lag, theory of, 15
Culture, difficulty of self-analysis, 26

Danish 1990 retrospective study, 78–93, 102, 105, 117–118, 124, 128–129, 189, 193
Darwinian theory, development of, 11
Death, 188
    fear of, 57–58, 73, 105–106, 166–167, 188
    near death experiences, 58
Defensive coping, 84, 166
Depression, 80, 90–91
Deprivation, 33
Developmental theory of Erikson, 46, 142–145, 163–164, 194
Disengagement, 4, 8–9, 31, 34–37, 74–77, 156
    development beyond, 74–77
    gerotranscendence, distinguished, 91–92, 192–194
    negative overtones of, 32
    psychological, 32
    social, 32

Earlier generations, connection to, 56–57, 73, 163, 188, 196
Ego-integrity, 40, 63, 74–77, 145, 164, 188, 195
    developmental model, 40
Egoism, 62–63
    decrease in, 61–63, 74, 188
Einstein, Albert, 21, 41, 43
Emancipated innocence, 66–67, 74–75, 189
    characteristics of, 67
The Encyclopedia of Aging, 16
Erikson, Erik, 40, 55, 63, 76, 129. See also Developmental theory of Erikson
Everyday wisdom, 68–69, 74, 168, 189
Exercises, 196–198
Experimental thinking with alternate metatheoretical paradigm, 37–43
Extended family, concept of, 14

Fairy tales, analysis of, 42
False consciousness, concept of, 17–18

Fear of change, 26
Fear of death, 57–58, 73, 105–106, 166–167, 188
    near death experiences, 58
Freud, Sigmund, 43
Fromm, Erich, 38
Functionalism, 12

Galileo, 20–21
Gender differences, 96–99, 106, 111–113, 130–131, 140–141, 148–149, 190–191
Generation chain exercise, 196
Generations, earlier, connection to, 56–57, 73, 163, 188, 196
Gerontology
    myths within, 13–15
    need for new theories, 6–30
    reminiscence perspective in, 143–144
    scientific paradigm of, 19–21
    social, need for new theories, 6–30
Gerotranscendence, disengagement, differences between, 91–92

Handbook of Aging and Social Sciences, 18
Happiness, transcendental sources of, 59–60
Hebrew tradition, 13
Humanitarianism, research based on, 27–28
Hume, David, 22

Identity continuity, theory of, 18
Identity function, 149, 151–153
Identity reminiscence, 150. See also Reminiscence theory
Importance of relations, 188
Innocence, emancipated, 66–67, 74–75, 189
    characteristics of, 67
Integrity of ego, 40, 63, 74–77, 145, 164, 188, 195
    development beyond, 74–77
Interpretation of gerotranscendental behavior, 155–170

Job preoccupation, 44
Jung, Carl, 37–38, 43, 46, 60

Knowledge, sociology of, 11

Lack of perfection, as human beings,
    25–26
Language, constraints of, 58–59
Laslett, Peter, 14
Life crises, 9, 44–45, 71–72, 89, 112–
    113, 128–142
    defined, 139
The Life Cycle Completed, 76
Life review, 143
Life satisfaction, 80, 83, 87–88, 105–
    106, 124–128, 193
Life-span contextualism, 76–77
Low copers, 84

Magical mastery, 92
    cross-cultural tendency toward, 36
Mask of aging perspective of gerotrans-
    cendence behavior, 9, 156
Masks, social, 65–66
Masquerade perspective of gerotranscen-
    dence behavior, 9, 156
Material assets, attitude towards, 67–68
Meaning, changed, 74, 94, 188
Mental illness, 80, 90–91
Mid-life values, 22
Misery perspective, 10–13, 27, 138
    within resource perspective, 23
Model of personal development, devel-
    opmental perspective, relation-
    ship to, 76
Modern asceticism, 68, 70, 74, 164–
    165, 189
Modernization, supposed effects of,
    14–15
Multicopers, 84
Music, as transcendental source of hap-
    piness, 59
Mystery in life, discovery of, 58–59, 73,
    188
Myths
    function within science, 25–28
    within gerontology, 13–15

Nature, as transcendental source of hap-
    piness, 59–60
Near death experiences, 58
Need for new theories in social geron-
    tology, 6–30
The Need for Theory-Critical Approaches
    to Social Gerontology, 7
Neugarten, Bernice, 46
Newton, Isaac, 20–21
Nursing home environment. See also
        Nursing staff; Staff members
    introducing guidelines in, 184–186
Nursing staff
    educating in gerotranscendence,
        170–180
    impact of theory, 170–180
        impact survey, 172–173
        intervention group, 171–172
    interpretations of gerotranscendence-
        related behavior, 155–170
    practical guidelines for, 181–184

Obstacles to gerotranscendence, 69–73
Offensive coping, 84
Ofstad, Harald, 12–13
Old Age Depression Scale, 83–84, 90
Our Contempt for Weakness, 13
Owning as burden, 69–70

Passive mastery, cross-cultural tendency
        toward, 36
Pathological perspective of gerotranscen-
        dence behavior, 8, 156
Patterns of coping, 79–80, 84, 86–87
Perfection, lack of, as human beings,
        25–26
Phenomenological research approach,
        29–30
Piotrowski, Jerzy, 34
Pity, transformation of contempt into,
        13
Popper, Karl, 22
Positive solitude, 70–71, 75
Positivism, 22, 35
    defined, 22
Productivity, ideal of, 24–25

Profession, 118–120
Psychological disengagement, 32. *See also* Disengagement
Psychosocial development theory, 163. *See also* Developmental theory of Erikson
Psychotropic use, 80, 90–91
Ptolemaic cosmology, 21, 35–36, 39

Quantitative empirical studies, 78–154
Quantum theory, 21

Reality, transcendental change in definitions of, 38
Rediscovering of, transfiguring of important life events, exercise, 197
Rejoicing, 73, 160–162, 188
Relations, importance of, 74, 94, 188
Relativism, 76–77
Relativity, levels of, 9–10
Reminiscence, functions of, 194–195
Reminiscence theory, 142–154
Research objects, elderly as, 22
Residence, 113–115
Resource perspective, 10
  misery perspective in, 23
Retirement, 15–19
  negative effects of, hypothesis, 16
Retirement shock, 2, 17–18
Role playing, 16, 74, 189

Science, Order and Creativity, 20
Scientific paradigm of gerontology, 19–21
  misery perspective, 19–20
  resource perspective, 19–20
Scientific revolutions, 20–21
Scientific society, distinguishing characteristics of, 26
Self-centeredness, decrease in, 61–63, 74, 188
Self-confidence, increase in, 65
Self-confrontation, 60–61, 74, 167, 188
Self dimension of gerotranscendence, 60–63, 74, 165–166, 188
Self-transcendence, 62–63, 74, 165–166, 188

Shadow self, confrontation with, 60–61, 74, 167, 188
Signs of gerotranscendence, 73–74, 187–189
Social activity, 79, 85–86, 193. *See also* Activity theory
Social and personal relationships dimension of gerotranscendence, 63–69, 74, 188–189
Social breakdown syndrome, 22, 33, 44
Social contacts, importance during life phases, 64–65
Social disengagement, 32. *See also* Disengagement
Social gerontology, need for new theories, 6–30
Social integration, 15
Social isolation, 14
Social masks, 65–66
Social reconstruction, model of, 33–34
Sociology of knowledge, 11
Solitude, 70–71, 75, 101, 119, 123, 137–138
  increased need for, 64, 75, 189–191
Solitude dimension of gerotranscendence, 64, 70–71, 75, 94, 100–101, 107–108, 119–129, 137–138, 142, 159–160, 189–191
Staff members
  educating in gerotranscendence, 170–180
  interpretations of gerotranscendence behavior, 157–158
  practical guidelines for, 181–184
Status quo, solidification of, 26–27
Successful aging, concept of, 3
Swedish 1995 cross-sectional study, 78, 93–95, 107–111, 113, 115–124, 127–142, 145–152, 189–190
Swedish 2001 study (65+), 78, 107–108, 110–128, 133, 136, 138, 189–190, 193

Theory, definitions of, 8
Theory of relativity, 21
Time, transcendence of, 55–56, 73, 158–159, 188, 196

Time and place exercise, 196
Transcendence of self, 60–63, 74, 165–
    166, 188

Uncertainty, management of, 76–77
Unity of existence, 147–149, 151–153
Unity reminiscence, 150. *See also* Remi-
    niscence theory

Value-dependent theories, forcing upon
    elderly, 23

Weakness, contempt for, 12–13
    Our Contempt for Weakness, 13
Western culture, 43–44
Whitehead, Alfred North, 42–43, 89
Wisdom, 76–78, 194
    relativism, 76–77
Wittgenstein, Ludwig, 42–43, 89
Work, value of, 23. *See also* Retirement

Zen Buddhism, 37–39

Springer Publishing Company

Multidisciplinary Perspectives on Aging

Lynn M. Tepper, MA, MS, EDM, EdD
Thomas M. Cassidy, MA, Editors

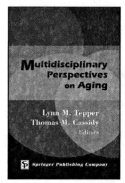

"This is an exceptional book that examines the key social, health, financial, legal and ethical matters with which aging-services professionals, and older persons themselves, must contend. For the new and experienced aging-services professional alike, here, in one volume, is a detailed overview and ready reference on a multitude of issues facing an aging society."

—William L. Minnix, Jr., D. Min.
President and CEO, American Association of Homes and Services for the Aging

In this multidisciplinary text, noted leaders from a variety of fields provide students and professionals with a big picture approach to the best possible care for today's growing aging population. Addressing the extensive concerns that have arisen out of an increased life expectancy and the "elder-boom" of aging baby boomers, the contributors point to changing care and housing needs; health, mental health, and wellness concerns; and financial, ethical, and legal issues in elder care.

Partial Contents:

- **Part I:** Changing Relationships, Changing Care Needs • Aging in America: Challenges and Opportunities, *L.M. Tepper, MA, MS, EdM, EdD* • Family Relationships and Support Networks, *L.M. Tepper, MA, MS, EdM, EdD* • The Nursing Home and the Continuum of Care, *W.T. Smith, MSW, PhD*

- **Part II:** Health and Wellness in Later Life • Medical Care of the Elderly, *R.H. Rubin, MD, FACP* • Health Promotion in Later Life, *C. Kopes-Kerr, MD* • Considerations for Oral Health in the Elderly, *B.M. Horrell, DDS, MS*

- **Part III:** Financial, Ethical, and Legal Issues in Elder Care from a Social Service Perspective, *S.S. Robinson, LMSW, PhD* and *L.M. Tepper, MA, MS, EdM, EdD* • Financing Health Care, *T.C. Jackson, MPH, CEBS* • Elder Law, *M.B. Kapp, JD, MPH, FCLM* • Elder Ethics, *E.R. Chichin, PhD, RN*

2005   304pp   0-8261-2575-1   hardcover

11 West 42nd Street. New York. NY 10036-8002 • Fax: 212-941-7842

$\mathbb{SP}$ *Springer Publishing Company*

Religious Influences on Health and Well-Being in the Elderly

K. Warner Schaie, PhD, Neal Krause, PhD
Alan Booth, PhD, Editors

This volume focuses on the ways in which religious institutions, religious practices, and religious organizations impact the health and well-being of older persons. Topics examined include the conceptualization and measurement of religion in late life; the relationship between religious coping and possible stress reduction; the role of forgiveness as an alternate mediator; and how social class, gender, and race can influence the specific effect of religion and religious institutions in a diverse aging society.

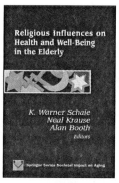

Contents:

- An Introduction to Research on Religion, Aging, and Health: Exploring New Prospects and Key Challenges, *N. Krause*
- Religious Observance and Health: Theory and Research, *E. L. Idler;* Commentary: Religion and Health: A European Perspective, *C. J. Lalive d'Epinay* and *D. Spini;* Commentary: Observing Religion and Health, *R. Finke*
- Prayer, Love, and Transcendence: An Epidemiologic Perspective, *J. Levin;* Commentary: Next Steps in Understanding the Prayer/Health Connection, *K. F. Ferraro;* Commentary: Prayer and the Elderly: Exploring a "Gerontological Mystery," *M. M. Poloma*
- Empirical Advances in the Psychology of Religion and Coping, *K. I. Pargament* and *G. G. Ano;* Commentary: Religious Coping in Later Life, *S. H. McFadden;* Commentary: Religion, Coping, and Health, *A. S. Willis*
- Religion Forgiveness, and Adjustment in Older Adulthood, *M. E. McCullough* and *G. Bono;* Commentary: Unforgiveness, Forgiveness, Religion and Health During Aging, *E. L. Worthington, Jr.;* Commentary: Multiple Forms of Forgiveness and Their Relationships with Aging and Religion, *M. A. Musick*
- Race and Ethnicity in Religion and Health, *L. M. Chatters;* Commentary: Race and SES Differences in the Relationship Between Religion and Health, *K. E. Whitfield* and *K. I. Jackson*
- Religion and Health in Life Course Perspective, *L. K. George, et al.*

Societal Impact on Aging Series
2004   320pp   0-8261-2404-6   hardcover

11 West 42nd Street. New York. NY 10036-8002 • Fax: 212-941-7842